Linguistic Minorities and Modernity:
A Sociolinguistic Ethnography

Real Language Series

General Editors:

Jennifer Coates, Roehampton Institute, London
Jenny Cheshire, Queen Mary and Westfield College, University of London, and
Euan Reid, Institute of Education, University of London

Titles published in the series:

David Lee Competing Discourses: Perspective and Ideology in Language
Norman Fairclough (Editor) Critical Language Awareness
James Milroy and Lesley Milroy (Editors) Real English: The Grammar of English Dialects in the British Isles
Mark Sebba London Jamaican: Language Systems in Interaction
Janet Holmes Women, Men and Politeness
Ben Rampton Crossing: Language and Ethnicity Among Adolescents
Brian V. Street Social Literacies: Critical Approaches to Literacy in Development, Ethnography and Education
Srikant Sarangi and Stefaan Slembrouck Language, Bureaucracy and Social Control
Ruth Wodak Disorders of Discourse
Victoria L. Bergvall, Janet M. Bing and Alice F. Freed (Editors) Rethinking Language and Gender Research: Theory and Practice
Anne Pauwels Women Changing Language
Monica Heller Linguistic Minorities and Modernity: A Sociolinguistic Ethnography

Linguistic Minorities and Modernity: A Sociolinguistic Ethnography

Monica Heller

with the collaboration of
Mark Campbell, Phyllis Dalley and
Donna Patrick

LONGMAN
LONDON AND NEW YORK

Addison Wesley Longman Limited,
Edinburgh Gate,
Harlow,
Essex CM20 2JE,
United Kingdom
and Associated Companies throughout the world.

*Published in the United States of America
by Addison Wesley Longman Inc. New York*

© Addison Wesley Longman Limited 1999

First published 1999

ISBN 0–582–27947–X CSD
ISBN 0–582–27948–8 PPR

Visit Addison Wesley Longman on the world wide web at
http://www.awl-he.com

British Library Cataloguing-in-Publication Data

A catalogue record for this book is available from the British Library

Library of Congress Cataloging-in-Publication Data

Heller, Monica.
  Linguistic minorities and the politics of identity / Monica
Heller, with the collaboration of Mark Campbell, Phyllis Dalley, and
Donna Patrick.
    p.   cm. — (Real language series)
  Includes bibliographical references (p.   ) and index.
  ISBN 0–582–27947–X. — ISBN 0–582–27948–8 (pbk.)
    1. Linguistic minorities. 2. Ethnicity. 3. Language and
languages—Political aspects. I. Title. II. Series.
P119.315.H45   1998
408′.9—dc21
                                              98–30249
                                                 CIP

Set by 35 in 10/12 pt Sabon
Produced by Addison Wesley Longman Singapore (Pte) Ltd.,
Printed in Singapore

Contents

Author's acknowledgements   vii
Publisher's acknowledgements   viii

PART I   1

1 **The transformation of linguistic minorities**   3
   1 The voyage: language, identity and
      hyper-modernity   3
      1.1 The *voyageurs*   3
      1.2 Linguistic minorities   7
   2 Linguistic norms, social institutions, and interest   11
   3 A sociolinguistic ethnography   14
   4 L'École Champlain   21
   5 The structure of the book   25

2 **'*L'Unité dans la diversité*'**   30
   1 Introduction   30
   2 1968: Schooling and minority language rights   33
   3 The consequences of mobilization   45
   4 Champlain and the politics of equity (1991–94)   61
   5 Champlain's 25th anniversary celebrations   67

3 **Norms and contradictions**   74
   1 Introduction   74
   2 The social organization of linguistic monitoring   77
   3 The construction and management of a
      monolingual ideal   91

4 *La qualité de la langue*   115
5 Normativity and strategic ambiguity   133

PART II   135

4 **Being bilingual**   137
  1 Playing the game   137
  2 Luc/Luke and Sandra   141
  3 Bilinguals rule   148
  4 *Les Québécois*   154
  5 *'Je ne comprenais rien'*   171
  6 Conclusion   187

5 **Girls and boys**   190
  1 Gender and public space   190
  2 Studs and Juliettes   193
  3 Ways in and ways out   198
  4 The 'Nerds'   202
  5 Conclusion   208

6 **Periphery to centre**   210
  1 Voices from the margins   210
  2 The phat boys   212
  3 A view from Africa   230
  4 Music and consciousness   242
  5 The Angels   248
  6 A hip-hop school   256

PART III   261

7 **The distribution of linguistic capital**   263
  1 L'École Champlain and the politics of identity   263
  2 Bilingualism, language norms and social selection   269
  3 Discourse at school and other sites   273

Bibliography   276
Author index   280
Subject index   282

Author's acknowledgements

As is usually the case with a project of this magnitude, there are many people and institutions whose contributions have been important. I want to start with l'École Champlain, its administrators, teachers, staff, students and parents, who shared so much time and knowledge with me and with all those who worked with me. I hope I have done justice to their honesty, commitment, energy, creativity and professionalism. The name of the school and the people associated with it have been disguised, but they know who they are.

The project was supported by two major sources: the Ontario Ministry of Education Transfer Grant to the Ontario Institute for Studies in Education (1991–93), and the Social Sciences and Humanities Research Council of Canada (1992–95). I gratefully acknowledge their support.

Many research officers and research assistants worked with me on this project over the years: Mark Campbell, Phyllis Dalley, Ellen Faulkner, Awad Ibrahim, Florian Levesque, Laurette Lévy, Claudine Moïse, Selina Mushi, Donna Patrick, Shelley Taylor and Robin Temkin all contributed in some way over part of the life of the project. Mark Campbell, Phyllis Dalley and Donna Patrick all collaborated with me on the production of this manuscript, especially with respect to sections of Chapter 4 (Donna Patrick), to Chapter 5 (Phyllis Dalley) and to Chapter 6 (Mark Campbell). Mark Campbell produced the illustrations. In addition to these three collaborators, Jürgen Erfurt, Michela Ferguson and Normand Labrie gave me a great deal of feedback on earlier versions. Timothy Kaiser patiently read draft after draft and provided insightful and stimulating comments, and careful editorial revisions. Whatever errors remain are, of course, my own.

Publisher's acknowledgements

We are grateful to International Music Publications Ltd for permission to reproduce one verse from the song 'Single' sung by The Pet Shop Boys. Words by Neil Tennant & Christopher Lowe © 1996 Cage Music Ltd/EMI 10 Music Ltd, London WC2H OEA.

PART I

1 *The transformation of linguistic minorities*

1 The voyage: language, identity and hyper-modernity

1.1 *The* voyageurs

The image of the *voyageur* (the voyager) is central to the construction of French identity in Canada. The first *voyageurs* were key players in the fur trade of the seventeenth, eighteenth and nineteenth centuries; their canoes followed the tracery of Canada's waterways, and their presence ensured European control of both political and economic life. Their story is familiar to all Canadians as part of the legend of Canada's origins, and is particularly important to French Canadians as part of the story of their specific contribution to building the country. But the *voyageurs'* image also has deeper resonances. It symbolizes the freedom to escape the constraints of an old way of life and to construct a new one, an interest in crossing boundaries between life-worlds, and the ability to create new identities. The voyageur. The image is a useful one for the story I want to tell here.

It is useful because of its force as a symbol of French Canada, certainly. But it is useful beyond that as a symbol of the larger story that French Canada has to tell us. This larger story is about linguistic minorities and their transformation in the world we know now, a world at the edges of what modernity has wrought. And the story of linguistic minorities is important because it sheds light on the ways in which hyper-modernity is transforming relations of power and the bases of identity in the Western world.

In many ways, hyper-modernity is about the voyage. It is about the transformation of an economic base from the extraction and processing of material resources, under the aegis of the nation-state, to an economy of service and information which is under the control of corporations, and unfolds beyond the confines of what states can impose. It is about the movements of people as they carry out the activities of the new economy, and as they position themselves socially to take advantage of what the new economy has to offer (or to resist what it is doing to them). This is particularly important for linguistic minorities, whose linguistic repertoires have value that is radically different from the value they had when a centralizing nation-state and a primary resource extraction based economy defined it. Linguistic minorities used the logic of ethnic state nationalism to resist that older form of power in order to enter the modern world. That modern world uses a different logic, and so linguistic minorities now have to redefine themselves in order to retain their economic and political gains, but without losing their legitimacy.

Different positions, different constraints; new ways of looking at resources and at players. The *voyageurs* are still with us; they show us how to find new paths across unknown territory, how to find what we want, and how to create what we might become.

This is the story of some of them. They work at and go to a school named after one of the most important French colonizers, Samuel de Champlain, a man who knew how to make extensive use of boats and waterways. Most of these modern-day voyagers use other modes of transportation, and in any case the voyage they are on is only partly geographic. They are members of what has become the linguistic minority of French Canada, and are living through a period of massive social transformation. Their identity has been shaped by political subordination to the conquering English, and by economic marginalization and exploitation. The past thirty years have seen collective mobilization to change this state of affairs; using the logic of national self-determination which came out of the ideologies of the nation-state of the past two centuries, francophone Canada has attempted to gain political power as a way to enter the modern world, and to participate fully in the new economy.

But the old politics of identity which situated them in the world, and gave them a basis from which to fight for what they wanted, is being challenged in three ways. First, it is being challenged from within, as unity gives way to diversity. Second, it is being challenged from without, as the old structures in which the politics of identity made sense, in particular state structures, give way to new forms of social organization and value, based on corporate capitalism. Third, it is being challenged by its own success, as the authenticity of its past gives way to entry into the modern world. What happens to these voyagers, that is, the path they choose to (and are able to) navigate into opportunities and around obstacles, the goals they set for themselves and their ability to achieve them, is part of the story of what is happening to minorities around the world, as the world changes shape.

Two elements of the story stand out. One is that linguistic minorities abandon the old politics of identity, and hence the problematics of authenticity, in favour of a new pragmatic position which allows them to take advantage of their access to multiple linguistic and cultural resources in order to participate in a globalized economy. This does provoke a crisis of legitimacy for minority institutions, which has to be managed, if only through discursive devices which neutralize the contradictions of claiming a new position on the basis of old values. Nonetheless, we shall see here the beginnings of the construction of a new basis of legitimacy, one founded not on authenticity and tradition, but rather on pluralism, on the extensiveness of the minority's social networks and on the quality of the linguistic resources the minority possesses. These values emerge as important because of the nature of the new economy, in which the ability to cross boundaries is important, but so is the construction of new global, international norms. Languages are still seen as autonomous systems; what is valued is multilingualism as a set of parallel monolingualisms, not a hybrid system. What is valued also is a mastery of a standard language, shared across boundaries and a marker of social status.

The second notable element of the story is that this shift has unforeseen consequences. The major consequence is that it depends on the existence somewhere of monolingual zones with respect to whom minorities can act as brokers. It foreshadows the emergence of a new bilingual, even multilingual élite. This élite builds a position which marginalizes both those bilinguals whose linguistic resources do not conform to the new norms, and those who are, simply, monolingual.

The story has many facets. Think of it as a kaleidoscope. There are several sets of patterned colours, each one representing a facet of the story. One pattern is linguistic nationalism, and in particular the role of the ideology of national self-determination in the politics of minority struggles for social, economic and political power. Another is the pattern of the economic conditions which underly such minority struggles, and in particular the transformation from national industrial/agricultural to globalized service and information economies. A third is the social institutions which serve to produce and reproduce, as well as distribute, valued resources, and hence contribute to the production and reproduction of relations of social difference and social inequality. The next patterns each represent one of the social categories which serve as the basis for the social organization of symbolic and material labour; the ones that concern us here are, at the broadest level, ethnicity, race, class and gender, but in other places other categories might be more important. Similarly, these broad social categories permutate at the local level into specific social categories of relevance to any specific community; here, we will need to understand the ways in which class, race, gender, ethnicity and language combine in the specific categories of 'nerds', 'popular kids', 'multiculturals', 'smokers' and 'Somalis'. Looked at one way, the colour of linguistic nationalism is in the foreground, and the colours of changing economies and dynamic identities form the backdrop. Give the kaleidoscope a turn, and linguistic nationalism moves to the background, and economic changes come to the fore.

At the same time, none of these patterns is fixed. Each is constantly changing, as a result of interactions among patterns, and as a result of the fact that each is, in the end, socially constructed rather than determined. Look closely at the patterns and what you see is people interacting with each other, drawing creatively on their linguistic and cultural resources to position themselves and each other as they struggle to redefine what it means, in this case, to be francophone and to speak French, as well as to define the value of the linguistic resources each possesses. At the heart of this book is a close examination of the discursive processes which allow us to understand the broad picture of the transformation of linguistic minorities in the current conditions of hyper-modernity. While the presentation in this chapter is top-down, in fact it has been the bottom-up analysis of life at Champlain which has led me to these conclusions, and it is the bottom-up analysis to which the bulk of the book is devoted. Nonetheless, in order for that bottom-up analysis to make sense, I shall indulge myself in this chapter in a consideration of the nature of linguistic minorities, and their experience of nationalism and of political mobilization through language, as a way of setting the stage. I shall, finally, describe the structure of the book, that is, the way I have chosen to tell the particuar story I want to tell here.

1.2   Linguistic minorities

What is a linguistic minority? The notion assumes that there is a whole of which a group is a minor part, and it assumes that what makes the difference between that group and the majority has something to do with language. But where does this notion come from? And where is it going? The concept of a linguistic minority only makes sense today within an ideological framework of *nationalism* in which language is central to the construction of the nation (Anderson 1983). The association of language and nation has a long history, which I shall trace briefly below. The most important parts of that history have to do with the ways in which, especially from about the end of the eighteenth century, language has been seen as central to nation-building, and with the ways in which that process has created minorities. Language has been central to nation-building in two ways. The first has to do with the construction of unity: a shared language permits the construction of shared values and practices. The second has to do with legitimizing the nation, and works in ways that are exactly the opposite to the first; that is, it is possible to argue that a group legitimately constitutes a nation because it shares a language. Not that language is the only terrain on which nations are built; but language is important precisely because it works in both these ways, while cross-cutting any other forms of social difference which might otherwise undermine solidarity.

Linguistic minorities are created by nationalisms which exclude them. At the same time, the logic of linguistic nationalism is available to minorities as a way to resist the power of the majority. Language revitalization movements are replications on a demographically smaller scale of the nation-building movements in Europe in the nineteenth and early twentieth centuries. And, of course, they

create their own minorities, since groups are never perfectly homogeneous (Marcellesi 1979).

It is hard to say when the tradition of associating monolingualism
with nationalism began, or that of legitimating nationalism on the
basis of shared language. Certainly these ideas have taken a variety
of forms and have had varying degrees of salience from one place
to another. Perhaps an appropriate place to start is with the combined effects of the French Revolution and German Romanticism,
at least for the shape that linguistic nationalism (not to mention
nationalist linguistics) takes today.

Language became important for the Revolution in two respects.
First, the revolutionaries were concerned to make sure that the
values of the Revolution spread, and that everyone would have
access to them. For a while, the preferred strategy was to bring
the message of the revolution to the people in their own language
(a strategy adopted by Christian missionaries in the Americas
and Africa since the seventeenth century). Later, the policy shifted
to a preference for ensuring equity of access through French, and
ensuring loyalty through monolingualism. The concerns of state-
building and the tense political relations with surrounding countries (and even within France) shifted the focus towards this other,
monolingual, vision of France. This vision of France is still strongly
associated with the linkage between the centralized state and the
values of the Revolution (Higonnet 1980; Grillo 1989). For German Romanticism, as understood particularly through the work
of Herder, the process worked the other way around. The notion
that language was the essence of a people served to legitimate
arguments for the construction of the German state (Sériot 1997).

Linguistic state nationalism has, then, two connected facets:
one which brings the people to the state by giving them the state's
language, and one which brings the state to a people which defines
itself in terms of shared language. Of course, these ideological
visions of language and nation construct a way of evaluating specific situations, which can then be seen as more or less perfect or
imperfect realizations of the linkage between language, nation and
state, necessitating action to achieve the fullest realization possible.
Sometimes this means arguing that a nation needs a state; or countering that argument on the grounds that the so-called 'nation' isn't
really a nation, that its language isn't really a language, or that it
is too weak to survive on its own as a state (Hobsbawm 1990).

Sometimes this means arguing that citizens need to become more competent in the language of the state; or countering that argument on the grounds that the state is crushing emergent nations by imposing its language on them. Of course, the relationship between state and linguistic hegemony is usually complex. As Marcellesi (1979) points out, it is necessary in each case to specify the groups (typically the bourgeoisie) interested in building a nation-state, those who construct linguistic hegemony, and the relationship between the two (they may coincide or overlap, they may collaborate or they may even conflict).

French Canada has occupied a variety of positions on this ground. It first manifested itself through a nationalism based on the association of language, nation and religion, in an explicit rejection of Revolutionary values. The French-Canadian nation was not tied to specific geographical territory, but rather to an ideological and social one. It survived by virtue of socioeconomic and political marginalization, supported by its own institutions, the most important of which was the Catholic Church. And yet, from the beginning of life under the British, there was a dissenting view, although this view did not come to the fore until well into the twentieth century. This view held that French Canadians needed to find a way into sharing the structures of power with the English; it was promoted, and acted upon, by a variety of members of the lay élite, sometimes with the support of the clergy. After the Second World War, more specifically towards the end of the 1950s and into the 1960s, the élite moved more clearly towards this second set of goals, but split in its view of how to pursue its aims (cf. Martel 1997; Bock 1996; Boudreau 1995). Some sought to achieve its goals through existing structures of power, notably through the federal government. Wedded to the idea of a French-Canadian nation, these people tried to transform Canada into a country in which francophones would have a better place. Others, based mainly in Quebec, argued that this was futile. They embarked instead on a project of ethnolinguistic state nationalism, intent on using the power of the Quebec state to achieve their goals, that is, to create a zone for themselves inside which they could wield power, rather than trying to gain access to their share of power controlled by anglophones. These two competing views of the place of the French in Canada are still current, and shape a large part of the Canadian political landscape. Language has become increasingly important as a defining characteristic of French Canada as the Church has lost power, and as the embracing of a democratic ideology as a way to achieve social, political, and economic goals has forced a shift away from talk of blood towards talk of citizenship (since language is something that can be learned). Nonetheless, in current discourses, one can still hear and feel the presence of layers of experience and orientation, which co-exist despite often being contradictory (cf. Boudreau and Nielsen 1994).

Current economic, political and social developments are undermining the logic of linguistic nationalism. Old nations group together to produce supra-national associations, like the European Union. The expansion of capitalism under corporate, rather than national, auspices (Lash and Urry 1994; Wolf 1982), creates communities of economic interest and corporate culture which cut across national (and linguistic) lines (although the expansion of English as a global language is, of course, embedded in this process; Pennycook 1992; Phillipson 1992; Kachru 1992). And economic and political migration account for major changes in the cultural and linguistic composition of both areas from which people move, and those to which they move. These conditions of hyper-modernity (Giddens 1990) create a crisis for the ideology of nationalism (Blommaert 1996) and for the methods of constructing identity that have for so long been linked to it (Billig 1995; Giddens 1991). They also create a crisis for the institutions of nationalism, that is, institutions devoted to reproducing the idea of the nation, and to making it function. This includes political institutions like the State, and also cultural ones, like the media and schools.

The crisis plays itself out in many ways, in many arenas, but language is an important one in part because of its role in processes of nation-building. This central role, and the values attached to the linguistic forms and practices that are tied to ideologies of nationalism and to national values and identities, are called into question by competing ways of organizing the production and distribution of important material and symbolic resources (Gee *et al.* 1996). At the same time, these competing ways are themselves constructed through ideologies which include linguistic ideologies; they are constructed through social interaction, and hence largely through language (Gumperz 1982) in ways which are mediated by our ideas about language in the world (Schieffelin 1997). We reconstruct our ideas about the world and our relationships to it

and to each other on the terrain of language, repositioning ourselves with respect to our old ways of thinking, being and doing,
and trying out new ones.

2   Linguistic norms, social institutions, and interest

Deborah Cameron has observed (1995: 95–6):

> [. . . C]onservatives use 'grammar' as the metaphorical correlate
> for a cluster of related political and moral terms: *order, tradition,*
> *authority, hierarchy,* and *rules.* In the ideological world that
> conservatives inhabit, these terms are not only positive, they
> define the conditions for any civil society, while their opposites
> – *disorder, change, fragmentation, anarchy* and *lawlessness* –
> signify the breakdown of social relations. A panic about grammar
> is therefore interpretable as the metaphorical expression of
> persistent conservative fears that we are losing the values that
> underpin civilization and sliding into chaos.
>
> This metaphor supplies the missing link between bad grammar
> and bad behaviour. If conformity to the rules of orderly speech
> signifies conformity to the laws of society, acquiescence in its
> traditional hierarchies and acceptance of legitimate authority, it
> becomes easier to see why disregard for 'nice points of grammar'
> should be construed as leading inexorably to disrespect for
> persons, property, institutions (. . .) and finally the law itself.

Linguistic nationalism involves much more than struggles over
whether a state and its institutions can be monolingual or multilingual, or whether a people can be a people and speak more than
one language. In addition, the imagining of the nation includes ideological struggles over its most central values, and these struggles
take place not only with respect to what monolingualism and multilingualism represent, but also with respect to the very shape of
the language to be privileged. Ideologies of the state are therefore
partly constructed through ideologies of language (Gal 1993; Kuzar
1996; Blommaert, forthcoming).

Part of this process of construction unfolds through processes
of regimentation, which generally take the form of control over
the construction of linguistic norms (cf. Balibar 1985). (France, of
course, is famous for doing this, but it is not alone.) The fact that
anyone exercises such regimentation, and that anyone takes this
regimentation seriously, is in itself significant, as Cameron points

out above. It implies the exercise of symbolic domination, and the acquiescence to a certain 'régime of truth', to use a term derived from the work of Foucault (cf. Fairclough 1992: 37–61). That is, it implies agreeing that somebody's idea of how to do things is the right, normal, natural way to do things for everyone, despite the fact that only certain people get to make up the rules, and hence profit from the fact that they do so, while putting everyone else at a disadvantage (Bourdieu 1972, 1982; Gramsci 1971).

The other dimension of regimentation has to do with the details of what counts as 'proper' language (Cameron 1995; Crowley 1991; Bourdieu 1977a, 1977b). Here, it is possible to see more clearly what values are attributed to language forms and practices, and how those values are attached to ideologies connected to social categories and social relations (like ideologies of the state, but also, say, ideologies of gender). Thus, for example, Swiggers (1990) points out that the French like to think of their language as a model of rationality, clarity and precision, and this is held to be revealed in particular in word order, as well as in the (related) use of prepositions. Thus people should speak French because it is inherently a better language than others, and especially insofar as it provides the speaker access to the best of French civilization's values (the idea is that just speaking French makes you more rational). Cameron (1995) has pointed out that lowering the pitch of your voice, in English, makes you sound more like a man, and therefore more authoritative (although a woman speaking with too low a voice risks sliding over the edge of what is considered legitimate appropriation). French Canadians consider that their preference for the use of the more informal second-person pronoun (*tu*) over the more formal *vous*, along with their ready acceptance of newly constructed norms for feminizing occupational titles (*le professeur/la professeure*, for example), signal a more egalitarian, more flexible society than the one found in France. We have all kinds of ideas about the values revealed in linguistic practices, and how they relate to our idea of our society and to its fundamental values. But the specific ideas we have depend a great deal on why we imagine our community the way we do, and on what we stand to gain or lose by imagining things that way.

Both these activities of regimentation have to occur somewhere. They can occur in the ebb and flow of everyday life; but they also occur in institutions. There are many institutions involved, of course, including those set up expressly to undertake the work of linguistic regimentation (the *Académie française* may be the best known of these). Among the most important of the other institutions which do the work of linguistic regimentation and the production and reproduction of linguistic norms, are the family, the media and the school (cf. Martin-Jones and Heller 1996; Jaffe 1993; Urla 1995).

In French Canada, the question of linguistic norms has become increasingly important for two reasons, one having to do with legitimating new nationalisms, and the other with developing linguistic resources which have a value in the new global economy. The essence of political mobilization requires the construction of linguistic forms which show local authenticity, that is, which reveal Canadian French, or better, Québécois, as a legitimate language variety on its own, in order to show that the Québécois truly are a people (Heller 1996). Indeed, the past thirty years have witnessed the founding of an institution responsible for regimenting language, the *Office de la langue française*, an institution which, among other things, has had a large role to play in constructing the authenticity of Québécois. In addition, the past thirty years have witnessed a great deal of activity oriented towards the codification of Québécois, partly through descriptive linguistics, and partly through the making of dictionaries.

By the same token, the specific goals of French-Canadian nationalism require an attention to policing the boundaries of this authentic variety. It is important that this variety be not only local (that is, not Parisian), but also purely French. Thus a great deal of attention has been paid to what are considered *canadianismes de bon aloi* (legitimate Canadianisms), which include French words invented in Canada to describe things that do not exist in French, or words of indigenous origin borrowed into French. A great deal of attention has also been paid to expurgating *anglicismes*, which are considered marks of the power English has exercised over French, and hence to be resisted, shaken off. Third, since another aim of nationalism is entry into the modern world, attention has been paid to forming a French which sounds and acts like a standardized, codified language, and which does not bear traces of the situation of oppression in which French Canadians lived for so long and from which they wish to escape. Finally, the language is held to be the place where the new Québécois (or French Canadian, or Acadian, or Franco-Ontarian, etc., depending on your point of view) will emerge. There is no consensus yet; but many conversations are given over to discussing whether or not certain ways of doing things (like transforming the pronominal system, or expanding morphological feminization) are good or bad, that is, in our image or not.

We must also ask, however: whose image actually is this? Behind the image is an interest. If the 'conservatives' to whom Cameron refers are interested in law and order, it is presumably because they stand to gain something from the maintenance of the status quo. If others are busy inventing new words, new pronunciations, new syntactic structures, it is presumably because they have other interests to advance. As we shall see, the question of linguistic norms is such a terrain of struggles over the advancement of sometimes competing interests in French Canada. Those who argue for the kind of norm I described above are representatives of the new middle class who have profited from nationalism in one way or another. Now there are new players in the game who want to play a role, without being able to lay claim to the kind of authenticity the first group can. One way to do this is to argue for a norm which allows them to exploit the linguistic capital they do possess, and to downplay the importance of the cultural capital they do not. In part, this is a process of shifting emphasis from the legitimizing function of language in this context, to its function as a way of constructing social distinctions (Bourdieu 1979). In addition, by virtue of their new-found power, those whose interests are best represented in institutions of social and cultural reproduction can leave aside others whose linguistic capital has failed to become valuable in the new social order. Those who find themselves marginalized are left to try to find a way in, to resist, or to bail out altogether. As we shall see, these positionings are largely informed by class and ethnicity, although they are also gendered; but the focus on language and culture which is at the heart of linguistic minority ideology and action obscures everything else.

3   A sociolinguistic ethnography

There are many ways of understanding these things that are happening around us, and that we are making happen. The method I have chosen here is sociolinguistic ethnography, that is, a close look at language practices in a specific setting. I have made many choices, and each one is motivated by a long list of reasons.

First, I have chosen to enter this danger zone through the question of what is happening to politically mobilized, nationalist, linguistic minorities. The major reason for this is that linguistic minorities occupy that interesting area between the 19th and 21st centuries. As I said earlier, they are the product of 19th- and 20th-century nationalism, and so linguistic minorities experience in particularly sharp ways the changes in the political conditions which gave them a name in the first place. Unlike the nation-states in which they are minorized, they do not carry around an institutional and ideological baggage which can sustain itself long after the life-support system has been turned off. They have long been critical of centralizing nation-states in particular, and have long searched for those interstices which give them a glimmer of hope for freedom and self-determination. And now the interstices become great gaps, huge doors through which it might just be possible to simply get up and walk. And yet, linguistic minorities are faced with the problem of their own legitimacy. Having based their claims on the logic of linguistic identity, on the right of a people, identified by its common language, to self-determination, it is difficult to imagine the basis on which these minorities would be able to reproduce themselves outside of the logic of linguistic nationalism altogether. Linguistic minorities thus illustrate particularly clearly the crisis of legitimacy that hyper-modernity has brought us.

By the same token, the situation of linguistic minorities clearly reveals some of the reasons why we engage in the politics of identity in the first place. The political mobilization of such communities (as in Wales, Brittany, Corsica, Catalonia, Quebec and many other places) was based on a struggle between local élites and members of the dominant, ruling groups of the centralized state over access to and control over local resources (McDonald 1990; Woolard 1989; Heller 1994a; Jaffe 1993). Globalization, the rise of corporate capitalism and the relative disengagement from public life of neo-liberal states makes it less clear now who controls what, and what is at stake, and this calls into question what the politics of identity might be about, or even whether such a politics makes sense any more.

Finally, linguistic minorities are suddenly fashionable icons of the new hybridity. Long accustomed to making bridges among worlds, and resolving tensions and contradictions among them (Heller 1988), linguistic minorities discovered borders long before cultural studies did. Their practices help us understand a phenomenon that is no longer so confined to the periphery; more and more people share the minority condition of multiple identities and constant border crossings.

Second, I have chosen the particular case of a francophone minority community in Canada. And not just any francophone minority community, as one might find somewhere in Quebec, say, but one which is minorized even within Canada by virtue of being located outside Quebec, in the predominantly English-speaking province of Ontario.

The first reason for this choice has to do with the fact that francophone Canada has followed the logic of nationalism in the same ways that many other linguistic minorities have done. This nationalism began as resistance to English domination after Britain conquered Canada in 1763. It only fully took the form of modern state nationalism, however, in the early 1960s, when Quebec fragmented the francophone population of Canada along territorial lines. Quebec has since then followed the logic of its territorial state nationalist movement, arguing that francophone Quebec forms a nation, and therefore has the right to an independent state. Quebec further argues that only a monolingual state will serve to protect its cultural and linguistic distinctiveness. This leaves Quebec with its own contradictions to resolve; namely, how to make itself a credible authority to those who live in Quebec but who do not share in the authenticity of francophone origins (these include indigenous groups, descendants of British and Loyalist settlers and more recent immigrant groups); or, conversely, how to invent a new basis of legitimacy founded on something other than national authenticity. This problem is compounded by the contradiction inherent in this, as in other similar movements, which is that the past, which is the guarantee of the legitimacy of current political claims, is precisely what mobilization aims to escape. Francophones have mobilized to enter the modern world in order to enjoy its fruits, not to maintain the marginalized and difficult life which was the basis of their solidarity, but which was not much fun.

While the situation of Quebec is complex and fascinating in itself, looking at this process from the perspective of the francophones of what is now fondly called the ROC (Rest of Canada) is in many ways even more illuminating. The francophone minority communities of Canada share in Quebec's experience, indeed, have learned much from it. Most importantly, they share Quebec's agenda of a politics of identity aimed at emancipation in order to part-icipate in the global economy, and Quebec's strategy of seeking to create monolingual zones through access to state-controlled institu-tions. They have also shared in the fruits of political mobilization, which has helped francophones to gain both political and economic power. This, together with the value accorded to multilingualism in the globe-trotting hyper-modern world, has considerably enhanced the value of French as a form of linguistic capital (Bourdieu 1977a, 1977b, 1982). But unlike Quebec, the francophone minority com-munities of the ROC cannot lay claim to any territory or to any completely autonomous government (although this idea has had an airing in one area of Eastern Canada in which francophones form a significant majority). They are therefore forced to imagine other forms of struggle, and to develop other discourses, other ideas, through which to resolve the contradictions of their condi-tions and through which to confront the changing conditions of their lives. This gives us a broader range of strategies to observe than might be available in such places as Quebec, where things are somewhat clearer. It also gives us a better chance of observing the process of discursive struggle, that is, of discovering ways in which people develop the strategies and ideological positions that they do develop, and reasons why they do so.

In addition, the extreme minority condition of these communities makes their experience of multiple identities and border crossings that much sharper. Very few francophones outside Quebec can lead a life removed from others, whether these others are members of the dominant anglophone majority or members of other minorities.

Of all the francophone communities in the ROC that I could have looked at, I chose to concentrate on Toronto. The city repres-ents an extreme version of the various processes to which I have referred, and which are central to the problem I want to address. The francophone community in Toronto is intensely urban, and made up of many elements, some drawn from older, more tradi-tional, unmobilized communities, others from highly politically conscious ones; some are from Canada and many are from else-where around the world; francophones here are found all up and down the economic scale and in a wide variety of occupations;

and Toronto itself represents a movement towards economic advancement through globalization and neo-liberalism, as well as towards multicultural hybridization.

I chose to look at the problem of nationalism, identity and minorization through the lens of schooling. Schools are important sites of social and cultural reproduction, and over the course of the nineteenth and twentieth centuries have come under state control in order to accomplish state agendas. As a result, they have often been sites of struggle over state versus local control; for linguistic minorities, this has often taken the form of struggles over policies concerning the language of instruction. This has clearly been the case in francophone minority communities in Canada, in which struggles over the right to use French as a (or the only) language of instruction, and over community control of educational institutions, have both a long history and a pressing currency.

Because the state does still (for the moment) control schools, schooling must also respect at least certain elements of the democratic ideology which is at the heart of government legitimacy in Canada. A combination of such ideological and more purely bureaucratic constraints flowing from state control (such as how many students are required in order to get funds to open a school), together with the historical changes in the value accorded to French, results, in Toronto's French-language schools, in an extremely socially, culturally and linguistically heterogeneous student body.

Finally, I chose a high school, because high school students are thinking both about the culture of their institution as well as about life outside of and after school. More so than elementary school students, they live a life which stretches in both time and space beyond the boundaries of home, school and neighbourhood. The struggles they engage in are relevant not just to what schools do to produce or reproduce social identities and relations of power in the short term, but also to what the students take with them outside school and after they graduate.

I would not want to argue that the school which welcomed me and my research assistants is exactly representative of linguistic minorities everywhere, or even of francophone minorities in Canada. Nor would I want to argue that what went on in that school will single-handedly change the direction of francophone society. However, I do want to argue that, by taking a close look at what goes on in this school, we can get a sense of the kinds of condition which make certain kinds of strategy and discourse possible, meaningful and influential. We can also get a sense of the consequences of those kinds of strategy and of the discursive struggles they entail, consequences for certain kinds of people, as well as for the institution in which they participate.

This book is therefore about what it means to be francophone, and to speak French, as seen through the life of a French-language minority high school in Toronto, Ontario. It is about the ways in which the school, as an institution, constructs and implements its linguistic norms, norms which only make sense if understood as part of the school's political, nationalist, mission – a mission which itself can only be understood as part of a minority's struggles for power. It is also about the ways in which students are positioned with respect to the school's public discourse on language and identity, and about how they take up, collaborate with or resist this discourse.

The contradictions of the minority condition produce a specific discursive struggle. The school, as a key site for the production of the nation, must create within its walls a monolingual zone, in order to produce bilinguals (who are, in effect, meant to be double monolinguals, that is, people who can act like monolingual francophones as well as monolingual anglophones). It manages the tension between fictive monolingualism and real bilingualism by creating a barrier between the monolingual, public discourse of the school and bilingual marginal discursive spaces. School representatives also adopt a range of conversational and discursive strategies, such as codeswitching, which allow them to manage these tensions in the heat of the action in the classroom. The school also pays close attention to linguistic norms within French, aiming at resolving a tension between valuing the authenticity of Canadian French while constructing a form of a standard which is seen as more appropriate to the modern world. The school does this largely by including French-Canadian content in the curriculum, and tolerating a certain, albeit limited, range of accents and vocabulary. The difficulty of constructing this ideologically motivated norm is seen in the lack of consensus as to what precisely it consists of.

Students are divided in how they live with this. One group of students, who are used to life in bilingual Toronto (having been born or brought up there), academically successful, economically comfortable, and ambitious, collaborate with the school's agenda and strategies for managing contradictions. However, they are not wedded to the legitimizing function of purely monolingual practices: they are bilingual, and proud of it. Nor are they wedded to the legitimizing function of Canadian French, and work actively to marginalize this dimension of school life. Recent immigrants, especially those from francophone Africa, contest the comfortably bilingual practices of the first group, and the locally based authenticity of the school's ideology. They argue for their place in the image of the school, as part of a new *francophonie internationale*. Their argument is heard, since it corresponds both to the ideology of monolingualism promoted by the school, and its commitment to democracy (here in the form of anti-racist efforts) and entry into the globalized modern world. These discourses marginalize the working-class speakers of vernacular Canadian French; they are the guarantee of the school's authenticity, and in many ways of its legitimacy, but they also represent the past from which the school is trying to help its students escape. Cross-cutting these divisions are divisions based on gender; the discourses on language are discourses produced mainly by males, and are fraught with processes of reproduction of gender stereotypes. The result is that academically successful males on the whole have the best chance of actually becoming bilingual in the way envisaged by the school; older female recent immigrants have the most difficulty gaining access to English; working-class males often stop speaking French altogether; and working-class females are silenced by linguistic insecurity and a lack of other arenas in which to speak.

By the time we left the school in 1994, the tension between *la francophonie internationale* as a model for the school's identity, and *la francophonie de souche* (local communities with 'roots') was being resolved in favour of the first. Ethnocultural diversity was being integrated into a new way of imagining the community, but in ways which obscured class and gender inequalities. Most significantly, this shift moves the school away from its traditional arguments regarding its legitimacy, and towards a new vision of French, not as an inalienable dimension of individual identity, but as a valuable form of linguistic capital; not as an emblem of collective identity, but as the mark of an international, pluralist élite.

4   L'École Champlain

The book takes the form of the story of one school, l'École Champlain, in the early 1990s. The research I conducted there was ethnographic, and sociolinguistic in that it concentrated on describing and explaining the language practices in everyday life at the school, as a way into discovering the nature of the social interests at play in the school.

My research assistants and I worked in the school for over three years, from September 1991 to March 1995. We aimed at understanding the perspectives of the institution and of its clientele; this meant paying attention to what all the relevant categories of players were doing, whether they were school board and school administrators, teachers, other staff, parents, or students. We began by looking at things from the perspective of the school, and this is reflected in many ways in the nature of the analysis and the structure of the book. Things might have looked different had we begun somewhere else. However, perhaps more importantly, that choice had consequences for how we were seen by teachers and students. In any school, an adult is more likely to be understood as some kind of teacher-figure than as a student, and this constrains the kinds of relationship one can have with students. Many researchers, in attempting to get around this problem in high school ethnography, have chosen to focus only on the students, carefully avoiding any association with teachers or their activities or their spaces (cf. Eckert 1989). This was not an option for us, since the focus of the project was on the school as an institution of social and cultural reproduction of a linguistic minority. Fortunately, some graduate students joined the project after we had finished with the first, school-focused stage, and they were able to conduct a set of relations with students relatively free of association with school authority. Still, we had to pay a price; this tension was always present.

Looking at things from the perspective of the school meant a number of things. It meant interviewing administrators (seven in all, including elected trustees and full-time administrators at both the board and the school level), teachers (the six teachers of the six classes we observed the first year; see below) and non-teaching staff (five, including guidance counsellors and social workers), and reading the various documents the school and its board publish about their activities and their philosophies, or which they use to organize themselves (these include monthly bulletins sent by the board to parents and any other interested parties; public minutes of board-level monthly meetings; the school's course calendar and yearbook; enrolment, discipline and other forms; published collections of student literary work in English and French; wall murals and various textual displays in the front hall and corridors of the school). It also meant spending about two days a week at school over the duration of the project, in classrooms, in the teachers' lounge, and at school-wide activities.

We chose classrooms that represented a range of situations, by level and by subject matter. Ontario has a policy of streaming students in high school. More precisely, courses are offered at four different levels, the top two leading to university study, the bottom two not. Champlain grouped courses according to the two middle levels; observing both advanced and general level courses gave us a sense of what kinds of practice were valued, and what kinds of practice were not. We chose to begin with Grade 10 classes, since that is where streaming begins. (This group contained about forty-five students out of a total enrolment of about four hundred students in Grades 7 to 13.) While we spent some time over the years with other students, this group became our major focus. We also chose to go to *Français* classes, since that is the most highly charged subject matter for the issues that concerned us. We then balanced that by looking at classes where language was important to the subject matter without being the focus of study, like *Géographie*, and where language might be less important (like *Sciences*). It also turned out that *Français* classes, especially at the advanced level, relied little on real-world knowledge, whereas classes like *Sciences* and *Géographie* did; this is important as, in a place like Toronto, real-world knowledge tends to come in the majority language. Over the course of the following years we were able to observe an even wider range of classes, including Drama, Accounting, Mathematics, English, English as a Second Language, Family Studies, Computer Science, and History. We observed many classes (each lasting 90 minutes) over the years; we tape-recorded an average of six each (minimum four, maximum eight) for the six classes we observed during the first year (1991–92). We also interviewed most of the students in each of the *Français* classes to get a sense of how they felt about the class, of their own sociolinguistic history and repertoire, of their ambitions, and also of how they felt about being at

Champlain. In 1994, we also tape-recorded four English as a Second Language classes, and student presentations in Accounting (two classes; individual presentations) and Family Studies (five classes; group presentations).

The second year we spent time (the amount varied, between three weeks and three months) with fifteen students, chosen on the basis of our observations the prior year as representative of a range of linguistic practices and social positions (boys and girls; advanced- and general-level students; students who spoke mainly French, or mainly English, or mainly Somali, or some combination of these; students who had been born or brought up in Toronto; and students who had recently arrived). We followed them around school, spent time with them outside school, and interviewed them. We also interviewed the parents of eight of them, sometimes with the students (in two cases), but usually separately. Student interviews continued throughout the rest of the project; in all, we tape-recorded interviews with forty-six students, most of them once in a one-on-one interview, some of them several times and some of them in sets of two or three students together.

In the third and fourth years we focused on groups of students who formed friendship networks, again focusing on a range of students occupying different social positions in the school. These included general-level students who defined themselves as 'smokers' and who were academically, socially and linguistically marginalized; groups of black students, mainly African, but also Haitian; a group of academically successful but socially marginal girls who called themselves variously the 'nerds' or the 'rejects'; a small group of boys of a variety of backgrounds who identified themselves as the 'multiculturals'; and academically successful and discursively dominant students who were identified by the 'nerds' as the 'popular group' or 'the cute kids'. These groups also identified themselves largely through music: hiphop, reggae, heavy metal and house provide the major fault lines. We tape-recorded some of these groups in a variety of ways. We invited some of the smokers to lunch on two occasions, and taped our conversations there; we did the same with some of the male African students. We also taped conversation in the smoking area on two occasions. I taped five conversations (lasting about half-an-hour) on school grounds (in the cafeteria, in the library, on the grass in front of the school) with a group of six African girls, conversations which occurred spontaneously as part of the group's activities, but at which I was present. I also tape-recorded conversation with them at lunch at my house. Mark (a member of the research team) taped similar conversations occurring among the 'multicultural' students on school grounds, in classes (mainly during group work in Drama class) and in breaks between classes. Phyllis (another member of the team) met on five occasions with the 'nerds' at school for conversations lasting about half-an-hour; she and I also invited the nerds to dinner one evening and taped that conversation. It was more difficult to tape-record the 'popular' students; they were, not surprisingly, less welcoming to us. Nonetheless, we were able to spend time with them without a tape-recorder, and two of them agreed to carry a tape-recorder around with them during two successive lunch breaks each. Two African students also did this for us.

Finally, throughout the three and a half years of research, we attended all public events at Champlain. Champlain used the public stage extensively as a way to construct its image, and to conduct its discursive struggles. Who had control of public discourse, and what they did with it, was thus a very important part of understanding the social construction of Champlain as a Franco-Ontarian minority school.

Public discourse took a number of forms. The most important type of event, and the most frequent, was the *réunion générale* (general meeting). These meetings were called by the student council on a regular basis, in order to prepare for upcoming events. They almost always took the form of skits. They also were held in order to prepare for annual student council elections. These events were the ones which were most extensively controlled by the students themselves. In addition, the school would sometimes call an assembly. One principal did this on a variety of occasions (perhaps two or three times a year), in order to talk to the students about his plans and concerns. Other assemblies were focused on themes, and tended to be preludes to workshops; these included, for example, workshops on combating racism (there were two while we were there; one school-wide, the other closed to a small group of selected students; we attended both) and on combating domestic violence and violence against women. There were also public performances given mainly by students. Every year, these included a *Soirée cabaret* (cabaret night), which consisted of short artistic performances by students and adults (songs, dances, dramatic monologues); a *Café littéraire* (literary café), which was organized by one or two teachers of Français, and consisted of recitals of literary works in French; a play or other public event organized on the occasion of Black History Month; and a fashion show. There were also shows brought into the school as part of its activities of *animation culturelle*, a programme designed to make students aware of francophone culture. These were mainly music performances, and tended to include a wide cultural range in keeping with the board's (and Ministry of Education's) policies of anti-racist education and ethnocultural inclusiveness. Every year there was also a *Déjeuner multiculturel* (multicultural lunch), organized by Family Studies teachers and students, to which students were encouraged to bring a sample of the national dish of their country or region of origin. During our stay there, Champlain also celebrated its twenty-fifth anniversary, which generated a number of public displays. Most of the public events at Champlain were recorded on video-tape by student members of the audio-visual club, and we had access to many of these tapes, in addition to having attended the events ourselves.

There were some sports events, notably in volleyball, but Champlain is not a sports-oriented school, unlike so many mainstream, majority schools. This is, in fact, largely a result of being a minority school, with a small enrolment, limited physical facilities, and a student body drawn from such a wide geographical range that after-school activities have to be kept to a minimum.

Finally, we were able to attend some public events outside school in which some students, parents or teachers participated, such as a student-run radio show on a local university station, and an annual community-wide francophone festival.

Clearly, there were other activities in which we never participated. Perhaps most importantly, we never got a real sense of what students' daily lives were like outside school. Nonetheless, in the time we spent there, we were able to get a close reading of a broad range of sites where public discourse was constructed, presented and contested, and of a broad range of social positionings with respect to the definition of the school.

5   The structure of the book

In order to tell the story of Champlain, I shall have to turn the kaleidoscope several times, and examine closely the dynamic processes which produce the patterns that emerge at any given turn. I shall begin, in Chapter 2, by showing where the school came from, and why it is so heavily ideologically invested in a certain image of French Canada. The emphasis here is on the tension inherent in the minority condition, and which is encapsulated in the school's motto: '*l'Unité dans la diversité*' (Unity in diversity). The unity is built on shared language, culture and identity, and on a common front of resistance against the attempts of the English-speaking majority of Ontario to deny francophones their rights, and to assimilate them into their ranks. The diversity is addressed both to the majority, in the form of an alternative vision of Ontario as a pluralist society, and to the community of the school itself, made up as it is of people from all over the world. Managing the tension between the two poles is central to Champlain's under-standing of itself, and to our understanding of the role it plays in the construction of the linguistic minority it represents.

Chapter 3 takes a closer look at the linguistic ideology of Champlain. Here we see its adherence to the two main threads of current nationalist ideology: the insistence on French monolin-gualism within the school as a form of institutional territorial autonomy (on the model of Quebec's geographical state territori-alism), and the concern for the production of *un français de qualité*. This adherence is manifested in a variety of expressions of the linguistic conventions the school favours, and in a variety of prac-tices engaged in by school staff. At the same time, Champlain staff must cope with the evident contradictions between the unified world it wants to create within its walls and the very real diversity which keeps creeping in. Staff members must also address the contradictions between the stigmatized but authentic vernacular which legitimizes the very existence of the school, and the emerg-ing standard which marginalizes vernacular-speakers but which opens the doors to economic advancement. They manage to adopt a range of discursive strategies which are available to them by virtue of the social organization of the school, as it reflects prevail-ing ideas about how teaching and learning should be conducted. These strategies serve to neutralize these contradictions, but do not resolve them in any way.

The next three chapters focus on the students. Chapter 4 looks at the ways in which students occupying different social positions take up the discourse of the school. The dominant group in the school at the time we began the study, the 'popular' students who controlled the structures of power (like the student council) and the use of social space, consisted of students who constructed themselves as bilingual. They came from families in which the parents had engaged in struggles for the kind of values Champlain represents, or who had come to share in those values and to want to share in the particular forms of symbolic capital only a school like Champlain distributes. These are, then, families who value education and social mobility, or, more often, want to make sure that their children maintain what their parents have managed to acquire. The children share these aims, but they do not share the experience of the school. They are bilingual, not monolingual, francophones. They therefore collaborate with the school's ideology by not overtly challenging its norms; they resist the school's practices by covertly using English. School is the only place, after all, where they can display the bilingualism of which they are so proud.

The bilingual practices of these students are a profound shock to newly arrived monolingual francophone students, as well as to immigrant students from former colonial areas who are used to accepting, uncritically, the use of French as the dominant language of communication. These students either keep themselves on the margins of school life, or contest the bilingual practices of the 'popular' students. The students from former colonial countries are best placed to be heard, because they share the school's linguistic norms both with respect to language choice and with respect to 'the quality of the language'. Students who are bilingual speakers of English and the French Canadian vernacular are also marginalized, since they speak a stigmatized version of French.

The different practices and perspectives of these groups are played out in the public arena in a number of different ways. Chapter 4 details the discursive struggles for control of public space, in which speakers of the vernacular are marginalized (and then marginalize themselves), and the other groups promote two competing visions of the school and its population: a vision of French Ontario as fundamentally bilingual, and anchored in local realities as a springboard from which they can gain access to global success; and a vision of the school as one small piece of a broadly defined, pluralistic *francophonie internationale*. Here the crucial elements include ethnic and racial inclusiveness, and the valuing of bilingualism as parallel monolingualisms (in the way the school does), as opposed to the accordance of value to bilingual practices which mark the identity and privileged position of bilingual students.

Chapter 5 demonstrates the ways in which these discursive positionings and struggles are profoundly gendered. For the most part, males control the construction of these discourses and discursive struggles. In addition, these discourses contain elements which are fundamentally about the reproduction of gender stereotypes, which, of course, permits the males to continue to dominate public discursive space. One small group of marginalized girls contests this state of affairs; while they are not able to achieve anything in the way of a transformation, they are able to achieve academic success, and therefore to show that it is possible to achieve what all students are after without engaging in the prevailing discourse on gender. At the same time, their acceptance of their marginalization forces them to deal on their own not only with academic success, but with their feelings about what it might mean to be French. They can only gain access to what the school has to offer in the way of such linguistic capital by virtue of getting a high-school diploma there; they cannot engage actively in debates over what the school might mean.

Chapter 6 documents more closely the development of the major visions of the school laid out in Chapter 4. Over the course of the research period, the 'multiculturals' and the African students began to develop an increasingly coherent alternative vision of the school, and began to understand their common interests. They were able to do this in part because of discursive spaces opened up for them by educational policies of racial and ethnocultural inclusiveness prevalent across North America. They began to develop a discourse of inclusiveness, which specifically aimed at taking over the legitimacy of the bilingual group, since it included them too. In the last student council election we witnessed before leaving the school, this platform put into power a group of heretofore marginalized 'multicultural' students, defeating a slate of candidates from the 'popular' group.

Chapter 7 takes a step back from the details of the story of Champlain to consider what this tells us about the politics of identity among linguistic minorities today, as well as what we might learn about the role of schooling in these processes. The nature of the politics of identity over the past thirty years, with its focus on ethnocultural solidarity above all else, has served to obscure both gender inequalities in the mobilization process, and emerging class inequalities as mobilization begins to achieve some of its goals. Schools, as a key site of mobilization, have helped this process along by adopting ideological positions in keeping with the goals of the mobilizing élite, and by serving as grounds for the development of discursive strategies which help to mask the contradictions inherent in the particular type of politics of identity we are witnessing.

On the other hand, the very conditions which gave rise to linguistic nationalism among minorities are shifting. Minorities are now in a good position to market their linguistic capital; but they continue to try to do so on an increasingly outmoded basis of ethnic authenticity. At Champlain we shall examine some ways in which the student body has helped move the school away from a politics of blood towards a politics of capital. This ought to provoke a crisis of legitimacy; in some ways this crisis is averted by the discursive strategies adopted by staff and students and which serve to neutralize the contradictions which might trigger such a crisis. It may also be averted by the slow development of an alternative vision of *la francophonie*, one which places an emphasis (a) on the value and quality of the resources that the school, as an agent of the community, produces and distributes, and (b) on its role in helping to position community members advantageously in the new internationalizing political and economic order. What we have not yet seen is whether that new vision will take hold, or whether those who are marginalized by these shifts will accept what is happening to them.

2 'L'Unité dans la diversité'

1 Introduction[1]

L'École Champlain has a variety of symbols, all revealing facets of its evolving identity. One of them is its name, one its mascot, and one its motto. When the school was founded in 1969, the new principal undertook to search for a name. It was his idea to call the school Champlain, after the 17th-century French explorer and colonizer who played such a large role in the establishment of a francophone presence in North America. The name seemed to him to reflect the school's situation and calling, since Champlain was a *voyageur* and explorer, a pioneer open to discovering the world and interested in building something new, like those who had fought for and would help build the new school. Champlain also represented the French contribution to the development of Ontario, a role the founders intended the school to continue to play, and one that legitimized its existence; naming the school after Champlain was a way of reminding the English-speaking authorities that francophones had a long and important history in the province too. Finally, Champlain is a figure around which all members of the francophone community could unite, no matter what their religious or ethnocultural background, since he represents values (and a history) which could be seen as general to the francophone world, belonging as

---

[1] This section and the next draw heavily from Haché (1976) and interviews conducted in November 1996 with four people who were closely involved with the establishment and early years of l'École Champlain. For reasons of confidentiality, they remain anonymous here.

he did to that era of French colonialist expansion which created the linguistic ties uniting the modern-day francophones of Toronto.

About a year after the school was founded, this same former principal recounts, several students got together with one of their teachers to choose a school mascot. While these particular students were not themselves of francophone origin, they were fed up with being called frogs outside the school. This frustration led them to choose precisely that symbol as the school mascot. As a surprise for the principal, they unveiled the mascot at a school assembly, at which the student body collectively swore allegiance to the frog, whom they promptly named after the principal himself. Despite the disapproval of some community members, who saw nothing funny in this attempt at appropriation of what still seemed to them to be a fundamentally negative symbol, the mascot stuck. For a while, the school ran a lunch-time radio show, called *Radio Frog*. Today, members of school sports teams still run around the gym in shorts bearing a smiling green frog logo. The image was even taken up by some other francophone organizations, both local and provincial.

The third significant symbol of Champlain is its motto: '*L'Unité dans la diversité*' (Unity in diversity). Champlain students are united, but the framers of the motto understand them (or want them) to recognize diversity in two ways. First, francophones are meant to unite not only to fight oppression, but also to take their place as one element of a plural society. Their goal is supposed to be to get the majority to recognize their right to '*vivre notre différence*' (to live our difference), and to then constitute one important and productive element of a pluralist society.

Second, the motto indicates that francophones should recognize that their unity is only one aspect of the reality of their lives. Their common cause serves to unite an otherwise disparate group. The francophones of Toronto wanted to make clear that they saw themselves as part of an international, world-wide francophone community, some of whose diversity was already manifesting itself within the school's clientele, as immigration processes brought francophones from around the world to Toronto.

This motto encapsulates the struggle of Champlain, of the francophone minority population in Canada in general, and indeed of many Western minorities, to strike a balance between unity and diversity, between the construction of homogeneity and the vision of pluralism. People involved in the early days of Champlain focused even then on different dimensions of the relationship between unity and diversity; for example, one says now that the purpose was to show the desire of Franco-Ontarians to take their place in the Canadian mosaic, while at the same time '*on voulait que l'école reflète l'universalité de la civilisation française*' (we wanted the school to reflect the universality of French civilization). Another founder says that for him it represents the diversity of the student body and its openness to the rest of the world. The tensions were thus there from the beginning.

These three symbols also encapsulate the paradoxes at the heart of the minority condition: using the logic of the monolingual, monocultural nation-state, mobilized minorities seek to break apart the monolithic identity of the state within which they search for a legitimate place. However, in order to do so, they must construct a fictive unity, which effectively produces internally structures of hegemony similar to those against which they struggle.

In the rest of this chapter, I shall describe the ways in which l'École Champlain has lived these paradoxes, as a way of setting the scene for a closer analysis of its institutional practices and of the ways in which students collaborate with or contest them. In the next section, I shall describe the political significance of Champlain, as one of the first publicly funded French-language high schools in Ontario. Here, I shall focus on the investment in a unity based on language that was a key dimension of the logic of mobilization in the 1960s, the years when Champlain was fought for, and eventually won. I shall also examine the ways in which the movement of national autonomy translated into the construction of a monolingual French-language school.

In the subsequent sections, I shall discuss some of the ways in which Champlain, as an example of the experiences of French-Canadian society, has experienced the consequences of francophone mobilization. The key issue here is the confrontation of unity and diversity, as mobilization and globalization have led to increased social and cultural differentiation, as well as to the need for those who are newly powerful to come to grips with the fictiveness of the unity which legitimizes their power. It is in the centre of these paradoxes that Champlain now finds itself, and, as we shall see in Part II, the ways in which those who participate in school life navigate their way through them will help us to understand how minorities everywhere find new ways of achieving equality and justice, new ways of organizing power, and new ways of understanding who they are in an increasingly complex world.

2 1968: Schooling and minority language rights

The year 1968 stands as a potent symbol in most of the West, a symbol of a moment in history when the idea of democracy seemed to take on a new significance, a moment when the mundane became fraught with political significance, a moment when no one could remain indifferent to the struggle for rights and for representation on the part of the marginal, the different, the oppressed. The most dramatic experiences of the 1960s in Canada revolved around the issue of francophone rights; while little happened that is remembered in the pages of international retrospectives (we see pictures of Chicago and Paris, not Montreal or Toronto), events of the 1960s were a turning point in francophone nationalist mobilization, and have marked political processes in Canada ever since.

After the British conquest of New France in 1759, francophone resistance to British authority took the form of a spiritual, messianic nationalism, in which language, 'race', and the Catholic religion were intimately related (Choquette 1987). Despite the very different visions of some members of the francophone élite (Martel 1997), and some moments of organized resistance (such as the Métis rebellion of the late 1800s), for most of the nineteenth century and much of the twentieth, francophone life was oriented principally towards the reproduction of a society on the margins of power. The 1960s saw the development in francophone Canada of a new nationalist ideology, one that turned away from spiritual messianism and took on, instead, the goal of gaining control of state apparatuses of power in order to create the conditions necessary to facilitate francophone access to the modern world – that is, full participation, as francophones, in the prevailing structures of economic, social and political power. This new ideology centred on constructing Quebec as a nation-state in which French would be the dominant language (and indeed, since 1974, French is the only official language in Quebec).

In order to counter Québécois state nationalism, the federal and other provincial governments attempted to show that a Québécois nation was not essential to the preservation of the French language and culture in Canada. In part, this attempt involved granting francophones in their provinces rights for which they had long struggled and which they had long been denied. Francophones outside Quebec thus had much to be grateful to Quebec for, and saw it as in their interests to support nationalism in Quebec (despite the obvious contradiction of supporting a movement which is strengthened by your own weakness).

In addition, the new perspective adopted by Quebec had the effect of shattering the old French-Canadian nation. If Quebec was now Quebec, what was to become of French Canada? While in many ways there has yet to emerge a consensus on what the answer to that question might be (see Juteau-Lee 1980; Grisé 1995), it is certain that one initial move involved the importation of Quebec's strategy into minority areas of other provinces. In Ontario, as elsewhere in Canada, mobilized francophones transformed Quebec's territorial nationalism into a form of institutional nationalism; it may not be possible to establish monolingual territories in areas where francophones constitute a geographically dispersed minority, but it is possible under such conditions to establish institutions run by and for francophones, in French. It is also possible to think of the population involved in those institutions, in that social (not geographical) space, in terms of the state; and so the term 'Franco-Ontarian' spread.

Education had long been the focus of struggle for francophone rights in Ontario, largely because it represented the major institution of social and cultural reproduction over which the (English-dominated) state exerted a concerted effort to gain control (see Welch 1988; Heller 1994a). It is therefore not surprising that the centre of the struggle of the 1960s was the establishment of state-funded French-language schools.

The history of francophone struggles for French-language education in Ontario is long and complicated, but I shall try to summarize the essential elements here (see Haché 1976; Sylvestre 1980; Choquette 1977, 1987; Welch 1988; or Heller 1994a for greater detail). First, it must be noted that the education of francophones was largely controlled by the Catholic Church, and this system persisted even after the state took over control of education for the province because of the peculiarities of the Canadian constitution. This constitution, initially elaborated in 1867, guarantees the rights of Catholics to education according to the dictates of their religion. (This right is enshrined in large part due to the efforts of the French-speaking population, who responded to their élite's call for mobilization, focusing on religion as the most important element of their identity; Labrie, personal communication.) Since education in Canada is under provincial, not federal, jurisdiction, each province has developed its own system for respecting this constitutional proviso. Ontario set up two parallel school systems; in most areas of the province there is a Protestant-inspired (but by now in fact non-denominational) 'public' system, and a parallel Catholic 'separate' system. (There are, of course, anomalies, such as cases where the separate system is Protestant, or where *de facto* Catholic schools found themselves in public school boards.) French-language education was almost entirely within the separate system.

In the course of the twentieth century, two problems arose with respect to this state of affairs, both of which are germane to the story of Champlain. The first has to do with the funding of the separate system. Initially, secondary education ended at Grade 10 (students are now usually about 15 years old in that grade). Eventually, the high school system was extended to Grade 13. However, the Protestant-dominated provincial government did not wish to supply additional funds for Catholic education. As a result, it became possible to attend public high schools free of charge to Grade 13, while state funding for separate schools remained frozen at Grade 10. Catholics who wished to pursue their education had either to transfer to public schools (all English) or to pay fees for private Church-run education (available either in English or in French).

The second problem had to do with the language of instruction. Provincial policy over the course of the nineteenth century wavered over the best way to handle French-language instruction; sometimes it was tolerated, sometimes attempts were made to suppress it, but in either case the strategy was principally aimed at facilitating francophone assimilation into English-speaking Ontario society. In 1912 an attempt was made to eliminate French-language schools through a regulation which, while not banning French outright as a language of instruction, made it next to impossible to run a French-language school. The regulation was suspended in 1927, although it was not officially repealed until 1944.

In the 1960s, the French-language school system in Ontario consisted for the most part of elementary separate (Catholic) schools, with some high school programmes of which the first two years only were covered by state funding, with the remaining run as private education. The result was that many francophones never completed their high school education, and others were assimilated to English through the English-language educational system.

As a result of nationalist mobilization in Quebec, and the consequent collective debate over the future of Canada which crystallized around Canada's centennial in 1967, the Ontario government began to look for ways to counter the Quebec nationalist movement by increasing francophone rights within its jurisdiction. Haché (1976) points out that John Robarts, then premier of Ontario, explicitly linked these efforts on the part of his government to the goal of preserving Canadian national unity, although one can assume that there were reasons other than the purely sentimental for wishing to do so. While other provinces engaged in similar debates, the issue was felt most acutely in Ontario and in New Brunswick, the two provinces bordering Quebec and including the major proportion of francophones outside Quebec. In addition, these two provinces may have had the most to lose from federal fragmentation, for both political and economic reasons.

Francophones in Ontario had also been influenced by the nationalist awakening in Quebec, and were mobilizing again to fight for their rights; the major issue on their agenda was the establishment of French-language high schools financed by the state through to the end of Grade 13. While the government of Ontario was clearly interested in extending this right, it encountered the obstacle of religion. Since most francophones in Ontario were Catholics, and their children mainly enrolled in the Catholic school system, it would have been logical, from a francophone perspective, to keep their high schools within that system. However, the government could not extend this funding for francophones without doing the same for English-speaking Catholics, of whom there were (and are) many, and this it was still very reluctant to do. The only way around this problem would be to fund French-language high schools through all five years, as long as the schools were in the public (non-denominational) system.

This situation left both the Catholic Church and the francophones of Ontario with a dilemma. While the Church had long defended the rights of francophones, it was difficult to give precedence to language over religion. Indeed, members of the Catholic clergy did not always agree on what position to take, although there did develop a broad consensus among francophone clergy across the province that public French-language high schools should be supported. At the same time, the modernization movement had already weakened the ties many francophones had with their Church, and language had come to the fore as the principal symbol of identity and belonging. Faced with a choice, most francophones preferred to have access to schools as good as those available to anglophones within the public system, than to continue with the situation in which they currently found themselves.

In 1968, the Robarts government finally passed a law permitting the establishment of public secondary schools which would use French as the (or a) language of instruction. This decision was to influence the development of the Franco-Ontarian community in many ways. It certainly contributed to redefining the institutional tie between the Catholic Church and the Franco-Ontarian community. It also provided a basis for gaining educational credentials which would place Franco-Ontarians in a better position to achieve their goals, as well as an institutional power base from which Franco-Ontarians could redefine their position in Ontarian, Canadian and international society. In these respects, 1968 marks a moment of great significance for Franco-Ontarians, as bureaucratic and boring as that moment may appear to be at first sight.

The passage of the law, of course, did not solve all problems. Individual school boards had to be convinced to open new schools made possible by the legislation. In some communities, there were bitter battles over the refusal of the anglophone-dominated board to comply with the requests of francophone parents. There were often also disputes within the francophone community over whether the schools should be English–French bilingual, or French monolingual institutions. Working-class francophones tended to favour the creation of bilingual schools in the belief (or hope) that this would give their children the kinds of skills in standard English that they would need for future success and social mobility. Middle-class parents wished to maintain their class standing through the maintenance of bilingualism, but since they usually already had access to English in the workplace, their concern was the creation of places where French could be preserved and developed. Monolingual schools were consistent with the logic of institutional territorialism, and with an ideology of bilingualism as parallel monolingualisms. The idea of monolingual schools also meshed well with the long-standing French-Canadian ideology of *la surviv-ance* (survival), shared by middle class and working class alike. The middle class therefore argued that French language and culture could not survive without the creation of monolingual zones – preserves where French, and French alone, would be practised. The most important of these preserves were schools. In the end, it was this middle-class viewpoint that won the day. Across the province, with the assent of local francophone clergy, *collèges classiques* closed. They were replaced by public system, French-language secondary schools.

Toronto experienced at least as great a struggle with anglophone authorities (including those of the Catholic Church hierarchy) as elsewhere, although its class-based struggles seem to have been attenuated. In the mid-1960s, as in other localities, in Toronto there already existed state-funded Catholic French-language elementary schools. There was also one Catholic high school, École Sainte-Marie, which had been founded by a religious order based in Quebec earlier in the decade as a school for girls; while eventually boys were also admitted, in 1968 there were still more girls than boys in the school. According to a member of Champlain's staff who had studied at that school in the 1960s, on the whole, Toronto's francophone families were more likely to send their daughters to a French-language school, and their sons to an English-language school or out to work. This was due to the way in which the gender division of labour intersected with the nature of Toronto's job market: girls were expected to act as the guardians of the language and the culture of their community through their responsibility for the socialization of children; boys were expected to get the technical and linguistic skills necessary for them to compete in Toronto's English-dominated job market. However, Sainte-Marie was having financial difficulties; not enough parents could, or chose to, pay the fees necessary for the completion of high school (perhaps considered unnecessary for girls in some cases). In 1967, the enrolment was only slightly over 100 students.

In 1967 the organized local francophone élite decided to undertake the project of getting a local public school board to agree to open a French-language public high school. These were people who occupied powerful positions in private enterprise, in unions, in professions and in the media, mainly in workplaces where the daily language of communication was English. They thus had a major interest in developing an institutional base for the kind of bilingualism that was becoming valuable at that time. They were also able to exploit their professional positions in a variety of ways in order to gain support for their cause, since through those positions they had access to important resources (whether time, connections, publicity or material resources).

The newly organized committee struck to lobby for the establishment of a French-language high school was strong in some ways. Its members were professionals with access to resources and with knowledge of how to exploit them. They were also able to capitalize on the prevailing climate, and preparations for the Robarts government legislation. However, they had to fight some disadvantages. For example, they were largely marginal to the major Franco-Ontarian power structures, and thus had to work largely alone. The francophone population was dispersed and heterogeneous. In addition, in the end, the legislation only made it possible in low francophone density areas like Toronto for a local public board to open a school, rather than mandating such a gesture as necessary. Local political and educational institutions were completely dominated by anglophones, who for the most part were either staunchly assimilationist or more concerned about anglophone access to French than about francophone minority concerns.

The local Church hierarchy was also dominated by anglophones, who were not supportive of an attempt to abandon Catholic institutions; they would have preferred to use the case to fight for extension of state funding in Catholic high schools to Grade 13. The small group of activists seeking to mobilize support for a public French-language high school felt strongly that extended funding of the Catholic system was unlikely to happen in the near future, and were unprepared to sacrifice their desire for a high school for the Church's goals. On the other hand, the local francophone clergy, including the school's principal, were prepared to support the group's efforts, despite having to do so in secrecy for some time.

Since the lobby group knew that the issue of monolingual versus bilingual education was already stirring emotions elsewhere in the province, they took steps to confront the question directly as they engaged in the process of mobilizing the population. One of those directly involved now says that the issue never came to the fore in Toronto as it did elsewhere precisely because the lobbyists were able to anticipate the arguments for bilingual education and to provide persuasive arguments for their point of view. It may also be possible that the relative weight of the middle class in Toronto may have been greater, thus enabling it to establish its goals and gain support for them with relatively greater ease than in areas with larger proportions of working-class families. Another contributing factor may have been that most Toronto francophones did in fact work in English, thus removing the concerns about access to English that may have prevailed in other, more francophone, regions.

The local committee then quickly established that it wanted a monolingual public school, in the most innovative board in the area, and it wanted a school which would draw from the region beyond the traditional board boundaries, in order both to serve the area's francophones, and to develop a large enough student base to be able to provide precisely the range of programmes that made public schools so interesting to local francophones in the first place. For 18 months, from January 1967 to September 1969, this group waged a constant campaign for the establishment of Champlain. Starting from its local organizational power base (such as a local francophone lobbying association, parishes, Parent–Teacher Associations, social clubs, benevolent societies), the committee established allies among the anglophones in the educational sector and francophones in the ecclesiastical sector, fought reluctant anglophone-dominated educational structures, and mobilized community support to increase the pressure on the school board.

In the event, the Toronto public board which had been the target of mobilized efforts finally agreed to establish the school in an area chosen because of its relative ease of access from all parts of the city and surrounding suburbs. Sainte-Marie closed, despite initial attempts on the part of the Catholic board to keep it open. Some of those involved at the time say that they felt that during that period the board, once its initial resistance was overcome, '*nous a permis de rêver*' (allowed us to dream). Although the school started life in September 1969 in portables (temporary outdoor classroom structures), within a few years a new, modern building was built, designed to reflect the openness of the school and its close ties to the community. In its programmes, the school attempted to reflect its cause by including within the curriculum mandated by the provincial Ministry of Education such material as French-Canadian literature and history. It had a large budget for building the library. While some of the staff members from the Catholic school (including several nuns) were hired to teach in the new school, it was still necessary to recruit staff from elsewhere. Toronto was not such an attractive destination for people from northern Ontario, who saw it as too anglophone, but teachers from Quebec and Europe tended to see it as an interesting, dynamic place. Certainly the province was rich at the time, compared to other parts of Canada or other parts of the world, and could provide resources to educators at levels they rarely saw elsewhere.

The school's origins thus place it squarely in the tradition of Franco-Ontarian struggle for rights and recognition. For many years the only French-language high school in the Toronto area, Champlain was and remains a symbol of the right of francophones to live their difference, in the province's capital and in Canada's major English-speaking city. At the same time, it is important to recognize the specific characteristics of the Toronto situation, with such a large proportion of the francophone population from elsewhere than Toronto itself, and a disproportionate representation of educated and prosperous members of the middle class. Champlain was thus born in conditions which represent an extreme case of the tensions that have come to characterize linguistic minority education elsewhere since then, in the form of tensions between both the minority and the majority with which it is in contact, and among members of the minority itself, along the lines of class, gender and race or ethnocultural origin.

When Champlain opened its doors in 1969, it was clearly a minority institution, physically located in the backyard of a major English-language high school, and the only French-language school in its board. Over the years, the conditions of its existence changed, however, as Franco-Ontarians built on the successes of early mobilization to fight for ever-increasing autonomy in the control of their educational institutions. At the same time, it is important to emphasize that mobilization occurred within state bureaucratic, political and legal processes. The kind of autonomy Franco-Ontarians sought was thus not a kind of alternative world, but rather the establishment of structures parallel to mainstream anglophone structures, broadly subject to the same kinds of constraint and value, while restricted in terms of participation in decision-making and free to a certain extent to adapt guidelines and constraints to the perceived needs of francophones.

The history of Franco-Ontarian mobilization from 1968 to the present is thus essentially a history of lobbying and legal action aimed at the establishment within the state-funded education system of institutions run by and for francophones, in French, but subject to the fundamental conditions of education in effect across the province. The state was thus the principal interlocutor for mobilized francophones, and the discourse of militants focused on acquiring schooling at least as good as that provided to anglophones, from pre-school to university. The point was not to opt out, or to be radically different; the point was to be allowed a slightly different path to the same goals.

Slowly over the course of the 1970s and 1980s the francophone educational system grew, often at the expense of painful and costly struggles (see Sylvestre 1980; Welch 1988; Heller 1994a). These struggles were by and large versions of the struggles of the 1960s, that is, struggles for the expansion of the French-language educational system at all levels, struggles for the establishment of institutions in areas which still did not have them, and struggles for increasing autonomous control over those institutions. By the mid-1980s, Champlain was part of a growing network of French-language minority educational institutions in the Toronto area, with legal guarantees accompanying the recognition of French as an official language of education in Ontario. The local Toronto French-language educational network included daycare centres, Catholic and public elementary and secondary schools run by three different boards of education, and a bilingual undergraduate university college.

In 1982, the Canadian government brought the national constitution, heretofore considered an act of the British parliament, back to Canada from London, thereby making implementation and changes the sole responsibility of the Canadian, rather than the British, parliament. The move opened the door to renegotiation of some of the most fundamental terms of existence of the Canadian state, and this has been the focus of struggles between Quebec, the other provinces and the federal government ever since. Central to these concerns is the status of Quebec within Canada, and related to that matter, the status of linguistic minorities across the country. One attempt to address this issue was the inclusion of

an article in the new Canadian Charter of Rights and Freedoms
defining parental rights of access to minority-language education
(English-language schools in Quebec, French-language schools elsewhere), which had as a principal aim to protect the rights of English
speakers to access to English-language education in Quebec, rights
felt to be threatened by Quebec's language legislation (Labrie, personal communication). Whatever its main goals, this article provided a legal basis for efforts in francophone communities outside
Quebec to continue their own battles. In 1986, legal action was
brought against the governments of Alberta and Ontario, arguing,
on the basis of this article, that francophones were not being
allowed a sufficient degree of control over their own institutions.
The decisions in those cases were favourable to the francophone
cause. One immediate result for Champlain was the establishment
of an autonomous French-language public school board, which,
as of 1989, brought together the elementary and secondary public
schools of Toronto, including Champlain, which had hitherto fallen
under the jurisdiction of two different anglophone-majority boards
of education (the Catholic French-language schools declined to
join the new structure, although there have been efforts at cross-
board collaboration). Champlain is now no longer the only French-
language high school in its board. In addition, Ontario passed
separate legislation in 1984, providing funding of all grade levels
in Catholic high schools. As a direct result of this legislation, three
new Catholic French-language high schools opened in the late
1980s and early 1990s in Toronto and surrounding suburbs. One
of these schools was presented as the re-opening of Sainte-Marie,
the first Catholic French-language high school in the city, and the
one that Champlain had effectively replaced in 1969. Champlain
lost clientèle as a result; from a high of over six hundred students,
it now has fewer than four hundred, including junior high school
students who were moved to Champlain from a nearby elementary school in the early 1980s. However, while it is in many ways
embattled, Champlain still stands as a symbol of everything Franco-
Ontarians have fought for over the years: the right to enter the
modern world as francophones, to have high schools just as bright,
and clean, and well-equipped as the anglophones, to have a direct
say over what goes on in those schools, and to have access to all
the resources the State puts at the disposal of its educational system.
As such, Champlain also embodies one of the central paradoxes

of francophone mobilization in Canada, that is, that the goal of mobilization is, somehow, to be the same and yet simultaneously different.

In many ways, Champlain also stands as a monument to the logic of that mobilization. The institutional nationalist strategy adopted by minority francophones entailed a commitment to a monolingual institution, that is, to the exclusive use of French as the language of instruction (with the obvious exception of classes where English was taught as a subject). The legitimacy of Champlain rests on the notion that one reason that francophones suffered from their minority status was because they had no place to be themselves, no paths to social and economic mobility or to political power in which they could use their language and act in a way in which they felt comfortable. A school like Champlain is meant to provide francophones with a place to be themselves, and to use what they know in order to be successful in the modern, wider world.

Champlain thus set itself two tasks from the very beginning: to provide a safe haven for Franco-Ontarians, and to prepare them to confront the wider, diverse, and English-dominated world successfully on its own terms. Champlain provides a place to maintain unity in order to allow francophones to take their place in a diverse world (and will do so principally by creating a monolingual francophone zone where curriculum content, including the language of instruction, reflects universally recognized standards of excellence). It is this dimension that predominated in the school's early years, when energies were focused on solidarity in the struggle for rights to be won from the dominant, English-speaking majority. At the same time, Champlain is also there to build unity out of the diverse elements that make up the francophone community. Of course, this aspect of Champlain's reality was present even at the beginning, since the conditions of its birth entailed a reassessment of what it meant to be francophone, and the necessity to face the issues of inclusion and exclusion, to decide what kinds of students would be welcome in the school, what kinds of teacher to recruit, how to involve parents, and on what basis. Nonetheless, once Champlain became established, the struggle with external bodies became less intense, and the very success of mobilization led to major shifts in the student body in the direction of diversification, leading to new struggles over how to define the nature of the school and its clientèle. It was more or less inevitable that this aspect of the paradoxes of minority education, over the years, should come to the fore in the life of Champlain.

3   The consequences of mobilization

Haché (1976) cites a variety of memos exchanged between school board authorities and the francophone lobby group in the period 1967–69; in almost all of them, the potential client population is referred to as 'Franco-Ontarian'. One can read this usage as a reflection of a consensus on the strategy of institutional territorialism, calqued on the state territorialism of Quebec, and, like Quebec, focusing on the state apparatus at the province level as the major mechanism for the extension of rights and resources.

In 1991, I asked Johanne, a school board trustee, how she came to decide to run for the position. She said:

(...) et là j'ai je suis simplement d'abord c'est la communauté qui m'a demandé de me présenter, pour qu'i ait représentativité euh de euh (pause) de ce que moi je suis, ou ce que je représente, alors euh que ce soit qu'on les mette comme franco-ontarienne, ou comme euh canadienne au Canada, ou francophone canadienne ou, alors (...)

(...) *and so I did I was simply first it was the community who asked me to run, so there would be representativity uh of uh (pause) of what I am, or what I represent, so uh whether you categorize them as Franco-Ontarian, or as uh Canadian in Canada, or francophone Canadian or, so (...)*

Johanne's problem is typical. The consensus underlying unified labels has dissolved, attacked from the outside as exclusionary and from the inside as limiting. The evolution, or multiplication, or fragmentation of labels reveals ways in which the tensions inherent in the conditions of Champlain's origins evolved over the years, in concert with social processes connected to the relative success of francophone political mobilization in the 1960s and early 1970s. The relative success of mobilization entailed an increasing social diversification of the francophone population of Toronto, in terms of class, ethnocultural origin and sociolinguistic repertoire. The result has been that the unified image of the Franco-Ontarian school has given way to struggles over the nature of the school, and over whose interests it is meant to serve. Those who once thought of themselves unproblematically as Franco-Ontarians have had to reassess what that means for themselves and for others involved in their institutions. These processes are at the heart of Champlain's development over the first twenty years of its existence, and help explain the centrality and specific characteristics of the politics of identity it lived through in the period of the early 1990s, when our research was conducted.

Class divisions were already growing in the 1960s, and continued to do so, especially as Toronto attracted more and more private sector head offices through the 1970s, especially from Montreal. It is hard to disentangle the economic and political reasons for this shift. Clift and Arnopoulos (1979) argue that Quebec nationalism can be seen as an organized attempt by middle-class, well-educated francophones to take over the private sector within Quebec, a move made possible, or at least plausible, by the existing shift westward of Canadian capital. This existing shift, in turn, they claim, can be explained by the relatively greater post-Second World War growth of industrial infrastructure in southern Ontario (itself the product of a combination of economic geography and politics), as opposed to that in Quebec, and by some astute decisions on the part of Toronto's financial élite which allowed it to out-distance its Montreal counterpart in some key domains. These conditions, Clift and Arnopoulos claim, created a vacuum at the management level of the private sector in Quebec, which indeed newly trained francophones were uniquely equipped to fill, given the continued importance of the largely monolingual francophone market in that province. At the same time, while it became possible for francophones to accede to management positions in Quebec, it also became necessary for many of them to spend time in Toronto, either on temporary assignment, or in order to work in their desired fields, since more and more of the kinds of job to which they aspired moved out of Quebec and into Ontario, or more of them were simply created in Ontario, and in particular in Toronto. It is also likely that developing francophone nationalism in Quebec subsequently contributed to the steady flow of head offices out of Montreal and into Toronto from the late 1970s onwards.

In addition, successful mobilization led to the passage of legislation, both at the federal and at the provincial level, guaranteeing government services in French (federal legislation was first passed in 1968, while Ontario's was passed in 1986). This led to the creation of public sector jobs at both levels for which French–English bilingualism was vital. Finally, this growth of the francophone economic sector also spun off a linguistic service industry (mainly translation, but also production of teaching, promotional and other types of material), and other services for the increasing numbers of francophones working in these various kinds of job (notably education for their children, media and entertainment).

It is principally this new middle class which, as we have seen, led the struggle for the establishment of Champlain as a free-standing monolingual French school, on the basis of solidarity with the longer-established working-class (Maxwell 1977), with whom they shared a long history (and indeed, from which many of them may have come). It is this group that Johanne represents; it has remained centrally involved in the school and in other community issues over the years. While working-class parents continue to send their children to Champlain (although many of them now remain in the suburbs where they live, and where new Catholic French-language high schools have opened), they are less involved in leadership positions themselves.

Class positions with respect to Franco-Ontarian education tend to differ in important ways. Middle-class parents tend to focus on the preparation of their children for university studies and professional careers, in which domains they assume that bilingualism (as parallel monolingualisms) will be valued, whether their children study in French or in English at the university level. They also are concerned to maintain French-language schools as part of the institutional power base many of them have actively sought to establish for the francophone community. Working-class parents are more concerned about the exigencies of the job market, which, in the Toronto area, is dominated by English. Their tie to French has more to do with family identity than with the social, political and economic interests of the middle class.

In keeping with these different orientations, middle-class families tend to be preoccupied with acquiring the kind of French that will be valued in the global marketplace, although they recognize the authenticity and solidarity value of the French-Canadian vernacular. Their compromise tends to lie along the lines of the development of a standard Canadian French (typically called *le français international*) which differs only slightly from European French (mainly in phonology and intonation, somewhat also in vocabulary), and which can be salted with flagged (but authenticating) uses of English or of vernacular forms, which everyone understands, but few people want to be seen as responsible for using. The working class tends to master mainly the vernacular, which is important for solidarity, but about which they are also very insecure: they have internalized the élite's stigmatization of their linguistic forms and practices. The main area of concern has to do with uses of French which bear traces of contact with English, whether in the form of codeswitching (and certainly many working-class people will say outright that they speak *bilingue*) or other phenomena like calques or loanwords, although certain phonological features (notably vowel diphthongization), morpho-syntactic features (like verb paradigm regularization), discourse features (notably the use of *là* as a discourse marker) and lexico-syntactic ones (the choice of certain relativizers over others) are also marked. The major class issues then have to do with differing ways of practising bilingualism (as parallel monolingualisms, or as mixed registers) and different positions with respect to what counts as good French, which the middle class defines in normative and relatively purist terms, and which the working class does not speak.

In addition to the increasing class differentiation, successful mobilization has brought ethnocultural diversity to schools like Champlain. One of the signs of the success of francophone mobilization has been the development of an interest in learning French on the part of assimilated francophones, who now decide they want to recapture their identity and their language, at least for their children, if not for themselves. Also, anglophones who previously wished to have little to do with French began in the 1960s to express an interest in that language. This is reflected in the French immersion programmes for which Canada is now well known, and also in the presence of anglophones in French-language schools like Champlain. The anglophones who choose French-language minority schools like Champlain over immersion programmes may do so because they feel the experience is more authentic, and therefore better, than immersion, and they may also do so out of a commitment to francophone rights (some send their children first to immersion schools, and then have them switch to Champlain; here admission is regulated by tests). French-language schools have accepted them because they needed to boost enrolment (one of the consequences of being part of the State system is that the same enrolment thresholds apply to minority and to majority schools), because of a feeling that anglophone interest in the francophone community should be welcomed, and because, frequently, anglophones have joined francophones in the struggle for their rights out of political solidarity. Legally, since the Canadian Charter of Rights and Freedoms defined rights of access to minority language schools across Canada in 1982, those who attended such a school prior to 1982 now have entrenched rights, even if they do not fit the other criteria and could be refused admission now.

Ethnocultural diversity within the school population is also the result of the relatively high rate of linguistically mixed marriages. Sometimes, this is simply the result of the conditions of adolescent and adult life in Toronto, which scarcely prevent one from encountering non-francophone potential mates. This may be especially true for young single immigrants, who find themselves alone in a city which has little in the way of a francophone community infrastructure to offer the new arrival. In the years that I have been living and working in Toronto, I have encountered countless women from Quebec or New Brunswick who all tell the same story: they came to Toronto for a year to learn English and see the world, met and fell in love with someone here, and, well, ten, twenty, thirty years later, here they still are. (I still haven't figured out where all the francophone men are.) Their children are bilingual or even trilingual from an early age, and their identity is less francophone than it is bilingual. For some students, being sent to a French-language school may represent their francophone parents' attempt to reproduce an identity they feel they are losing in the family, where frequently a spouse's inability to speak French imposes English as the language of family communication.

Mobilization has also therefore brought to schools like Champlain students whose major language of communication outside school is English. The presence of such students, whether products of mixed marriages, assimilated families, or families with no kinship ties to the francophone community understood in an ethnic sense, has been a source of problems for Franco-Ontarian education. In some sense, the problem they pose can be understood as a result of the ambiguity between the ethnic authenticity which legitimizes these schools, and the institutional and democratic discourse which the mobilization movement has adopted. As a result, the debates about the problem have carefully avoided treading on ethnic territory, but translate the problem instead into technical and linguistic terms. Thus no one would argue that specific groups should be excluded on ethnic grounds, and it is morally difficult to exclude students of francophone origin, or with one francophone parent, on the grounds of linguistic deficit. Instead, concerns have been expressed about the effect the presence of students whose first language is not French may have on the students whose first language is French, leading to debates revolving essentially around the question: Who are French-language minority schools for? As we shall see in Chapter 3, a good deal of energy has been invested both at the level of the provincial educational bureaucracy and at the level of the school in resolving the tensions which flow from the structural ambiguities inherent in the schools' ideological foundations.

A third kind of diversity has become increasingly important in recent years: ethnocultural and racial diversity stemming from a combination of mobilization success and immigration processes. The contribution of mobilization success lies, in part, simply in the establishment of schools like Champlain, and in part in the increased value attached to French–English bilingualism in Canadian society. The result is that, in Toronto, schools are now available to immigrants who are francophone or who come from countries with a tradition of French-language education. These and other immigrants concerned with success in their new country may also, like their middle-class anglophone counterparts, see attendance at a French-language minority school to be the best and most authentic path to bilingualism for their children.

The contribution of immigration processes lies in the fact that Canada depends greatly on immigration to provide sufficient labour to keep the economy going. Despite many ways in which the immigration regulations are flawed and discriminatory, Canada provides a better chance at immigration than many other industrialized countries, and has a more open policy regarding refugees. Recent changes in Canadian immigration policy have resulted in selection from a broader range of countries than before. Thus Canada has become a destination of choice for many immigrants from a wide variety of regions. Within Canada, immigrants are drawn to economically viable urban areas, of which Toronto is perhaps first on the list for those arriving from anywhere other than the Pacific

Rim (for whom Vancouver may be the most attractive destination). Some, however, go first to Quebec, which tends to favour immigrants from countries which have French as a first or second language. Since 1977, Quebec's language legislation obliges immigrants in any case to send their children to French-language schools. While many move to Toronto after a few years in Quebec, because of economic conditions, they frequently choose to continue to send their children to a French-language school.

As a result, because Champlain happens to be in Toronto, it has attracted over the years a wider and wider variety of ethnolinguistic groups, as immigration processes have shifted. Some come directly to Toronto, some come through Quebec; some have French as a first language, some as an additional language; some speak French at home, some do not; some have been educated in French already, others have not; some have knowledge of English; others do not. In addition to the various paths to Champlain described above, some of these students also arrive through French immersion, along with other English-speaking students (of course, if anything, Toronto's English-language school system is even more ethnolinguistically diverse than its French-language system).

Students with origins outside Canada come from a wide range of countries. Many are Europeans (mainly from France, but also from Belgium and Switzerland), who tend to provide a constant trickle of students over the years. Most Europeans come directly to Toronto, rather than through Quebec. Some come on temporary business assignments. Over the years, there have also been a number of immigrants from Vietnam and Lebanon during the years of war there; there is also a long (for Canada) history of immigration from other countries of the Middle East (such as Syria) and of North Africa (notably Morocco and Egypt). More recently there have been arrivals from the francophone Caribbean, especially Haiti; from Asia; from sub-Saharan Africa (notably Somalia, Djibouti, and Ethiopia, but also Zaïre, Cameroun, Burundi, South Africa, Tanzania and Kenya); and from the French territories of the Indian and Pacific Oceans. Students from many other areas are also represented in Champlain's population, including such countries as Israel, Chile, Peru, Guyana, Iran, Afghanistan, Russia, Poland, Turkey, Britain, Romania, Sweden, Italy, Hungary, China, Australia, and India. In many cases, waves of immigration correspond to economic and political crises in the countries of origin. The diversity of national origins, of course, also corresponds to religious diversity.

A member of Champlain's staff put the question of student origins like this (note Mireille's use of possessive pronouns: *our* schools, *their* children):

Mireille: (...) on a passé tous les, toutes les guerres civiles et tout le reste. Parce que tout d'abord le premier groupe c'était les Vietnamiens, et puis après ça le Moyen-Orient, les Iraniens, les Libanais, les gens de l'Afrique du Nord, il y avait à un moment donné, euh, beaucoup de gens, c'étaient pas tous des francophones, mais c'étaient des gens qui parlaient français, et espagnol, et d'autres langues, mais pas l'anglais, du Maroc, des années 70, il y avait toute une vague de Juifs (...) parce que dans l'Afrique du Nord et au Moyen-Orient, c'est une tradition depuis quelques générations que la langue de l'éducation c'est le français, ça n'a jamais été la langue du pays, la langue de la rue, c'était la langue de l'éducation, et je pense que ça va continuer, parce que on voit des fois des jeunes qui viennent d'un autre pays, ils parlent pas français à la maison, mais ils veulent inscrire *leurs* enfants dans *nos* écoles parce que l'école, c'est là où on apprend le

(...) *we've been through all the, all the civil wars and all the rest. Because at first the first group was the Vietnamese, and then after that the Middle East, the Iranians, the Lebanese, people from North Africa, at one point there were, uh, many people, they weren't all francophones, but they were people who spoke French, and Spanish, and other languages, but not English, from Morocco, in the 70s, there was a whole wave of Jews (...) because in North Africa and the Middle East, it's a tradition a few generations long that the language of education is French, it was never the language of the country, the language of the street, it was the language of education, and I think that will continue, because sometimes we see young people who come from another country, they don't speak French at home, but they want to enrol their children in our schools, because school is where you learn*

français, alors, il y aura toujours de ça. (. . .)	French, so, there will always be that. (. . .)
Monica: est-ce qu'il y a beaucoup de Québécois qui arrivent aussi?	*are there many Québécois who also arrive?*
Mireille: il y a des vagues. Ça dépend de l'économie. (. . .)	*there are waves. It depends on the economy.* (. . .)

For the story I wish to tell here, it is important to note three things. One is that the varying forms of diversity have brought sociolinguistic heterogeneity to the school, in terms of students' experience of and access to different forms of French, English and other languages, and in terms of the values they accord these linguistic forms. This makes it difficult to establish a consensus over the kinds of bilingualism, and the kinds of French, to value. Adrienne, a school board member (herself from France, but long established in Toronto), resolves the dilemma by positing a French-language education which prepares students to be part of global society ('*citoyens du monde*' – citizens of the world) through providing excellent education. Part of that education, for Adrienne, includes the inculcation of a French which, while tolerating differences, also unites francophones through a common language:

(. . .) qualité du français euh je pense que ça c'est dans notre volonté d'avoir une éducation excellente euh qu'ils s'expriment mais qu'ils s'expriment en français pas puis là je vais utiliser quelque chose qui va être peut-être interprété comme racisme, comme on disait autrefois (xx), il faut que ça soit un français normal, il faut que ça soit un français point, ce qui ne veut pas dire un français sans accent, euh y a y a le français correct qui est le français normal, mais qui peut être utilisé avec x nombre d'accents, ou même x nombre de variations de vocabulaire qui [est] aussi riche et aussi important.

(. . .) quality of French uh I think that that is in our will to have an excellent education uh that they express themselves but that they express themselves in French, not and here I'll use something which will perhaps be interpreted as racism, as we used to say (xx) in the old days, it has to be a normal French, it has to be a French full stop, which does not mean a French without accent, uh there is there is correct French which is normal French, but which can be used with x number of accents or even x number of variations of vocabulary which [is] just as rich and just as important.

However, Adrienne's hesitations and reformulations betray once again the contradictions of unity in diversity. Adrienne needs to posit some neutral, universally recognized 'correct' and 'normal' French in order to maintain the unity, but also, at some level, recognizes through her concern that charges of racism may be levelled against her, that perhaps such a thing does not exist, perhaps all varieties of French are socially located and fulfil partial, social interests. This tension is endemic to the situation of Champlain and of other linguistic minority schools, and will be taken up in greater detail in Chapter 3.

Second, much of this immigration process has involved small groups or individual families (or even individual students), arriving over a fairly drawn-out period. As a result, it was not always the case that a student would be part of a large group of the same background, who could rely on each other for social relations and social support. In many cases, one or two students would find themselves alone in a class of other individuals from different origins, ranging from other immigrants, to children of mixed-marriages, to Québécois, to Franco-Ontarians, to former immersion students, and so on. In some ways, as we shall see, the amount of time spent in Toronto, or class background, or gender, could be just as important as anything else about them, in terms of their ability to form friendships and to take part in school life.

At the same time, there have been moments when parents and students from outside Canada have challenged the prevailing ethnolinguistic ideology of the school, and made Champlain a site of struggle over access to power and control. Initially, Champlain had been the privileged terrain of those who had fought for its establishment, the group Johanne claims to represent. However, in the mid-1980s, a group of parents who had arrived more recently from such places as Lebanon, Egypt and Haiti, lobbied for greater access to decision-making bodies. They successfully mobilized support from families who were feeling marginalized, and established inclusiveness as an important principle in the culture of the school. Concretely, this group managed to elect representatives (indeed to completely take over) the advisory committee on French-language education which acted as the principal means for the francophone community to influence the English-dominated school board which governed Champlain at that time. In 1989, when Champlain became part of an autonomous French-language board, some of the same individuals were elected trustees. (In addition, this process may have had repercussions well beyond Champlain and its school board. According to some accounts, the issue may have crystallized around representation on this specific advisory board, but quickly spread to the issue of representation in a wide range of Franco-Ontarian organizations.)

The following is an account provided by Armand, one of the participants in this movement, and it is worth quoting at some length:

(. . .) il y avait une très grande bataille entre la communauté ethnique francophone et la communauté franco-ontarienne à Toronto, et ça a été une très grande bataille parce que la communauté franco-ontarienne de Toronto a toujours s'est toujours sentie mal à l'aise avec les groupes avec le concept euh des groupes ethniques francophones parce que ils ont toujours eu peur que eux, parce que eux ils sont minoritaires, un groupe minoritaire, alors ils ont eu peur qu'on les fasse eux passer pour un autre groupe minoritaire, alors ils ont toujours eu une peur bleue dès qu'on leur parle de multiculturalisme, ils disent nous n'avons pas de multiculturalisme ici, allez voir les anglophones, alors que nous-autres Francophones on venait d'ailleurs, on s'est senti rejetés (. . .) en 90 l'ACFO [l'Association canadienne-française de l'Ontario] a passé une résolution, dans cette résolution é il a été proclamé que le terme 'Franco-Ontarien' s'applique à tout francophone

(. . .) there was a very big battle between the ethnic francophone community and the Franco-Ontarian community in Toronto, and it was a very big battle because the Toronto Franco-Ontarian community always felt ill at ease with the groups with the concept uh with the ethnic francophone groups because they have always been afraid that they, because they are a minority, a minority group, so they were afraid that we would make them seem like another minerity group, so they have always been terribly afraid, as soon as you talk to them about multiculturalism, they say we have no multiculturalism here, go see the anglophones, so us francophones we came from elsewhere, we felt rejected (. . .) in 1990 the ACFO [Association canadienne française de l'Ontario] passed a resolution, in this resolution w it was proclaimed that the term 'Franco-Ontarian' would apply to any francophone living in Ontario. But before that resolution, the term

qui vit en Ontario. Mais avant cette résolution, le terme 'franco-ontarien' ne s'appliquait qu'aux autres Franco-Ontariens de souche 'pure laine', et alors il y a eu toute une bataille autour de ceci, et nous n'avons pas été acceptés à bras ouverts. (. . .) nous sommes des francophones venus d'ailleurs, mais nous nous sommes toujours dits que nous étions des Franco-Ontariens, nous étions des Franco-Ontariens de choix, nous avons fait le choix de vivre en français en Ontario, nous avons fait le choix d'envoyer nos enfants dans les écoles françaises, nous avons fait le choix de ne pas intégrer à la communauté anglophone, nous avons préféré nous battre pour nous faire accepter par la communauté franco-ontarienne (. . .) parce que nous on a apporté ici eh avec nous un bagage culturel francophone, un héritage francophone et qu'on voulait garder ce bagage culturel, on voulait pas le perdre, on voulait pas être assimilés, comme ça arrive à beaucoup de Franco-Ontariens (. . .) (. . .) Moi je me suis fait un peu, je me suis fait é é je me suis fait é élire, puis j'ai participé à l'élection parce que je pensais plus le groupe de Franco-Ontariens de l'époque traitait les institutions publiques comme un domaine privé, c'est ce qu'on avait appelé la privatisation du

'Franco-Ontarian' only applied to the other Franco-Ontarians of origin 'pure wool', and so there was a whole battle about that, and we weren't accepted with open arms.

(. . .) we are francophones from elsewhere, but we always told ourselves that we were Franco-Ontarians, we were Franco-Ontarians by choice, we made the choice to live in French in Ontario, we made the choice to send our children to the French schools, we made the choice not to integrate into the anglophone community, we preferred to fight to be accepted by the Franco-Ontarian community (. . .) because we brought here uh with us francophone cultural baggage, a francophone heritage and because we wanted to keep that cultural baggage, we didn't want to lose it, we didn't want to be assimilated, like what happens to a lot of Franco-Ontarians (. . .)

(. . .) I got myself a bit, I got myself e- e- I got myself e-elected, and I took part in the election because I thought more the Franco-Ontarian group at the time treated public institutions like a private domain, that's what we called the privatization of the public domain, for example, the

domaine public, par exemple, l'école, c'étaient leurs écoles, 'nous nous sommes battus pour cette école, ça nous a pris cent ans à avoir, et c'est *notre* école', et j'ai dit 'non, c'est une école publique, et c'est pour tout le monde', nous nous sommes battus, et nous avons réussi à percer ce bouclier là qui voulait pas (xx) 'allez trouver les anglophones, ce sont eux qui ont le multiculturalisme', y a pas de place pour nous, alors c'est pourquoi nous nous sommes organisés et pis nous avons élu nos (xx) pis on s'est fait, nous avons été élus (...)

school, they were their schools, 'we fought for this school, it took us a hundred years to get it, and it's our *school', and I said, 'no, it's a public school, and it's for everybody', we fought, and we succeeded in piercing that shield which did not want (xx) 'go find the anglophones, they're the ones with the multiculturalism', there is no place for us, so that's why we organized ourselves and then we elected our (xx) then we got ourselves, we were elected (...)*

Armand's account reveals the ways in which the institutional embedding of the school in state structures prompts the fundamental questions of who the schools are for, and who counts as a francophone. Establishing francophone schools as public schools does raise the issue of access. It also provides political mechanisms for engaging in debates over these questions, and for wielding or seizing power. This account also reveals how the challenges posed by people like Armand make those challenged reassess their positions. As Johanne's representation of herself shows, the question is whether those in power can construct themselves as truly representative of the school population (with a label designed mainly to distinguish this school population from that of the majority), or whether they are revealed as representative of more sectarian interests (as Armand and his group have claimed).

The struggles that Armand describes have continued in a variety of forms. There have been more moments of the kind of crisis Armand describes, the most recent one triggered by the arrival in the early 1990s of a large group of Somalis. While the debates flowing from this demographic change will be taken up in greater detail later, it is important to note here that the Somali students joined the challenge begun earlier by others, insisting on the necessity of redefining the school in the direction of greater inclusiveness.

In 1992, in the midst of this debate, Charles, a member of Champlain's staff, had the following to say about the different perceptions various groups have of the school:

(. . .) on dit que du côté francophone traditionnel on renvoie en général à l'excellence, excellente école, c'est formidable ce qu'on fait, etc., tout ce discours là, euh côté disons multiculturel ou minoritaire, mais minoritaire dans la minorité, euh à ce moment là on dit y a rien à faire, on n'y arrivera jamais à changer ce qui se passe là-dedans, là c'est l'inverse, mais complet. Et si on si on s'adresse aux communautés disons aux communautés anglophones, elles n'ont pas de position, à bien des égards on dit ça ressemble plus à une école privée qu'autre chose. (. . .)

(. . .) they say that on the traditional francophone side they generally refer to excellence, excellent school, it's wonderful what they do, etc., that whole discourse, uh on the let's say multicultural or minority side, but a minority within the minority, uh, at that time they say there's nothing to be done, we'll never succeed in changing what goes on in there, it's the inverse, but total. And if you if you speak to the communities let's say the anglophone communities, they have no position, in many respects they say it resembles a private school more than anything else. (. . .)

According to Charles, these perceptions are as follows: the 'traditional francophone community' sees no problems, it is invested in and feels solidarity with the school. This can be taken to reveal the extent to which this group's interests are advanced through the way the school currently operates. The 'multicultural' or 'minority' community still sees itself as outside trying to break into a closed circle (despite the successes of Armand's group in the mid-1980s), and with interests not served at all by the status quo. The 'let's say the anglophone community' is not touched by these struggles, but gratefully sees itself as profiting from access to privileged resources (like 'a private school'). This account accords substantially with that provided by Armand, Johanne and Adrienne, as well as by others. Others might object that 'anglophones' may not feel privileged; they may feel simply, in the way that Armand does, that a public school is for everyone, no matter who you are.

A comparison of the labels used in Charles' account with those used by Armand, Johanne and Adrienne, also provides a clue as to the different perspectives at play. For all of them, labels are problematic (they provide multiple labels for the same notion, they hedge, they hesitate), and none of them uses the same labels (with the exception of *'communauté de souche'* – community with roots, as it were – which is used by both Armand and Adrienne, although not in the same way). They have a sense that they are talking about identifiable groups, but none of them is really sure how to characterize those groups; they are aware at some level that the labels in circulation, or any label they could invent, indexes a perspective. No hegemonic perspective has been established, in other words; the labelling confusion betrays a moment of Bakhtinian heteroglossia (Crowley 1996).

For example, Charles talks about the *'côté francophone traditionnel'* (traditional francophone community); Johanne refers to the community as *'franco-ontarienne, (. . .) canadienne au Canada (. . .) francophone canadienne'* (Franco-Ontarian, or Canadian in Canada, or francophone Canadian). For Armand this is the Franco-Ontarian *'communauté de souche, pure laine'*, which he opposes to 'ethnic francophone' or 'francophones come from elsewhere'. Adrienne opposes *'la communauté de souche'* to *'la communauté visible'* (the visible community), and to *'notre population multiculturelle'* (our multicultural population). She also sometimes talks about race explicitly as the most salient distinction to be made (the 'white community' as opposed to the 'visible community'). For Charles, in addition to the 'traditional francophone community', there is the 'multicultural' or 'minority' community, and the 'let's say the anglophone community'.

Two concepts are at work here: race or ethnicity as a biological notion ('visible', 'white', *'pure laine'*), and roots or traditions (*'communauté de souche'*, 'Canadian', 'traditional', 'multicultural') (Only Charles appeals to a notion of power, with his use of the term 'minority'.) Both concepts index criteria of inclusion and exclusion, uncomfortable notions for a public school which subscribes to the principle of democratic education (even 'anglophone' and 'francophone' in Canada can have ethnic connotations, precisely because the terms emerged as a way to talk indirectly about the explosive subject of ethnic identity). But they are also necessary elements of a discourse which recognizes that these concepts do act as principles of social organization which reveal a varied set of social positions and interests with respect to the school, positions and interests which must be understood if we are to grasp what is at stake in the explicit struggles and 'battles' (to use Armand's word) which affect the life of the school. Opinions which are linked to specific interests are thereby linked to social position. The crucial element of positioning has to do with families' access to knowledge of French and English, and in particular to the kinds of French and English valued at school and in the workplace (according to the principle of authority or prestige), or in families or the community (according to the principle of authenticity). This access to what a social scientist would call linguistic *capital* (Bourdieu 1977) influences families' hopes and expectations of what school might do for them, especially as regards maintaining or increasing the value of the capital they already have, or as concerns facilitating their access to capital they want to acquire.

At the same time, it is important to remember that groups are not monolithic and do not operate by consensus. Even individuals may hold contradictory opinions at the same time, or may change their minds. It is perhaps, then, most useful to say that the following covers the major (and in some ways mutually incompatible) interests people express:

- Champlain represents a monolingual haven, a place to preserve valued elements of a threatened language and culture.
- The school is a place in which to gain access to the skills and knowledge that will facilitate participation in the modern, globalized world.
- It is a place in which to gain access to French, either of the authentic Canadian or of the placeless 'normal' kind.
- It is a place in which to participate in the redefinition of *la francophonie*.

These interests flow from the wide variety of social positions occupied by members of Champlain's student population and their families. This variety is a direct result of mobilization, which contributed to the diversification of the population, and hence to the multiplication of economic, social and political interests with respect to French-language education. Further, the paradoxes inherent in this specific mobilization (and others like it) are aggravated by this diversification. The result is a long debate, punctuated by crises, focused on the politics of identity.

Champlain was established on the basis of an argument that the different cultural identity of Franco-Ontarians, and their specific social position, warranted institutions, programmes and pedagogies adapted to their specific interests and the specific cultural and linguistic resources they wished to control and to which they wished to gain access. Once established on such a basis, a school like Champlain then raises by its very existence the question of who counts as Franco-Ontarian, all the more so since the material conditions of its context blur the boundaries from the beginning. Struggles over the definition of what is going to count as knowledge at Champlain, over what the school will teach and what it expects students to know, and over who can legitimately gain access to it, all become struggles over language, culture and identity.

From 1968, through the 1970s and 1980s, the ground was thus in many ways prepared for the battles that were to ensue in the early 1990s, battles over who the school was for, and what its fundamental nature should be – battles fought principally on the terrain of language and identity: who is a francophone? what is French? what is bilingualism?

The beginning of our fieldwork period (1991–94) coincided with the arrival of a large group of Somali-speakers, causing a demographic shift which was to trigger another of the crises in the politics of identity the school has experienced over the years. It also coincided with the early years of an ill-fated leftist provincial government (1990–95), sensitive itself to the politics of identity. The combination led to a specific set of structural circumstances which were to dominate the public life of the school during the fieldwork period, as the school navigated the consequence of the complex interplay of the different forms of diversity present in the school, within the context of its historical unifying mission, and of the ideological domination of a class of francophones for whom the politics of language and identity have brought economic gain and political power. In the section that follows, I shall discuss some of the institutional processes that have proved to be central to the most recent manifestations of the struggle between unity and diversity, over the various visions of what Champlain can and should be, and over whose interests Champlain can and should promote.

4 Champlain and the politics of equity (1991–94)

As a state-run school, Champlain could scarcely fail to be influenced by the educational politics surrounding it. Ontario was certainly not alone in North America and Europe in being concerned with equity issues in the early 1990s, but the social democratic party which came to power in the autumn of 1990 (for the first time in the history of a province long-dominated by social and fiscal conservatives) was, for ideological reasons, especially interested in promoting equity, notably (although by no means exclusively) through education. In practical terms, this meant a focus on race, gender and class.

The new provincial government's focus on class was concerned mainly with structural means through which education tends to reproduce social stratification. In Ontario, this occurs largely through high-school streaming practices. Ontario has four streams: enriched, advanced, general and basic (in French, the streams are referred to as *niveaux de difficulté,* or levels of difficulty, which helps to obscure the social dimensions of the selection process they operate). The first two prepare students for university entrance; the last two prepare students for direct access to the lower end of the job market, or to post-secondary vocational and technical training (for example, through the state system of community colleges). The new government had an ideological commitment to destreaming; however, probably because of opposition among educators, the only destreaming to occur was implemented for the ninth grade in 1991.

Champlain is the only one of the three Toronto French-language high schools to offer the lower level streams (although in practice almost all its classes are either advanced or general level, with enriched and basic levels offered on the basis of individually adapted programmes; this is simply because of the low numbers of students involved). There are more advanced level students than general level students, however; indeed, the success rate for university entrance is quite high. (Most university entrants remain in Ontario for university; while some choose to attend the University of Ottawa, the largest bilingual university in the province – Ontario has no French-language university, a subject of some concern for militants – many choose one of the province's major English-language universities, notably the University of Toronto. A few choose to attend McGill University in Montreal, which can be seen as another way of choosing bilingualism, since McGill is an English-language institution in a mainly francophone province.)

The division between advanced and general level students is principally concerned with class. Working-class students, many of them of French-Canadian origin, dominate the general level classes, while middle-class students of varied backgrounds dominate the advanced level classes. Most of the Somali students were placed in the general level when they arrived; initial placement was difficult, since so many arrived without records of any kind, and it was only as a result of this wave that the guidance office worked at developing placement tests. Mireille explained to me that the decision to place most Somali students in the general level was based on the assumption that the system they came from would not have, could not have, prepared them for the Canadian school system, simply because it was so different. The school thought it would make more sense to try the students out at that level, and move them up if they did well, rather than trying the reverse. This placement was considered objectionable by many of the Somali students, who mainly came from well-educated families, and considered their education to have been in many ways superior to that offered in North America.

While students are placed in individual courses rather than in levels (that is, it is possible to take, say, advanced level Science, English and History, but general level French), in most cases students take all their courses at the same level. Also, while it is theoretically possible to go into advanced level courses from general level courses, in practice it is extremely difficult to do so, if only because the curriculum differences do not in fact prepare students for the shift. Staying in general level courses only means that you fall farther and farther behind, or at least that you diverge more and more from what advanced level students are learning. Thus despite an ambient discourse regarding destreaming, and some support for destreaming among school administrators, streaming was in fact well entrenched at Champlain. While many teachers recognized the difficulties associated with it, they were also concerned about the lack of support for dealing with the mixed level classrooms that destreaming would produce.

The government's concern for equity also encompassed gender issues, principally with respect to employment equity, but also with respect to issues of harassment. At Champlain this was reflected mainly in special events designed to promote awareness of gender-based violence and harassment, and to provide techniques for dealing with it. Champlain's school board did have a committee on women's issues. Administrators were particularly concerned with employment equity, but generally felt that the efforts they had engaged from the beginning of the board's history were paying off, and that women were well represented at the higher levels of school administration. At Champlain, it was frequently pointed out that almost all the science teachers were women, as were some of the mathematics teachers. Female students, numerically dominant since the school's founding, had frequently been involved in student government (although not in the sports hierarchy). Nonetheless, some concern was expressed about whether female students were gaining equal access to non-traditional fields of study (by which was meant principally Science and Mathematics), although to the best of my knowledge no official action was ever undertaken in this regard.

Finally, the province's Ministry of Education paid a great deal of attention to anti-racist education initiatives, within the general context of the government's efforts towards establishing social equity. For some time, educators across Canada had been struggling to move beyond the politics of multiculturalism, the federal government's initial contribution to pluralism, dating from the early 1970s. For many, the federal vision of multiculturalism, which posited Canada as a peaceful mosaic (in counter-point to the American roiling melting pot), was too stifling and too superficial. In practical terms, it seemed to focus on folkloric dimensions of identity (dress, food, song, literature), while suppressing the more troubling issues of inequality and violence. The Ontario government took up this trend, and promoted anti-racist education initiatives across the province. Some of these initiatives were structural, and provided, as we shall see, opportunities for new perspectives on Champlain to be expressed, despite the fact that the opportunities may initially have been intended for something quite different.

In the period 1991–94, that is, the period of our fieldwork, it was possible to see at Champlain a sort of sedimenting of multiculturalist and anti-racist policy initiatives. On the one hand, Champlain (along with many other schools) held such events as annual multicultural lunches (the first was held in 1991) – events that are usually pointed to by critics of multiculturalism as folkloric and superficial, but which in any case many students and staff members at Champlain seemed to enjoy. These lunches were typically organized by a volunteer group of students (almost always female) under the supervision of a (female) teacher. Students were invited to bring a dish representing their country or region of origin (those who brought dishes received free admission; everyone else had to pay). They were also invited to attend in 'national' costume, and the gymnasium where the lunch was held was decorated with banners created by the students and representing their country or region of origin. (One lunch that two of us attended was clearly run mainly by a group of Somali young women. There were a very large number of Somali dishes, and a vast number of *tourtières* (a meat pie considered typical of Quebec), alongside dishes from another twenty or so countries, arranged more or less geographically by continent along the buffet tables.)

In addition to the multicultural lunches, Champlain had imported a tradition of recognizing February as Black History Month. Originally an American invention, Black History Month is intended to highlight information traditionally absent from the classic History curriculum, namely the contribution of African Americans and African Canadians to the development of their respective countries, and, in a slightly different perspective, the privileging of the study of the history of the black population of North America for its own interest and importance. For the most part, this is a history of speakers of languages other than French; however, for Champlain, it opened doors to the examination of the situation of francophones of African origin, and was seized as such an opportunity in particular by the African-born students at the school. It thus became a means through which to attain some visibility, and to gain a voice. Thus while for some Black History Month had multiculturalist connotations, in that it could be used simply to note and 'celebrate' specific attributes of the African-Canadian community, it also became available to more radical reinterpretations and views, an institutionally structured moment in which to facilitate (if not force) the examination of the situation of black students in our schools.

More clearly radical have been initiatives specifically designed to support anti-racist education. During our time at Champlain, two in particular stand out. One was a government-run programme designed to provide school-board-based support for black students who, in the English system, statistically run the greatest risk of all student groups of being streamed into the lowest streams, and of dropping out of school altogether. Champlain and its sister high school were able to benefit from this programme in the form of a school-board-based youth worker who organized meetings and activities in which students could participate on a voluntary basis. While the black student profile of French-language schools is strikingly different from that in English-language schools, the necessity of providing equal access to similar resources across the provincial system made available an institutional space which black students could use for addressing their specific interests. In some ways, it is possible that this group also helped to create, or at least foster, a political consciousness that may otherwise have lain dormant or taken a different form. Certainly, it brought together students from Haiti and from east and west Africa on a basis which gave them something in common and a place in which to understand and act on it. Some of the major efforts at contesting prevailing visions of *la francophonie* and at establishing a new voice in the public space of Champlain had their origin in that group.

The second major initiative was part of one principal's efforts to raise Champlain's profile and to carry out a broad campaign for innovation. I believe that his concern was that the arrival of the Somali students might precipitate (from his perspective, may have already precipitated) a crisis due to the lack of match between programmes and policies designed for one, now historical, understanding of the school, and the reality of a new and different student body. For him, anti-racist education had to be the centerpiece of a general strategy of reorganization and rethinking that would allow Champlain to grapple with the realities of its student body. Anti-racist education meant, to him, the organization of round tables and school-wide meetings with the topic of race relations as their focus. While these efforts were controversial (in particular it seemed that problems ensued over the relative authority of the principal, the teaching staff, the parents and the students), the principal did put anti-racism squarely in the centre of public debate at the school, although it was embedded in an overall ideology of innovation and effectiveness.

The period 1991–94 was therefore one in which the issue of diversity, and the challenge it poses for a particular vision of unity, was central to the life and culture of Champlain. Clearly, the seeds of the conflict had been sown in the early days, and were part of the contradictions inherent in the terms and conditions of Champlain's very existence. While this is not the first crisis Champlain has known (those over its founding, over the presence of English-dominant students, over the inclusiveness of the 1986 advisory committee, and over the founding of the new autonomous French-language school board, spring to mind), it is perhaps one of the most essential, striking as it does at the heart of the minority dilemma of modern, urban globalizing times. The discourse of the nation-state, so important to the legitimacy of the francophone mobilization movement, has run its course, its promise of equity given the lie by internal inequalities which can no longer remain hidden, its promise of keys to opportunity overrun by opportunities controlled beyond and in the interstices of the state. While in many ways the minority movement was itself a key element in fragmenting the state, it nonetheless also took the state as its model and most important interlocutor. The conditions of that conversation, while not entirely gone, are being forcefully challenged from within and from without. What Champlain does in the face of these challenges provides clues to what minorities elsewhere may do, and how they may contribute to the reinvention of the politics of identity.

5 Champlain's 25th anniversary celebrations

In the midst of these transformations came the occasion of the twenty-fifth anniversary of the founding of the school. Such events are traditionally opportunities for looking back on what the institution has accomplished, and for thinking about future directions. It is also an occasion for public display, a moment when an audience can be defined and an image created for that audience to fix in its mind, a moment when Champlain has possibilities for saying publicly what it is, for exercising some control over how it is imagined by those with an interest in the school, or by those whom Champlain would like to develop an interest in the school. It is a means by which to create the imagined community (Anderson 1983), not just of the school, but through the school, of *la francophonie*, and to establish its authenticating traditions (Hobsbawm and Ranger 1983).

Throughout the year there were special events. Most of them focused on cultural activities, designed to express in public space various elements of Champlain's identity. One important set of activities was a series of concerts held in the school's cafeteria-cum-auditorium. As we shall see later, while the school tended to categorize students in terms of linguistic repertoire or competence, ethnicity, race or national origin, the students themselves paid more attention to musical styles as a way of organizing their social networks. When the school sponsored musical activities, it was then moving onto the students' terrain.

Our own 1994 survey of students' musical tastes and practices showed that the school was about evenly divided between those who prefer some form of rock, and those who prefer hip-hop, reggae and rhythm and blues (based on responses from over half the student body from Grades 9 to 13). Based on interviews and observations (for example, of who dances to what at school dances; of who has the logos of which bands on their clothing or bags; or of who listens to what on the portable tape or CD players many students bring to school), it seems that these divisions are both class and ethnoculturally based, with economically comfortable and academically oriented students preferring milder forms of rock (or what they often revealingly call 'normal' music, or 'just anything'); other francophone students prefer heavy metal; and students of other backgrounds, especially those of African origin, tend to prefer hip-hop, reggae and rhythm and blues. If there was any possibility of cross-over, it may have been through reggae. In addition, students of all backgrounds almost always listen to music in English, whether or not they can speak it themselves (the survey showed that 85 per cent of the students listened to music only in English, with another 5 per cent listening to music in English and other languages). This background will help explain student reactions to the musical events of the twenty-fifth anniversary celebrations.

The first concert was devoted to Franco-Ontarian music, presented by young artists who were clearly attempting to fuse traditional and modern, and to use their Franco-Ontarian roots to carve out a special niche in markets (country and rock) dominated by the English-speaking world. Following concerts featured francophone music from other arenas, from Haiti, Africa and cabaret France. Each of these concerts received the most attention from students whom Rampton (1995) would call 'inheritors', students whose own families came from places where the music in question also claimed its roots (while the others slept, listened to their own music on portable cassette or CD players, or found some way to leave the room altogether). The major musical tastes of the students were, however, never included, and all the music was in

French, the language perhaps least used for musical purposes by anyone in the school (see, however, Chapter 7). On the other hand, this was not necessarily a problem from the students' perspective; as we shall see in Part II, many of them expect the school to construct this vision, and indeed the school would lose its value to them if it did not.

Champlain, then, was clearly committed to the vision of a school which touched on varying dimensions of *la francophonie internationale*, without losing sight of its Canadian and nationalist origins. Indeed, the school invested the greatest amount of time and energy in organizing the visit of a Québécois singer who is closely identified with the Quebec nationalist movement. He was one of the main artists to express the notion of authenticity in legitimizing the movement of the 1960s, and has continued to provide that note ever since. For such a figure to visit a minority French-language institution is an event obviously fraught with significance and danger. Other such visits have not turned out well; for example, a Québécois nationalist author used the occasion of a reading at a Toronto francophone institution to call his audience '*cadavres encore chauds*' (still-warm corpses). The problem is clearly that from a Québécois nationalist perspective, Franco-Ontarians should either already have disappeared or they should be well on their way to doing so, if the Quebec claim that francophone survival can only be guaranteed in a monolingual state is to be borne out. On the other hand, Franco-Ontarians also represent the selfsame fight for survival in hostile territory that the Québécois are engaged in, and Franco-Ontarians frequently have looked to Quebec for support and encouragement. This visit was presented in that last light, as inspirational attention from a man who knows what the fight is all about, and who represents many of the values of authenticity (and uniformity) that are present in Champlain's ideological universe. It was an occasion to reaffirm a certain historical view of what a Franco-Ontarian school is all about, namely a view in which centre stage is occupied by the historical struggle for cultural emancipation of francophones descended from the original settlers of New France.

Besides these events on the terrain of music, a variety of other events were organized, all designed to foster school spirit through collective action, and making physical marks on the landscape both inside and outside the school, to make manifest the school's existence and its community links. Some of these resemble the activities in which most Toronto high schools engage, such as garage sales or pizza sales, while others had more explicitly cultural aims, such as a *café littéraire* or a mural portraying multicultural students of Champlain from 1969 to the present. There is thus a balance, or perhaps a tension, between activities designed to show that Champlain is indeed just as much fun to be part of as any other high school in Toronto, and just as able to organize the same kinds of attractive spirit-building activities; and those designed to showcase its special cultural and linguistic attributes, which make it so different.

But the greatest amount of attention was paid to the most symbolically charged zone of the school, its entrance hall. For this significant space, the student council commissioned a statue of the school's namesake. The statue was commissioned from a Quebec sculptor who works in wood, and who proposed a fairly traditional, historically informed likeness. I read this as an agreement with a symbol which emphasizes traditional French-Canadian values; after all, Champlain himself was in many ways responsible for what is argued as being the prior claim of residence of francophones over anglophones on Canadian territory, and presenting a traditionally dressed and coiffed likeness of him simply serves to underscore that authenticity. In addition, wood as a material has strong connotations for francophones in Canada, who in the process of colonization cut their way through forests, ran through them, trapped in them, and later cut down their trees, floated their logs down rivers and worked in the mills which cut them into planks. The sculptor himself came from the French-Canadian heartland. However, the students drew the line at the sculptor's plan to grace Champlain's chin with a goatee; this can be seen as one symbolic stand against too slavish a devotional representation of the authentic past, an attempt to give the face of that past some semblance of youth, freshness and orientation towards the future.

Today Champlain stands in the foyer under a skylight. In front of him there is a plaque which provides a few biographical details (date and place of birth), and a summary of some of his most significant achievements as a pioneer in the area of what is now Ontario. It particularly focuses on Champlain's life among the native population. It then goes on:

L'École Champlain en 1969, fut le pionnier des établissements scolaires du Grand Toronto. Elle marque la célébration de son vingt-cinquième anniversaire, le 19 mai 1994, en inaugurant cette statue. Ainsi, les élèves, leurs parents et le personnel entier de l'école entendent renouveler leur engagement au respect et à la promotion de l'idéal commun dont on a pu dégager l'exemple dans la vie de notre patronyme, celui de 'l' Unité dans la diversité'.

L'École Champlain was, in 1969, the pioneer of the educational establishments of Metropolitan Toronto. She marks the celebration of her twenty-fifth anniversary, the 19th of May 1994, by inaugurating this statue. In this way, the students, parents and entire staff of the school intend to renew their commitment to the respect and the encouragement of the common ideal the example of which we have been able to find in the life of our patronym, that of 'Unity in diversity'.

Like so many of the students, parents and teachers at Champlain, Champlain was a *voyageur*. The school's account notes that he brought with him values which he sought to implant in the new world, but he also learned new things from those whom he found already here. This may be subject to historical debate, but that is not the point; Champlain serves as an authenticating tradition, a condensation symbol for the affirmation of values which legitimize the school's existence and its practices, and which help resolve the tensions flowing from the differences among its members. And so Champlain is meant to balance the pride of origins with respect for others.

This theme is taken up in the yearbook for 1994, a yearbook dedicated to the 25th anniversary of the school. The yearbook editor provides the following message:

L'École secondaire Champlain constitue un véritable oasis culturel au sein d'une société principalement anglophone. Elle se distingue parmi les autres établissements de la région par la fonction qu'elle occupe au sein de la communauté : celle d'offrir à ses élèves, tel qu'il est stipulé dans la déclaration de sa mission, 'une programmation de base, solide et unique, dans une atmosphère de respect mutuel entre tous et toutes'. Mais, plus important encore, Champlain réunit des jeunes gens en provenance des quatre coins de cette planète qui sont liés par un fait collectif, leur francophonie. Née de ce fait, la famille 'Champlainienne' fait hommage à la devise de l'école qui est celle de 'l'Unité dans la diversité'. (. . .)

Champlain High School constitutes a veritable cultural oasis in the midst of a society which is mainly anglophone. It distinguishes itself from the other establishments of the region by virtue of the function it serves in the community: that of offering to its students, as is stipulated in its mission statement, 'a basic programme, solid and unique, in an atmosphere of mutual respect among all'. But, more important even than this, Champlain brings together young people from the four corners of this planet who are tied together by a collective fact, their 'francophonie'. Born from this fact, the 'Champlainian' family renders homage to the motto of the school, which is that of 'Unity in diversity'. (. . .)

Here we can see that, twenty-five years after the founding of Champlain, the two dimensions of the school's ideology are still in place, although it seems fair to say that one dimension of the school's motto has taken precedence over the other. While Champlain is still thought of as an *oasis culturel*, a francophone island in an anglophone sea, its motto, 'Unity in diversity', has come to refer mainly to a polyglot, multicultural student body, joined together by their mutual affinity with French, their shared belonging to an international *francophonie*.

Today, in the foyer, on the wall behind Champlain hang banners taken from the gymnasium after a multicultural lunch; Canada (represented by indigenous symbols), England (represented by Celtic symbols), Somalia, Libya, Hungary and China all surround the statue. In cases and on the walls there are also new plaques designating the winners of school awards over the years, awards mainly for excellence in French, but also in Mathematics and in Sports. On the facing wall, there are photo displays of each year's graduating class. The names on the plaques and the photographs on the walls change over the years, bearing witness to the changing population of the school. And so the *voyageur* Champlain stands, symbol of unity, in the midst of diversity.

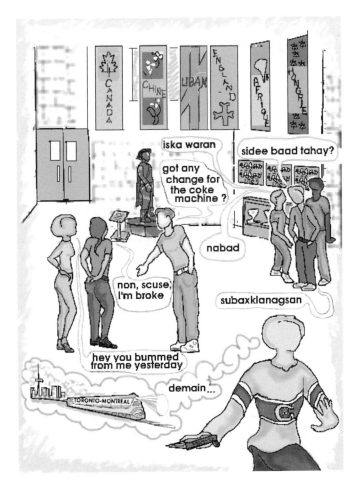

3 Norms and contradictions

1 Introduction

Anyone who sets foot in a French-language minority school will immediately notice tensions that arise from the fact that, despite the school's expectations that students will speak French on school grounds, many students speak something else among themselves. Most of them speak English by preference when among their peers. This is a widespread convention, consistent since at least the 1970s, and might simply pass unnoticed just because it is so prevalent and routine. However, what brings it so forcefully to the attention of even the most casual passer-by is the strength of the school's resistance to this use of English, the school's fierce attempts to eradicate it, and the depths of despair experienced by francophone educators who often ask themselves if they are battling a lost cause. A closer look only serves to uncover more and more ways in which the school tries to come to terms with this flouting of the norm in which it has invested itself. Some of these ways are overt, indeed hard to miss, but others are more subtle, and are closely integrated into the processes of daily life at school.

This chapter examines the school's language norms: what they are, how they are manifested in daily life in school, where they come from and how teachers cope with the contradictions that sometimes arise in trying to render them concrete. The first, and most important, norm has to do with the clear expectation that the school should function as a monolingual French-speaking island in an English-dominant sea. The second has to do with the nature of the French that the school thinks should be taught and used. This norm is less focused than the first; while there is a clear preference for European or Canadian standard French, it is not always clear exactly what the characteristics of those standards are. At the same time, there is a tension between the status and authority accorded to the standard, and the authenticity accorded to the Canadian-French vernacular. Both kinds of French are necessary to support the legitimacy of the school, the first in terms of the school's claims to prepare young francophones for the modern world, social mobility and access to global networks, and the second in terms of its claim to be uniquely able to respond to the needs of an oppressed, marginalized and distinct minority group. The two ideological domains, that of francophone monolingual-ism and that of language quality, overlap insofar as one dimension of language quality is its purity, that is, the extent to which the French spoken at school is free of traces of contact with English. In addition, for at least some participants in school life, the two are conceptually linked; concern for the quality of French is tied to pride and awareness of francophone identity as separate from (and a bulwark against) anglophone identity. As one student put it in an open forum on the school and its needs: '*la qualité du français devrait être plus élevée pour permettre de résister à l'assimilation*' (the quality of French should be higher in order to help resist assimilation). However, for purposes of clarity, I shall maintain a distinction between the two.

In this chapter I shall discuss the nature of the school's linguistic ideologies and their institutional history, notably with respect to French monolingualism and a focus on what is called *la qualité de la langue* (the quality of language). I shall also examine forms of social organization which make it possible for the school to produce and reproduce its linguistic ideologies; this includes the conditions which make possible strategies of ambiguity which allow staff and students to cope with contradictions and conflicts in ways that reduce their threat to the school's normative order. The focus here is on the linguistic and other interactional activities of school rep-resentatives, as well as on the legal, institutional and ideological underpinnings of those activities.

While there are clearly some explicit, overt ways in which the school conducts its work of ideological management (and these will be examined in the sections devoted to monolingualism and language quality), there are also subtler ways in which this work can be carried out. In order to fully set the scene, before discussing the specific ways in which the school constructs monolingualism as an ideal and works on the quality of students' linguistic production, I shall first focus, in the next section, on the social organization of linguistic monitoring (the school's ability to monitor and shape the linguistic production of its students).

Subsequent sections focus on the two major dimensions of linguistic production which are considered important. First, I shall discuss the school's attempts to create a monolingual French-speaking world within its walls, and the ways in which school personnel act to enforce that norm. Underlying the preference for French monolingualism at school is a hegemonic ideology of the monolingual condition as 'normal', an ideology, I have argued above, which serves the interests of the politically mobilized francophone class which forms a new élite. Efforts to render this ideology concrete in daily life at school are most visible in explicit policy statements, and in on-going interactional efforts in key arenas. These arenas are situations in which the school presents a public face, either to the outside world or to itself, and in any other place where school authority must assert itself. Among the most important of these arenas are classrooms where the teaching of symbolically charged subject matters is conducted. This is most clearly the case in the teaching of *Français* as a subject, but may also affect such areas as History. However, in some circumstances, conflicts between the linguistic norms of authority and authenticity, between linguistic and pedagogical goals, or between ideal and real versions of the sociolinguistic conditions of life at Champlain, create the necessity for strategies of ambiguity which blur these norms, or soften their edges (and which thereby help to maintain them). This can be the case, for example, in the teaching in *Français* classes of Canadian-French literary pieces in which the vernacular is used for both artistic and political purposes (as is characteristic of much theatre and song of the 1960s, which served to raise political consciousness and to advance the nationalist cause). It can also arise in classrooms (such as *Sciences*) where the subject matter is often tied to the pedagogical strategy of building on students' specific, practical (and usually English-mediated) real-world knowledge in order to facilitate access to abstract, universal knowledge constructed through French.

The fourth part of the chapter will examine the issue of what is usually referred to as *la qualité de la langue* (the quality of the language). Debates over language quality, which can be institutionally organized or which can also occur in the course of ordinary conversation, reveal a tension between authority and authenticity, a tension which becomes magnified as the two aspects of linguistic norms confront each other in daily life. This occurs, for example, when it comes to teaching French as a subject to speakers of the authentic vernacular, but also when speakers of the authentic vernacular find themselves teaching students trained in the standard. The tensions manifest themselves, and may be at least partially resolved, through the use of strategies like code-switching, hedging, flagging, translation and silence. All of these are discursive strategies which serve to signal the speaker's stance with respect to what he or she has just said, and in particular can help someone to say something without accepting full responsibility for having said it, or for having said it in a specific way (Heller 1988).

In both cases, norms can be reinforced or tensions managed through the exploitation of conventional ways of organizing school talk, which allow the teacher full access to students' linguistic production, and full authority to comment on it. Pedagogical practice makes linguistic surveillance possible and legitimate. What this means in practice is that teachers tend to retain control over the allocation of turns at talk, and prefer unified floors and sequential turn-taking – that is, everyone in class participates in the same conversation, and only one person talks at any one a time. As we shall see, this form of interactional organization is so important that it is assimilated to the fundamental social value of *'respect'*.

Before going on to discuss the various ways in which the school's linguistic ideologies of monolingualism and quality are manifested and reproduced, I shall show how the school produces and reproduces this fundamental mode of social organization which lies at the heart of teachers' ability to do interactional ideological work.

2   The social organization of linguistic monitoring

The school monitors the linguistic production of all participants in the school setting. What this means in practice is that staff monitor their own production as well as that of others, and that monitoring can be more or less tense, or more or less diffuse, depending on the symbolic charge of the activity, the investment of the participants, and the extent to which the activity is implicated in the construction of the school's public face.

In my data, monitoring was most diffuse in situations where the authority of the school was not well established, that is, in activities taking place in the interstices of institutional functioning. This was notably the case in interaction among students during breaks between classes, and in the liminal zones of corridor and grounds outside the school building (see also Rampton 1995 on the importance of liminality). (Once clearly *off* school grounds, students accordingly switched patterns. The student who might make a point of speaking English from the door of the classroom to the edge of the school grounds after school, might easily switch to French on the bus, to impress, and maybe even to shock, the other riders – all presumably non-francophone, although surprises do occur.) Also, while self-monitoring did occur among staff members even 'back-stage' (as in the staff room), it tended to be more diffuse there than when staff found themselves in the more public arenas, such as the classroom.

The surveillance was clearly most focused in situations where student behaviour came directly under the control of school representatives, the most important of these being the classroom. Among classroom settings, surveillance was more or less focused depending on the symbolic charge accorded to French in the subject matter; thus *Français* classes were clearly the most significant, while Mathematics, Art, Music and Science were among the least. In addition, some subjects lend themselves more easily to teacher monitoring of interaction than do others; for example, Science classes necessitate lab work, in which students tend to work in pairs or groups at tasks which may require them, or at least permit them, to move around the room. Finally, a certain amount of monitoring depended on the personal investment in the school ideology on the part of the teacher in question; often this is directly linked to the subject matter in which he or she specializes (so that a *Français* teacher will likely care more about these issues than will a teacher of Physical Education), but it can also have a great deal to do with the teacher's personal experience of varieties of French and of bilingualism. A teacher whose spouse or partner speaks no French, or who himself or herself grew up in a French minority setting and has been bilingual from early childhood, may well see things differently from one who speaks little or no English and the greater part of whose life was spent in a French majority setting. In what follows, I shall first describe the embedding of linguistic surveillance in the structure of verbal interaction, and then discuss how this may vary according to the conditions which influence the degree to which that surveillance is focused or diffuse.

The prevailing norm of interaction at Champlain included a preference for a unified floor (everyone talks about the same thing, engages in the same conversation) and for sequential turn-taking (one person talks at a time). In addition, teachers have the authority to control turns at talk. Finally, the prevalence in many classrooms of the canonical Initiation–Response–Evaluation (I-R-E) cycle provides an automatic interactional slot for feedback on form, not just on content. These conditions make it difficult for individual students to hide their linguistic production, and invest a great deal of power in teachers regarding the evaluation and shaping of that production. It also puts a great deal of pressure on teachers to conform to the norm.

These preferences, at least in part, are upheld through an ideology of *respect*. From the school's perspective, respect is a central value, and is manifested concretely through interactional means. Respect means listening to others until they have finished speaking their piece, and taking a turn only when authorized by the teacher to do so. This preference emerges, not surprisingly, most clearly where it is not respected. Example 3.1 is an evaluation sheet that is filled and signed by the teachers regarding students who are being disciplined.

Example 3.1   Disciplinary evaluation sheet (Feuille de route quotidienne), *1994*

1	Aux enseignant-e-s: Veuillez	*To teachers: Please evaluate*
2	évaluer dans les domaines	*in the areas indicated.*
3	indiqués.	
4	– Travaille de façon concentrée	*– Works with concentration*
5	et ne perd pas son temps	*and does not waste his or*
6		*her time*
7	– Parle que lorsqu'elle est invitée	*– Talks only when invited*
8	à le faire et cela avec respect	*to do so and with respect*
9	– Écoute attentivement et	*– Listens attentively and*
10	respectueusement lorsque son	*respectfully when his or her*

11	professeur ou un autre élève	*teacher or another student*
12	parle.	*is speaking.*

It is important to note here that this sheet focuses on the core behavioural expectations of the school. Three are mentioned; one has to do directly with work habits, and the other two with interactional propensities. Taken together, the two interactional concerns link the notions of sequential turn-taking and the unified floor to that of respect.

It is possible, however, to find cases where the links are made even more clearly, especially where the challenge to the normative order is most evident. The best example is the struggle of Lise, the teacher responsible for a 10th grade, general level, *Français* class in the autumn of 1991, to establish order in her classroom. The fact that it is general level is significant; for the most part, these are students who know already, three years before high school graduation, that they are not expected to go to university. However, almost half the class also consists of Somali-speakers who had just arrived in Toronto a few months before. From well-educated élite families, they had attended private European-run French-language schools in Africa, and were surprised and shocked to be placed for the most part in general level classes. The school had no preparation for their arrival, and little understanding at the time of their situation or background; similarly, the students found themselves parachuted into a world for which they were extremely ill prepared. The teacher, Lise, is not a *Français* specialist; her main areas of expertise are Physical Education and Counselling. Her fiancé speaks no French. Although she spent the early part of her life in Quebec, she moved to Toronto while she was still in school. In fact, Lise is a graduate of Champlain, and so is well acquainted with the school's culture and with the experience of its students. She has great experience with life as a francophone in an English-speaking milieu, and speaks fluent English.

The general level *Français* curriculum places great emphasis on sociolinguistic competence for the real world. (This in itself causes problems, of course, since Lise and the students all know that real-world sociolinguistic competence in Toronto – the real world they are likely to end up in – rarely involves monolingual-type competence in French, at least not for the type of job market the curriculum has in mind for them.) The programme consisted of six units, each focused on a different genre, in both oral and written modes: magazine-type articles, adventure narratives, imaginary / fantasy narratives, advertising, newspaper-type articles and the novel.

Almost all classes are set up with desks arranged in rows facing the teacher's desk and the blackboard (with the notable exception of laboratories, but also a few others). This is a sort of default mode, since, as a secondary school, classes do not stay in one place with one teacher all day, but rather students, and often also teachers, move from space to space during the day. The arrangement of furniture at Champlain already conditions the social organization of classroom interaction. Lise's classroom was no exception. For Lise it was important *not* to organize her classroom traditionally, as a teacher-centred classroom with students sitting in neat rows. As she told her students at one point, she had been taught like that, and she hadn't liked it. She tried as a result to challenge the strong expectations of a teacher-centred classroom conducted through an I-R-E format, notably by physically reorganizing the classroom space. From the beginning of the school year, every time she entered the classroom, she would ask the students to rearrange the desks into a U-shape. She decided that she wanted to teach at least the first unit through group work, so that most days, from the U-shape used for roll call and warm-up activities, students would shift desks into sets of three or four.

Within a week or so, however, Lise was already encountering difficulties with this mode of social organization. She often had to remind students to speak French, to do their work, and, perhaps most frustrating of all for her, to listen to her when she wanted to say something. She was particularly challenged by one student, who, she felt, interrupted her constantly (certainly the content of his interventions was challenging, including as it did frequent requests for explanations of why they had to do what they were doing). By early October, things had reached a crisis point with this student; Lise felt that it was no longer possible to try to continue to get things done the way she had originally intended. One day, this student's challenge was so direct and so severe that Lise sent him to the principal's office, and then stopped the on-going pedagogical activity in order to have a discussion about discipline. She said that she found things impossible; '*ça manque de respect*' (there is not enough respect), because the students were constantly talking and moving around. She said that she did not want to have to put them back into *'rangs d'oignons'* (literally, rows of onions) *'et être méchante'* (and be mean).

The next day, Lise devoted most of the class period to a discussion of the social order of the classroom. Lise had the students sit in a U, and asked them to tell her what 'respect' meant to them. After a long discussion, she summed up:

Example 3.2   10th grade Français général *1991*

1	*Lise:*	le respect selon moi vous	*respect in my opinion*
2		me direz si vous êtes	*you'll tell me if you*
3		d'accord ou non, il y a	*agree or not, there*
4		trois respects très	*are three very*
5		importants que tu sois à	*important respects,*
6		l'école, que tu sois au	*whether you're at*
7		travail, que tu sois à la	*school, at work, at*
8		maison.	*home.*
9		Premièrement, si tu veux	*First, if you want to*
10		te respecter toi-même	*respect yourself*
11	*Nathalie:*	oui la première chose	*yes, the first thing*
12	*Lise:*	te respecter toi-même, ça	*respect yourself, that*
13		veut dire faire attention	*means paying*
14		à toi, ça veut dire	*attention to yourself*
15			*that means*
16	*Mohamud:*	c'est contrôler	*it's controlling*
17	*Lise:*	(xx) que ton hygiène	*(xx) that your hygiene*
18	*Female student:*	c'est contrôler	*it's controlling*
19	*Mohamud:*	c'est contrôler alors	*so it's controlling*
20	*Lise:*	c'est te contrôler,	*it's controlling*
21		contrôler tes colères,	*yourself, your anger,*
22		contrôler tes peines,	*your sadness, your*
23		contrôler tes joies, c'est	*joys, it's also*
24		aussi respecter autrui,	*respecting others, that*
25		c'est-à-dire respecter les	*is other people, that*
26		autres, ça veut dire	*means when a person*
27		lorsqu'une personne qui	*is speaking, you have*
28		parle, tu dois apprendre	*to learn to be quiet*
29		à te taire	
30	*Mohamud:*	la dernière chose c'est	*the last thing is*
31		bon pour (xx)	*good for (xx)*
32	*Leïla:*	(laughs)	*(laughs)*
33	*Lise:*	tu dois aussi apprendre à	*you also have to learn*
34		écouter l'autre qui parle	*to listen to others*

35		(pause) okay tu dois	*when they speak*
36		aussi apprendre à ne pas	*(pause) okay you also*
37		fesser l'autre parce qu'il	*have to learn to not*
38		vient de dire quelque	*hit another person*
39		chose que t'aimerais pas.	*because he's just said*
40		Pis la troisième c'est	*something that you*
41		respecter tout ce qui est	*wouldn't like. And the*
42		matériel, c'est-à-dire	*third is respecting all*
43		c'est pas parce que t'es	*material things, that is*
44		fâché que tu vas envoyer	*it's not because you're*
45		un pupitre sur le tableau	*angry that you're*
46		par exemple, il y a	*going to throw a desk*
47		d'autres façons de régler	*against the board, for*
48			*instance, there*
49			*are other ways to settle*
50	*Female*		
	student:	madame, c'est bien (xx)	*madame, that's fine*
51			*(xx)*
52	*Lise:*	il y a trois respects selon	*there are three*
53		moi, toi, l'autre, puis	*things to respect in*
54		matériel.	*my opinion: yourself,*
55			*other people and*
56			*property*
57		(. . .)	*(. . .)*

The day after that, Lise wrote on the board:

Example 3.3   10th grade Français général *1991 (from field notes)*

1	– interruptions non-nécessaires	*– unnecessary interruptions*
2	– comportement peu désiré:	*– little desired behaviour:*
3	– parler sans raison	*– speaking for no reason*
4	– impolitesse	*– impoliteness*
5	– parler une autre langue que	*– speaking a language other*
6	le français	*than French*

Lise commented on this list, saying '*C'est une forme de respect, c'est bien, pour la première fois je parle et je m'entends*' (It's a form of respect, it's good, for the first time I talk and I hear myself speak), and '*Est-ce mon droit et celui des autres de s'entendre?*' (Is it my right and that of others to hear oneself speak?) For Lise, a unified floor and sequential turn-taking are clearly manifestations of respect. She would prefer to obtain them while permitting more democratic forms of social organization (notably group work), and so her first attempt was to make her expectations explicit. Eventually, though, Lise gave up, and reverted to the default mode of putting students' desks in rows, and using group or individual work on fewer and fewer occasions.

However, even in more teacher-centred modes she had difficulty establishing the modes of interaction she valued, requiring her on several occasions to make explicit again her fundamental expectations. Example 3.4 is taken from the beginning of a class in which individual students are to make oral presentations. Lise has asked each student to write a composition on an invention, and then to present it in class (the theme is tied to competence in technical language). At the beginning of the class Lise takes the roll as the students file in and engage each other in conversation. As is most often the case, the Somali-speakers talk to each other and use Somali, the others talk to each other in English. There are two networks within this class of about twenty students (the number fluctuated somewhat over the course of the semester), and they rarely meet. (This too makes it difficult for Lise to accomplish anything resembling sequential turn-taking or a unified floor.) Lise then tries to establish a unified, French-speaking floor in order for the presentations to occur. Indeed, these two conditions, characterized by her as manifestations of respect, are so important that the key communicative event of the class cannot begin until and unless they are satisfied (see especially lines 9, 50–3, 61–84 and 130–4).

Example 3.4   10th grade Français général *class, 1991*

1	Lise:	(. . .) euh ok alors les	(. . .) *uh ok the oral*
2		présentations orales	*presentations I wanted*
3		je voulais commencer	*to start with Stéphane*
4		avec Stéphane Nora	*Nora Stéphane at the*
5		Stéphane en ce	*moment is in detention*
6		moment est en retenu	*so we'll do it afterwards*
7		alors on le fera par	*Leïla Abdi are you ready*
8		la suite Leïla Abdi	*to start?*
9		êtes-vous prêts à	
10		commencer?	
11		(Many students talk	(Many students talk at
12		at once)	once)
13	Lise:	chut vous êtes prêts	*sh you're ready ok uh*
14		ok euh je vais passer	*I'll pass you pass around*

15		tu fais passer une	*a sheet to each Saïd (xx)*
16		feuille à chacun Saïd	*a sheet to each now (xx)*
17		(xx) une feuille à	*each one a sheet Saïd*
18		chacun là (xx) chacun	*ok*
19		une feuille Saïd ok	
20		(Many students talk	(Many students talk at
21		at once)	once)
22	*Lise:*	ouais la feuille qu'on	*yeah the sheet we which*
23		que Saïd vous passe	*Saïd is passing around*
24		en ce moment vous	*to you now you will give*
25		allez me la remettre le	*back to me*
26		nom c'est le nom de	*the name is the name*
27		Leïla et Abdi que vous	*of Leïla and Abdi that*
28		mettez et non pas le	*you write and not your*
29		vôtre (pause) vous me	*own (pause) you give it*
30		le donnez vous vous	*to me you remember if*
31		souvenez si si vous	*if you answered the*
32		répondiez par un oui	*question with a yes it*
33		à la question ça valait	*was worth one point if*
34		un point si c'est un	*it's a no it becomes zero*
35		non ça devient zéro et	*and if it's a maybe it's a*
36		puis si c'est un peut-	*point five ok*
37		être c'est un point	
38		cinq ok	
39	*Saïd:*	je vais les donner	*I'll give them afterwards*
40		après	
41		(Many students talk	(Many students talk at
42		at once; Lise explains	once; Lise explains the
43		the evaluation system	evaluation system to
44		to Monica)	Monica)
45	*Male*		
	student:	aujourd'hui c'est le	*today is the eleventh*
46		onze	
47	*Mohamud:*	non non non c'est	*no no no it's not eleven*
		pas onze	
48	*Female*		
	student:	c'est douze	*it's twelve*
49	*Mohamud:*	oui	*yes*
50	*Lise:*	on vous laisse deux	*you have two minutes to*
51		minutes pour vous	*prepare yourselves and*
52		préparer puis après	*after that we start*
53		ça on commence	
54	*Leïla:*	d'accord	*okay*
55	*Saïd:*	Leïla et Abdi	*Leïla and Abdi*

56	Lise:	Zahra (xxx) feuille	*Zahra (xxx) sheet Saïd*
57		Saïd tu lui as donné	*you gave it to to*
58		à à	
59	Saïd:	oh euh (xxx) (in	*oh uh (xx) (in Somali)*
60		Somali)	
61	Lise:	(xx) aujourd'hui vous	*(xx) today you speak*
62		parlez en français	*French*
63	Saïd:	d'accord je vais parler	*okay I'll speak French*
64		français	
65	Lise:	okay alors on écoute	*okay so we listen to*
66		Leïla et Abdi	*Leïla and Abdi*
67	Student:	chut	*shh*
68	Student:	*shut up*	<u>*shut up*</u>
69	Lise:	okay on recommence	*okay we start again*
70		quand on fait une	*when we do an oral*
71		présentation orale ou	*presentation or an*
72		un exposé on s'attend	*exposé we really expect*
73		vraiment à ce que à ce	*people to listen*
74		que les gens écoutent	
75	Rahman:	c'est quoi ça	*what's that*
76	Lise:	ok si vous avez déjà	*ok if you have already*
77		présenté on vous	*presented we then ask*
78		demande alors	*you to listen also we*
79		d'écouter aussi on	*listened to you yesterday*
80		vous a écouté hier	*(you?) do the same for*
81		(vous?) faites la même	*the people today ok I*
82		chose pour les	*repeat again for the*
83		personnes	*evaluation you are*
84		d'aujourd'hui ok je	*going to do there are*
85		répète encore pour	*nine questions so it's*
86		l'évaluation que vous	*out of nine if you reply*
87		allez faire il y a neuf	*yes to a question it's one*
88		questions donc c'est	*point no to a question*
89		sur neuf si vous	*it's*
90		répondez oui à une	
91		question c'est un	
92		point non à une	
93		question c'est	
94	Rahman:	(xxx)	*(xxx)*
95	Lise:	c'est zéro des peut-	*it's zero maybe or*
96		être ou moyen c'est	*medium is point five ok*
97		point cinq ok si vous	*if you have questions*
98		avez des questions	*ask them either during*

99		soit que vous les	or after
100		posez durant ou après	
101	*Leïla:*	après après	*after after*
102	*Lise:*	après	*after*
103	*Male*		
	student:	non durant	*no during*
104	*Lise:*	alors gardez toutes	*so keep all your*
105		vos questions	*questions answer*
106		répondez	
107	*Male*		
	student:	on oublie on va	*we forget we'll forget*
108		oublier Madame	*Madame*
109	*Lise:*	si t'as des questions	*if you have questions*
110		sur son invention	*about his/her invention*
111	*Saïd:*	Madame	*Madame*
112	*Lise:*	ok	*ok*
113	*Rahman:*	d'autre part si si on a	*on the other hand if we*
114		quelque chose à dire	*have something to say*
115		on (xx) parce que si	*we (xx) because if we*
116		on	
117	*Lise:*	non tu le dis après	*no you say it later (xx)*
118		(xx) tu l'écris quelque	*you write it somewhere*
119		part ok	*ok*
120	*Saïd:*	Madame	*Madame*
121	*Lise:*	oui Saïd	*yes Saïd*
122	*Saïd:*	(xx) il faut qu'ils	*(xx) they have to draw*
123		dessinent les le robot	*the (pl) the (sing) robot*
124	*Lise:*	mais ceux qui font la	*but the ones who are*
125		présentation c'est à	*doing the presentation*
126		eux de choisir	*it's up to them to decide*
127	*Leïla:*	(xx) là si tu veux	*(xx) there if you want*
128	*Saïd:*	alors mets-la ici	*so put it here*
129		(laughter)	*(laughter)*
130	*Lise:*	ok ok on les écoute	*ok ok we listen to them*
131	*Rahman:*	on on peut pas (xx)	*we we can't (xx)*
132	*Leïla:*	alors on commence	*so we start*
133		(The presentation	(The presentation
134		begins)	begins)

A similar problem occurs in Example 3.5, only this time it occurs on another day, in the middle of a different student's presentation. Here, Lise actually interrupts the event in order to re-establish interactional order (see lines 24–33).

Example 3.5   10th grade Français général, *1991. Mohamud is making a presentation about marriage practices in Somalia.*

1	Mohamud:	il y a une autre coutume	*there is another custom*
2		que j'ai entendu parler	*I've heard of it's it*
3		c'est ça existe en	*exists in Somalia like*
4		Somalie comme la fille	*the girl is born her*
5		est née son avenir est	*future is already*
6		déjà prédit il y a	*predicted there is*
7		comme un sorcier ou	*like a sorcerer or*
8		quelque chose comme	*something like that you*
9		ça vous ne comprenez	*don't understand (xx)*
10		pas (xx) un sorcier (xx)	*a sorcerer (xx) a*
11		un sorcier qui va venir	*sorcerer who will*
12		qui va dire à la fille tu	*come who will say to*
13		vas te marier avec ce ce	*the girl you will marry*
14		ce gars là (xx) elle va	*this this this guy*
15		se marier avec ce gars	*(xx) she'll marry this*
16		là sans obligation	*guy without obligation*
17		même si elle vit (xx)	*even if she lives (xx)*
18	Leïla?		
	Zahra?:	(xx) moi j'ai jamais vu ça	*(xx) I never saw that*
19	Mohamud:	et on paie rien	*and one pays nothing*
20	Saïd:	j'ai jamais entendu	*I've never heard of that*
21		dire ça	
22		(Many students talk,	(Many students talk,
23		laugh)	laugh)
24	Lise:	est-ce que tu sais	*do you know how (xx)*
25		comment (xx) un peu	*a bit of respect (xx) to*
26		de respect (xx) de	*show respect for others*
27		porter du respect pour	*to listen when someone*
28		les autres écouter	*talks this makes at*
29		lorsqu'une personne	*least five times that I*
30		parle ça fait cinq fois	*ask in five minutes*
31		au moins que je	
32		demande en dedans de	
33		cinq minutes	

Lise's struggles show how central the canonical mode of interaction was to her idea of classroom life, valuing it as she did as 'respect', and insisting on it to the point of sacrificing some important pedagogical principles. In the case of classes such as *Sciences*, the nature of the material imposed a form of social organization based on group or individual work, and sanctioned the kind of moving around the room that Lise found so difficult to tolerate. Nonetheless, even in Sciences there were limits to what was acceptable. In *Sciences général* there were occasional reminders; in one instance, the head teacher, Danielle, reminded her students about submitting work on time and '*en ordre*' (in order). This included handing in homework on time, homework cleanly presented ('*je vais regarder aussi la propreté*' (I shall also look at the cleanliness)), and with all questions answered in sequence. However, in the midst of her explanation (from line 14), Danielle also extends '*ordre*' to the organization of talk:

Example 3.6   10th grade Sciences général, *1991*

1	*Danielle:*	(. . .) C'est le deuxième	*(. . .) It's the second one*
2		que je ramasse puis je	*I've collected and I'm*
3		vous dis ce que j'aimais	*telling you what I didn't*
4		pas. J'ai beaucoup de	*like. I have a great deal*
5		difficulté à accepter que	*of trouble accepting that*
6		quelqu'un le fasse plus	*someone not do it in*
7		en ordre, parce que je	*order anymore, because*
8		vous ai tous dit dans	*I've told you all in what*
9		quel ordre. Si vous étiez	*order. If you were not*
10		pas correctes, je vous ai	*okay, I took points off*
11		enlevé des points la	*the last time. So you*
12		dernière fois. Alors	*should all be in order.*
13		vous devriez tous (tUt)	*Okay, like if you talk*
14		être en ordre. Okay,	*(like? with?) Fatima, you*
15		comme si vous parlez	*are not in order (. . .)*
16		(comme? avec?) Fatima	
17		alors vous n'êtes pas en	
18		ordre. (. . .)	

Here, Danielle not only explicitly equates talking sequentially on a unified floor, that is, refraining from holding other conversations while she is talking, with 'order', she also uses her position as controller of talk to interrupt herself to control the parallel conversations going on while she talks. In the structure and the form of her communicative action, Danielle shows how central these specific forms of talk are to social order.

In other classrooms the links, and the value, perhaps came out less clearly, but only because they were less directly challenged. Most other classes simply followed the required format, and if anyone stepped out of line a sharp (and completely implicit) 'Stéphane!'

or 'Sophie!' would usually do the trick. Nonetheless, Danielle's concern with interactional and other forms of order were echoed in other classes, where teachers insisted on work being presented in a certain order, handed in by seat order, and so on.

The school's routine organization of classroom space in ways supportive of teacher-centred classrooms, and its valuing as 're-spect' the use of a unified floor and sequential turn-taking, rendered available the social organizational means for teachers to monitor the linguistic production of students. I do not want to argue that this preference for specific forms of social organization of interaction was intended to support such monitoring. There are reasons to believe that that specific consequence may have (at least originally) been no more than fortuitous. For example, the insistence on unified floors and sequential turn-taking seems to me to be tied to broader concerns of social control in the classroom, of which the specific preoccupation with language in French-language minority schools only happens to be one, socially and historically contingent, example. In addition, the link between sequential turn-taking and respect seems also tied to the school's simultaneous efforts to engage in anti-racist education. Respect is, of course, a key concept in anti-racist education, and, at least in the way in which it was practised at Champlain, was held to be demonstrated through concerted efforts at listening to what the other had to say, in order to understand diverse points of view. The result though is that each of these threads (linguistic monitoring, general social control, anti-racist initiatives) reinforces the other, and may militate against the introduction of change in any one of these domains. For example, recent shifts in pedagogical ideologies have encouraged movement away from teacher-centred classrooms, but Franco-Ontarian schools' concerns with language may present obstacles to the introduction of new ways of organizing classroom interaction; despite an interest in the pedagogical benefits of group work, for instance, teachers have sometimes been reluctant to use it on the grounds that it would permit students to use more English (Heller 1994a).

In the following two sections, I shall take a closer look at the way in which institutional arrangements permit the production and reproduction of the twin ideologies of monolingualism and language quality. In both cases, I shall discuss overt and explicit strategies, as well as the kinds of linguistic monitoring rendered possible by the normative interactional order of the school. Finally, I shall also examine strategies which help to reinforce the dominant ideologies by diminishing tensions among conflicting interactional circumstances or conflicting ideologies.

3 The construction and management of a monolingual ideal

In Chapters 1 and 2, I discussed the nature of the ideological basis of francophone mobilization in Canada, and the ways in which the characteristics of the mobilization have entailed an investment in a form of territorial nationalism in Quebec, and institutional nationalism elsewhere in Canada (with the possible exception of the more ambiguous situation of Acadia), in an ideological structure tracing its origins to 19th century state nationalism, and which holds the monolingual nation-state to be the normal way to organize social, economic and political life. Translated into the circumstances of francophone minority life, this manifests itself as a preference for a distinct separation between the world of French and the world of English, and political lobbying for the creation of monolingual French institutional zones, of which the school has historically been the most important.

A large part of the energy invested in the creation of monolingual schools has gone towards fighting for their legal and institutional infrastructure (see Chapter 2). Somehow it was assumed that once it was possible to create such schools, they would simply function in the way they were intended to function, that is, monolingually. Perhaps this assumption came from lack of experience, perhaps it flowed logically from the guiding notions of the argument which led to the schools' establishment, it is hard to say which. Certainly, it would have been difficult to argue for the establishment of French-language schools on the grounds that French-speakers lacked the competence in English to function well in English educational milieux, while at the same time pushing for establishment in those schools of the means to ensure that those same students would indeed speak French. The legitimacy of monolingual state/institutional nationalism depends on the existence of a homogeneous nation with intrinsic and inalienable characteristics. The fact that another argument for the necessity of these schools was the galloping assimilation rate among young Franco-Ontarians does not vitiate this argument; it would have been possible to assume that, given the chance, these young people in danger of assimilation would remain within the fold.

However, the actual conditions in which the schools were established meant that it would frequently be very unlikely for legislators', educators' and community leaders' assumptions about school monolingualism to be borne out. As we have seen, three conditions militate against school monolingualism, in varying degrees depending on the precise location of the school: (1) the minority setting, which ensures student exposure to life in English outside school; (2) the linguistic assimilation of some portion of the student body; and (3) the necessity of accepting non-francophone students in order to maintain enrolment levels. Once the schools were established, it became necessary to cope with these realities. This has meant, on the one hand, a consistent reaffirmation of the monolingual nature of the schools, at least at the official, policy level, and, on the other, the development of strategies for dealing with the *de facto* bilingualism or multilingualism of school life.

The history of Franco-Ontarian schooling permits a view of the development of a variety of such strategies, most of which, at the policy or programme level, have involved discussions of admissions criteria and of programmes and pedagogies aimed at correcting the anomaly of bilingualism. More specifically, these programmes have aimed at creating a student body, all members of which are at least able to act as francophone monolinguals in school (whatever other languages they may master and choose to speak elsewhere).

I have documented the efforts of the late 1970s and early 1980s elsewhere (see Chapter 2; and Heller 1994a, 1994b). The 1990s saw a new round of efforts, cast in a slightly different spirit. While earlier initiatives focused on specific programmes for students who came to school without the knowledge of the kind of French that school expected of them, and/or of the means to display that knowledge, the initiatives of the 1990s were aimed at supporting the school itself as a monolingual site.

In this spirit, in 1991 the Ministry undertook the production of basic policy guidelines for Franco-Ontarian education. My knowledge of these documents comes both from the texts of the documents and from having participated in various phases of the consultation process involved in their production. Most versions of the text were prepared by a writer hired on contract to the Ministry; some elements were prepared by other writers, notably academics (including me; I wrote the first version of the Mandate statement discussed below as Examples 3.7 and 3.8). These drafts were then circulated to a core group of consultants, including academics, Franco-Ontarian educators, and representatives of relevant francophone interest groups (such as the association of parents) who furnished feedback either in written form or through occasional workshops and other discussion fora. Some of these discussions were heated, particularly those concerning the extent to which recognition should be given to the language and culture of the oldest established francophone communities, versus those of the diverse newcomers, and those discussions concerning the management of English and English speakers in the schools.

The initiatives were initially conducted under the heading of *Refrancisation*. This is not a term which lends itself easily to translation, but essentially connotes attempts to make French again someone or something that had initially been French but had subsequently at least partially lost that characteristic. It was the major (although not the sole) term favoured for this subject during the 1980s. However, problems with it immediately surfaced, especially the fact that some of the students in Franco-Ontarian schools could not be described convincingly as having been French in the first place. The term was then amended to *Refrancisation/Francisation*. Again problems surfaced as it became clear that the purpose of the schools was to serve a French-speaking clientèle who identified themselves as members of the francophone community, and it was difficult to openly accept – indeed, practically advertise – the fact that the clientèle included students who might not meet those criteria. Furthermore, this question raised the contentious issue of whose interests were to be given priority in this new initiative: those of francophones long-established in Ontario who were hoping the schools would help them repair the damage of generations of marginalization and oppression, or those of newcomers?

After three years of discussion and multiple revisions (ultimately all conducted by the single designated writer rather than by the original authors) these documents were eventually published in 1994 as a set of three guidelines: *Aménagement linguistique en français: Guide d'élaboration d'une politique d'aménagement linguistique* (Language planning in French: A guide for the development of a language planning policy); *Investir dans l'animation culturelle: Guide d'intervention* (Investing in cultural community development: An action guide); and *Actualisation linguistique en français et Perfectionnement du français* (Linguistic realisation in French and Perfecting French).

The three titles already reveal the Ministry's orientation. At one and the same time the Ministry focuses on the school's ability (indeed the school's need) to regulate language use within its walls and recognizes the interdependence between the school and the community which it serves. It provides guidelines for accomplishing the elusive goal of making the schools what they were intended to be (monolingual French institutions) with a population which, whatever its differences, has at least two things in common: some sense of affiliation with the concept of a Franco-Ontarian community (whatever that may be), and the mastery of whatever variety of French it is that would constitute having perfected it.

In developing these guidelines, the Ministry published, for the first time in the history of publicly funded French-language education in Ontario, a statement of the mandate of its French-language schools. As I mentioned, in 1991 I was asked to prepare a draft of this mandate, a draft which focused on the three objectives listed in Example 3.7.

Example 3.7   From: Draft version of Le rôle ou le mandat de l'école de langue française *(submitted to the Ministry of Education and Training of Ontario, 1991, p. 1)*

1 Les objectifs:	*Goals:*
2 1. Favoriser la réussite	*1. To promote the academic*
3 scolaire, de toutes et tous les	*success of all francophones of*
4 francophones de la province	*the province without regard to*
5 sans égard aux origines	*their geographic or*
6 géographiques ou	*ethnocultural origins, or to*
7 ethnoculturelles, à la race, au	*race, gender or social class.*
8 sexe ou à la classe sociale.	
9 2. Servir de lieu privilégié	*2. To serve as a privileged site*
10 pour l'évolution de la langue	*for the development of French*
11 et de la culture françaises en	*language and culture in*
12 Ontario. Ceci entraîne	*Ontario. This entails*
13 l'encouragement de débats	*encouraging debates*

14	concernant la nature des liens	*concerning the nature of the*
15	entre l'école et la	*ties between school and*
16	communauté, les variétés de	*community, concerning the*
17	langue et les formes	*linguistic varieties and cultural*
18	culturelles à favoriser dans le	*forms to be favoured at*
19	milieu scolaire et la	*school, and concerning the*
20	participation de divers	*participation of various groups*
21	groupes dans la population à	*in the population in French-*
22	l'école de langue française.	*language schools.*
23	3. Servir de lieu privilégié	*3. To serve as a privileged site*
24	pour la définition des	*for the definition of the social,*
25	objectifs sociaux,	*economic and political goals of*
26	économiques et politiques de	*the francophone population*
27	la population francophone de	*of the province. This includes*
28	la province. Ceci inclut des	*attempts at creating a*
29	tentatives vers un projet de	*pluralist and egalitarian society.*
30	société pluraliste et égalitaire.	

Quite frankly, I thought to myself that if the Ministry was going to ask me to draft a mandate for Ontario's French-language schools, I might as well at least respect my own social and political position; after all, they could always change what they didn't like. I am not sure how many drafts this text went through, but Example 3.8 shows the final version. What is most notable, from my perspective, is the shift from conceiving of the school as a site where on-going debate about social, cultural and linguistic values should occur, to precise statements about the nature of the values the school will prefer. Nonetheless, there is an attempt to preserve the pluralist and democratic perspective of the original.

Example 3.8   From: Aménagement linguistique en français: Guide d'élaboration d'une politique d'aménagement linguistique *(Ontario Ministry of Education and Training, 1994a, p. 9)*

1	Énoncé de principe: Le	*Statement of principle: The*
2	mandat des écoles franco-	*mandate of Franco-Ontarian*
3	ontariennes	*schools*
4	– Favoriser la réussite scolaire	*– Promote the school success*
5	et l'épanouissement de	*and personal development of*
6	l'ensemble des élèves, filles et	*all students, girls and boys,*
7	garçons, dans le respect	*respecting their characteristics,*
8	de leurs caractéristiques –	*be they physical, intellectual,*
9	physiques, intellectuelles,	*linguistic, ethnic, cultural,*

10	linguistiques, ethniques,	*racial or religious, and*
11	culturelles, raciales et	*whatever their socio-economic*
12	religieuses – sans égard au	*status.*
13	statut socio-économique.	
14	– Favoriser chez les élèves le	*– Promote the development of*
15	développement de l'identité	*students' personal, linguistic*
16	personnelle, linguistique et	*and cultural identity as well as*
17	culturelle et le sentiment	*their sense of belonging to a*
18	d'appartenance à une	*dynamic and pluralist*
19	communauté franco-	*Franco-Ontarian community.*
20	ontarienne dynamique et	
21	pluraliste.	
22	– Promouvoir l'utilisation du	*– Promote the use of French in*
23	français dans toutes les	*all spheres of activity at school*
24	sphères d'activités à l'école	*as well as in the community.*
25	comme dans la communauté.	
26	– Élargir le répertoire	*– Widen students' linguistic*
27	linguistique des élèves et	*repertoires and develop their*
28	développer leurs	*knowledge of and competence*
29	connaissances et leurs	*in French, while accepting their*
30	compétences en français, en	*spoken French and using it as*
31	acceptant et prenant comme	*a point of departure. This*
32	point de départ leur français	*acquired competence in the*
33	parlé. Cette compétence	*decontextualized use of French*
34	acquise dans l'usage	*will allow them to successfully*
35	décontextualisé du français	*pursue learning all their lives*
36	leur permettra de poursuivre	*in whatever field of study they*
37	avec succès leur apprentissage	*may choose.*
38	toute la vie durant, quel que	
39	soit le domaine d'études	
40	choisi.	
41	– Permettre aux élèves	*– Permit the students to acquire*
42	d'acquérir une bonne	*a good communicative*
43	compétence communicative	*competence in English, under*
44	en anglais, dans des	*conditions which promote*
45	conditions qui favorisent un	*additive bilingualism.*
46	bilinguisme additif.	
47	– Encourager le partenariat	*– Encourage a partnership*
48	entre les écoles, les parents,	*among schools, parents,*
49	les différents groupes	*different community*
50	de la communauté ainsi que	*groups as well as the world of*
51	le monde des affaires, du	*business, commerce and*
52	commerce et de l'industrie.	*industry.*

53	– Donner aux élèves les outils	– *Give students the tools*
54	nécessaires pour participer à	*necessary to participation in*
55	l'essor de la communauté	*the development of the*
56	franco-ontarienne et pour	*Franco-Ontarian community*
57	contribuer avec succès à la	*and to successfully contribute*
58	société, sur les plans social,	*to society, whether in the social,*
59	politique, économique et	*political, economic or scientific*
60	scientifique.	*domain.*

What we have in this text is a synthesis of long-standing goals regarding the role of schooling in the Franco-Ontarian community, principally to foster a sense of Franco-Ontarian identity alongside facilitating participation in the mainstream market (here referred to as 'society', and specified with reference to 'social, political, economic and scientific domains' – see lines 58–60). The Ministry also underlines the importance of the monolingual nature of the school for the survival of the Franco-Ontarian community (lines 22–5).

The text echoes this principle in its reference to 'additive bilingualism', a concept first used by the Canadian social psychologist Wallace Lambert, but made popular in francophone minority circles by Rodrigue Landry (cf. Landry 1982 for an early, but definitive, formulation). Landry argues that there are two ways to become bilingual: through subtractive bilingualism, in which one language replaces the other in an individual's or a community's repertoire; and additive bilingualism, in which one language is added to, but does not displace the other. Landry further argues, at least for the Canadian francophone case, that additive bilingualism is desirable, while subtractive bilingualism is not. For him, as for the Ministry, seemingly, the ideal bilingual is one who can act as a monolingual, but in two (or more) languages; ideal bilingualism is a kind of double monolingualism. What underlies this notion is the idea that true, real, good linguistic competence is that which takes as its model the way one uses a language in a monolingual setting. It is also important to note that the Ministry has no quarrel with the importance of learning English; as elsewhere we see that ideological differences emerge not over whether or not to speak English, but rather over how to manage one's bilingual repertoire. It also recognizes that the community may be heterogeneous ('*pluraliste*' in its terms), but stresses nonetheless the importance of a common affiliation to something called a Franco-Ontarian community; this is reflected in the definition of the term provided in the second document.

Example 3.9   From: Investir dans l'animation culturelle: Guide d'intervention *(Ontario Ministry of Education and Training, 1994b, p. 10)*

1 La communauté franco-	*The Franco-Ontarian*
2 ontarienne est formée des	*community is composed of*
3 descendants du peuple	*descendants of the French-*
4 canadien-français établis en	*Canadian people long-*
5 Ontario de longue date, des	*established in Ontario, of*
6 membres de la francophonie	*members of the Canadian and*
7 canadienne et internationale	*international francophone*
8 résidant en Ontario et leur	*community living in Ontario as*
9 descendance, et des	*well as their descendants, and*
10 autochtones s'identifiant	*of members of the Native*
11 à l'Ontario français.	*population who identify with*
12	*French Ontario.*

What is necessary here is a balancing between the ideological necessity of both constructing a commonality (the Franco-Ontarian community) and recognizing heterogeneity (described as 'pluralism' and specified as referring to a francophone community wider than the limits of Ontario). Since the definition rests on concepts that are social constructs themselves ('people', *'francophonie'*), what is important about it is that it accomplishes both the boundary-drawing that is key to the construction of identity, and the ambiguity and fluidity that render the definition workable in a world which will not sit still to have its picture taken once and for all.

The final element of the text of the mandate to which I wish to draw attention here is its focus on community as based not only on affiliation, but also on a common valuing of the decontextualized language taught at school. The Ministry also recognizes that there may exist a gap between the variety of French valued by the school and that mastered by the students. This aspect of the text will be taken up in the next section of this chapter.

The focus on the school as a monolingual French-speaking milieu is taken up at the school level in the way it publicly represents itself. The school makes an explicit point about this in one of its key documents, its annual course guide. While the document serves mainly to help students select courses for the coming academic year, and, as can be seen from the text below, is written directly for an audience of current and prospective students, it also serves as a general introduction to the school, featuring messages from key administrators and descriptions of school life alongside photographs and other material designed to create a public image of the school. However, the following text does not simply present the school as a French-language institution (in case, perhaps, a student might be wondering if it was a French immersion school, aimed at second language learners of French, for example). It goes beyond this to insist on the exclusive practice of French, an insistence which would not be necessary if it were already the prevailing convention.

*Example 3.10   From École Champlain course listing (*Répertoire des cours*) 1992–93, p. 3.*

1 Usage du français: L'École	*Use of French: Champlain*
2 Champlain est une école de	*School is a French-language*
3 langue française. Toutes les	*school. All activities, whether*
4 activités, qu'elles soient	*strictly academic, cultural or*
5 purement scolaires ou qu'elles	*recreational take place in*
6 soient culturelles ou récréatives	*French. We also expect of you*
7 se déroulent en français. On	*that you speak in French to*
8 attend également de vous que	*your teachers and fellow*
9 vous vous adressiez en français	*students; in class and during*
10 à vos enseignant-e-s et à vos	*all school and extra-curricular*
11 condisciples; en classe et	*activities. The Law on*
12 pendant toutes les activités	*Education stipulates that in a*
13 scolaires et parascolaires. La	*French-language school the*
14 loi sur l'éducation précise que	*language of administration*
15 dans l'école de langue française	*and communication is French.*
16 la langue d'administration et	*A French-language school, in*
17 de communication est le	*addition to being a teaching*
18 français. Une école de langue	*institution is also a source of*
19 française, en plus d'être une	*extension of this language and*
20 maison d'enseignement est	*of the culture it transmits. No*
21 aussi un foyer de rayonnement	*human being can develop in*
22 de cette langue et de la culture	*harmony, can develop his or*
23 qu'elle véhicule. Aucun être	*her full potential if he or she*
24 humain ne peut se développer	*does not master perfectly this*
25 harmonieusement, se réaliser	*tool of thought and of*
26 pleinement s'il ne maîtrise pas	*communication. Each teacher*
27 parfaitement cet outil de	*and each department will*
28 pensée et de communication.	*have a policy aimed at*
29 Chaque enseignant-e et chaque	*encouraging you to use only*

30 secteur auront une politique	*French in school and in the*
31 visant à vous encourager à	*classroom.*
32 n'utiliser que le français à	
33 l'école et dans les salles de	
34 classe.	

Here the justification for school monolingualism builds on the Ministry's notion that the school is responsible not just to itself, but also to the community. If the school is not French, the community will have difficulty retaining its identity, and the language and culture will not develop as they should. But more importantly, the notion of what French language and culture are rests on an ideology of monolingualism. Again, it is the state of monolingualism that is taken as normal, and therefore as essential to linguistic and cultural development both at the level of the community and at the level of the individual.

The school makes explicit its commitment to this ideology, an ideology which flows from the logic of the legal and policy foundations of Franco-Ontarian education and of the movement for francophone rights from which they have emerged. It also commits its teachers to working towards its realization, in the event that students (as the school is well aware) may not cleave to it automatically.

Because indeed, as we have seen, most students do not. This state of affairs thus puts the school and its staff in a state of constant paradox. On the one hand, the logic of the school supposes that students are speakers of French. On the other hand, the same logic presupposes that some of these students might be suffering the assimilative consequences of life in a minority setting. In addition, the sociological reality of the school renders necessary some acceptance of the fact that the student body actually includes an even wider range of linguistic repertoires than at first imaginable. The use of French by school representatives reflects this tension, as they move back and forth between frustration and bewilderment at the sociolinguistic reality of the school ('But they don't even speak their mother tongue!'), determination to construct the sociolinguistic reality to which the school is committed, and recognition and acceptance of the concrete sociolinguistic conditions of the classroom as they currently exist.

Elsewhere, I have documented some of the more evident ways in which teachers and other school representatives across Ontario's

French-language schools attempt to construct the school as a French-speaking monolingual milieu, notably through eternally repeated cries of '*Parlez français!*' ('Speak French!'), and through institutionally organized punitive or incitative campaigns (rewards for speaking French, punishments for speaking English; cf. Heller 1994a, 1995). During the time I was at Champlain, no school-wide punitive campaign was ever even discussed (such campaigns in any case tend to be found more often at the elementary rather than at the secondary level). However, several teachers used smaller-scale punishments. The most frequent one was to request, from a student caught speaking a language other than French, a composition on the subject of '*pourquoi on est dans une école de langue française*' (why we are in a French-language school). In Example 3.3 above, Lise includes speaking a language other than French on her list of behaviours she will not tolerate, and characterizes that one as '*le plus gros problème de la classe*' (the biggest problem of the class). Indeed, the ensuing class discussion focused on appropriate punishments for each type of infraction.

On the other hand, various kinds of school-wide incitative measures *were* discussed and sometimes implemented. One was proposed as part of a initiative to create an 'effective school' (the effective schools movement began in the United States in the 1980s, and is well documented in the educational literature); this proposal included a system of rewards (similar to ranked orders of merit) which included linguistic performance among its criteria. However, this system never saw the light of day. The major measure used during the research period was a literary contest (winning entries were published annually). In addition, the school began an annual literary and cultural fair. Students and visitors, during the two or three days of the fair, circulated among a variety of events. One such event was a kind of literary café; tables were set up in a large room, and admission was restricted to the number of seats at these tables. Drinks and snacks were available, and entertainment was provided by the students. This was organized through *Français* classes, in which students were generally obliged, individually or collectively, to select a piece (a prose reading, poem, skit or song) to perform. Two teachers then put together the programme from these student selections. In both cases, the promotion of French was conducted through the valuing of literary production. As we shall see in subsequent chapters, students responded in different ways to this association of French with the public display of high culture, some embracing and others resisting the opportunity presented to them to invest in this particular form of symbolic capital.

Otherwise, the major form of sociolinguistic control exercised by school staff took the form of linguistic surveillance through interaction. In this section I shall focus on surveillance of language choice, although what I have to say here will also bear on the discussion of language quality in the next section.

It is important to note that teachers actually monitor their own language use, perhaps almost as much as they monitor that of their students, or even, in some cases, more. This is true both in regard to monolingualism, and in regard to language quality. The issue of self-monitoring is not so pressing in classes where it is possible to establish a French-speaking world – that is, where teachers are not dependent on community resources or real-world knowledge, and where they themselves manifest a linguistic security that comes from having spent most of one's life in a majority setting (advanced level *Français*, with its focus on decontextualized language skills, is the best example of such a class). To the extent that it is necessary to make reference to the English-speaking world, most teachers in such circumstances deal with the problem by heavily flagging these references (see Examples 3.12 and 3.14 below, and Examples 3.17, 3.19, 3.20 and 3.21 in the next section). Students, especially those in advanced level classes who are more likely to collaborate with school efforts at social control (see Chapter 4), make sure their use of English remains recognizably off the unified floor of the classroom, notably by limiting it to whispered conversations at the back of the classroom or behind the teacher's back, or through passing notes. The use of English on the unified floor is recognized as a challenge to the teacher's authority, and usually occurs only when a student is simultaneously doing such challenging through the content, not just the form, of what he or she says.

The problem is more evident in classes like *Sciences*, where frequent reference is made to the local or regional environment, and where there is greater dependence on English-speaking networks and institutions for resources. The following example concerns an episode from a 10th grade advanced level *Sciences* class in 1991. Like Lise, Aline (the teacher), has an anglophone spouse and she herself comes from a francophone minority setting (although a more socially and culturally homogeneous one than Toronto). She makes

allowances for normative deviance in students' linguistic performances, as long as they do not occur on the public unified floor or
in interaction directly with her. Since the course involves lab work,
students' use of English among themselves is tolerated while they
work in small groups. Anything said loud enough to be heard by
all, directed to Aline, or said during lecture components of the
course, however, must be in French. Since this is an advanced level
course involving students who generally see it as in their interest
to collaborate with the school's agenda, Aline rarely has to make
her expectations on this count explicit.

The following example is fairly typical of Aline's class, and
of other advanced level classes. The unified floor, IRE format is
accompanied by the use of French with very few exceptions. The
sequence is taken from a review session near the end of the semester.
While the students' responses here are minimal, there are similar
sequences where their utterances are longer, although generally
teachers take much longer turns at talk than do the students.

Example 3.11   10th grade Sciences avancé, *1991*

	1	*Aline:*	(. . .) le deuxième cas	*(. . .) the second case*
	2		de lumière blanche tu	*of white light you put*
I	3		mets ah un filtre euh	*ah a uh cyan filter so*
	4		cyan donc quelles	*which colours will*
	5		couleurs vont traverser	*pass through*
R	6		(pause) aucune	*(pause) none*
	7	*Male*		
		students:	(xx)	*(xx)*
I	8	*Aline:*	cyan est formé de quoi?	*cyan is made of what?*
R	9	*Male*		
		students:	bleu	*blue*
EI	10	*Aline:*	cyan bleu et	*cyan blue and*
R	11	*Several*		
		students:	vert	*green*
E	12	*Aline:*	bleu et vert donc si	*blue and green so if I*
	13		je mets un filtre rouge	*put a red filter what*
	14		qu'est-ce qui va passer	*will go through that?*
I	15		à travers ça?	
R	16	*Male*		
		student:	aucune	*none*
E	17	*Aline:*	aucune troisièmement	*none third I have*
	18		j'ai deux couleurs deux	*two colours two rays*

	19		rayons j'ai un rayon	*I have a blue ray and*
	20		bleu puis j'ai un rayon	*I have a red ray if I*
	21		rouge si je mets un	*put a magenta filter*
	22		filtre magenta magenta	*magenta is formed*
	23		est formé de quelles	*from which two*
I	24		deux couleurs?	*colours?*
R	25	*Several students:*	bleu et rouge	*blue and red*
E	26	*Aline:*	bleu et rouge donc	*blue and red so which*
I	27		quelle couleur sera	*colour will be blocked*
	28		bloquée par magenta?	*by magenta?*
R	29	*Female student:*	bleu et rouge	*blue and red*
E	30	*Aline:*	magenta est-ce que le	*magenta will the blue*
	31		bleu et le rouge	*and the red be able to*
	32		pourront passer?	*pass?*
	33		magenta bloque quelle	*magenta blocks which*
I	34		couleur?	*colour?*
R	35	*Male student:*	rouge	*red*
E	36	*Aline:*	magenta regardez	*magenta look magenta*
	37		magenta est formé de	*is formed of red and*
	38		rouge et bleu donc	*blue so my first filter*
	39		mon premier filtre	*blocks what? so so the*
	40		bloque quoi? donc	*blue can pass right?*
	41		donc le bleu peut	*but cyan cyan is here*
	42		passer n'est-ce pas?	*formed of blue cyan*
	43		mais cyan cyan est ici	*green cyan cyan will*
	44		formé de bleu et de	*block uh the red and*
	45		cyan vert cyan cyan va	*so the blue will pass*
	46		bloquer euh le rouge	
	47		puis donc le bleu va	
	48		passer	

Aline herself is relatively careful to not use English, although there are times when it is hard not to, times when, due to the nature of the subject matter, references to English-based knowledge in the outside world are next to unavoidable, or, in any case, pedagogically advisable. In Example 3.12, Aline is reading from a flyer sent to all southern Ontario high school Science teachers by recruiters at a nearby English-speaking university. The poster details the kinds of jobs that are available to those holding undergraduate degrees in the natural sciences. The poster, is, of course,

in English. Aline had several options open to her (throw it away, pin it up without discussion), but chose to present it to the class before pinning it up. However, rather than read it in English, she chose the more difficult route of simultaneous translation. Even so, she was not able to translate everything (bilinguals in Toronto are good, but only human), which caused her to find a path around the obstacle. The path she found was to accept the appropriate word in English, but from a student, or to use it herself, flagging the word with hesitations, and, if possible, immediately self-correcting (see lines 30–1, 40–2 and 57–9).

Example 3.12   10th grade Sciences avancé, 1991

1	*Aline:*	(. . .) ok vous savez que	*(. . .) ok you know that*
2		l'an prochain euh vous	*next year you'll be at*
3		serez au palier senior là	*the senior level 11 12 13*
4		11 12 13 et c'est là où	*that's where the science*
5		les cours de sciences sont	*courses aren't like a a bit*
6		pas comme un cours	*of bio a bit of chemistry*
7		général où on voit un	*a bit of physics instead*
8		petit peu de bio un peu	*it's the bio course the*
9		de chimie un peu de	*chemistry course (xx) I*
10		physique mais c'est le	*received a kind of (pause)*
11		cours de bio le cours de	*form from Guelph*
12		chimie (xx) j'ai reçu un	*University anyway to*
13		genre de (pause)	*show you the kind of*
14		formulaire de l'Université	*career you can have with*
15		Guelph, en tout cas pour	*a bachelor's in chemistry*
16		vous montrer le genre de	*or a bachelor's in*
17		carrière que tu peux avoir	*biochemistry if you have*
18		avec un bac en chimie ou	*a bachelor's in chemistry*
19		un bac en biochimie si tu	*here's the kind of thing*
20		as un bac en chimie voici	*you can do if one of*
21		le genre de choses que tu	*these interests you (sing.)*
22		peux faire donc si une de	*you (pl.) come to see me*
23		ces choses ça t'intéresse	*to take the chemistry*
24		vous venez me voir	*course next year in 11th*
25		prendre le cours de	*and uh two years later*
26		chimie l'an prochain en	*(bio?) ok you can become*
27		11ᵉ et euh deux ans de	*an um analytical*
28		temps après (bio?) ok tu	*analytical chemist for a*
29		peux devenir um	*gas company you can*
30		*analytical* chimiste	*become a chemical*
31		analytique pour une	*engineer you can become*
32		compagnie d'essence tu	*uh a salesperson for*
33		peux devenir ingénieur	*chemical products you*
34		chimique tu peux devenir	*can work for Hydro-*
35		euh vendeur de produits	*Ontario you can work*
36		chimiques tu peux	*like the police as a*
37		travailler pour Hydro-	*chemist uh*

38		Ontario tu peux travailler	
39		comme les policiers	
40		comme chimiste euh	
41	Marcel:	*forensic*	*forensic*
42	Aline:	*forensic* ouais tu peux	*forensic yeah you can*
43		enseigner tu peux euh	*teach you can uh work*
44		travailler pour fabriquer	*to make products uh*
45		des produits euh produits	*beauty products you can*
46		de beauté tu peux avec	*with a bachelor's in*
47		un bac en chimie	*chemistry continue and*
48		continuer et devenir	*become a dentist you can*
49		dentiste tu peux devenir	*become a research*
50		directeur de recherche en	*director in industry with*
51		industrie avec un bac en	*a bachelor's in chemistry*
52		chimie tu peux aussi	*you can also become a*
53		devenir médecin scientiste	*doctor an environmental*
54		de l'environnement ou	*scientist or ecologist an*
55		écologiste scientiste des	*explosives scientist again*
56		explosifs scientiste encore	*for forensic for the police*
57		pour *forensic* pour la	*for the (xx) uh a lawyer*
58		police pour les (xx) euh	
59		un avocat	

Nonetheless, Aline seems to recognize that it would be odd for her to pretend she doesn't speak English, or recognize that English-mediated nature of much real-world experience. In Example 3.13, taken from the same review session as Example 3.11, Aline refers to an experiment on acids and bases in which the class used commercially available antacids, which of course in Toronto have English names. While it is possible to nativize the names through French phonology, Aline pronounces them in their language of origin.

Example 3.13   10th grade Sciences avancé, 1991

1	Aline:	okay on continue. Dans	*okay, we continue. In*
2		quel d'après votre lab	*which according to your*
3		laquelle est préférable,	*lab which is preferable,*
4		Alka-Seltzer, Eno,	*Alka-Seltzer, Eno, Rolaids,*
5		Rolaids, Tums?	*Tums?*

Example 3.14 is taken from the same session, and concerns the structure of polymers in natural fibres. Here, the students refer a great deal to their knowledge of natural fibres in the outside world,

sometimes in English. Not only does Aline tolerate this, she actively incorporates their strategy in her summary (see especially lines 9–12, 96–8, 157–67, 184–6, 204–12).

Example 3.14   10th grade Sciences avancé, *1991*

1	*Aline:*	okay on continue,	*okay, we go on,*
2		Objectif E et (posez	*Objective E and (put*
3		votre?) s'il vous plaît	*down your?) please*
4	*Male*		
	student:	(xx)	*(xx)*
5	*Aline:*	on fera ça quand je	*we'll do that when I do*
6		ferai les retards je vais	*the lates I'll (xx –* noise
7		(xx – noise of chairs	of chairs moving*) in*
8		moving) dans vos mains	*your hands (xx) okay*
9		(xx) okay qu'est-ce que	*what are fibres?*
10		c'est que des fibres?	
11	*Male*		
	student:	fibre	fibre
12	*Aline:*	ouais	*yeah*
13	*Two*		
	students:	(xx)	*(xx)*
14	*Aline:*	(xx) okay (xx) par quoi?	*(xx) okay (xx) by what?*
15	*Several*		
	students:	(xx)	*(xx)*
16	*Aline:*	okay (xx) quelle autre	*okay (xx) what other*
17		substance?	*substance?*
18	*Male*		
	students:	(xx)	*(xx)*
19	*Aline:*	le linge par exemple,	*clothes, for instance, so*
20		donc les fibres doivent	*fibres have to have what*
21		avoir quoi comme	*characteristics?*
22		caractéristiques?	
23	*Male*		
	students:	(xx)	*(xx)*
24	*Aline:*	assez stable okay	*stable enough okay next*
25		ensuite qu'est-ce (qu'on	*what (do we need what*
26		a besoin qu'est-ce qu'on	*do we need?) to make*
27		a besoin?) pour faire	*cloth?*
28		des tissus?	
29	*Kevin?:*	(xx) assez longs?	*(xx) long enough?*
30	*Aline:*	il faut que les molécules	*the molecules or the*
31		ou les composés sont	*compounds (mainly?)*
32		(principalement très?)	*have to be (very?)*

33	Marcel?:	longs	*long*
34	Aline:	okay donc (she begins	*okay so (she begins to*
35		to dictate) fibres (xx)	*dictate) fibres (xx) are*
36		sont des composés	*compounds* (pause)
37		(pause) longs et minces	*[which are] long and*
38	Irène:	sont des composés ou	*thin are compounds or*
39	Male		
	student:	'é-e-s' à 'composés'	*'composés' [is written*
40			*with] 'é-e-s'*
41	Aline:	sont des composés longs	*are long thin*
42		et minces (pause) utilisés	*compounds* (pause) *used*
43		pour (pause) fabriquer	*for* (pause) *making cloth*
44		les tissus (end of	(end of dictation)
45		dictation)	
46	Male		
	student:	(xx)	*(xx)*
47	Aline:	oui maintenant la	*yes, now the*
48		relation qu'il existe	*relationship which it*
49		entre les fibres et les	*exists between fibres*
50		acides et les bases c'est	*acids and bases is that*
51		que pour faire les fibres	*to make fibres we*
52		on a besoin des acides	*need acids and bases*
53		et bases donc la	*so the first part of the*
54		première partie du	*chapter was what were*
55		chapitre était qu'est-ce	*acids and bases, the*
56		que c'étaient que les	*title of the chapter is*
57		acides et les bases, le	*(xxation?) why we use*
58		titre du chapitre c'est la	*acids and bases. So*
59		(xxation?) pourquoi on	*fibres are things we use*
60		utilise les acides (les?)	*regularly to make our*
61		bases. Donc les fibres	*clothes for example to*
62		c'est des choses qu'on	*make [them] it takes*
63		utilise couramment	*acids and bases okay*
64		pour faire notre linge	
65		par exemple pour faire	
66		ça prend des acides et	
67		des bases okay	
68	Male		
	student:	(xx)	*(xx)*
69	Aline:	okay il y a deux sortes	*okay there are two kinds*
70		de fibres (pause) okay il	*of fibres* (pause) *okay*
71		y a deux sortes (pause)	*there are two kinds*
72		quelles sont les deux	(pause) *what are the*
73		sortes de fibres si je	*two kinds of fibres if I*

74		compare par exemple	*compare for example*
75		le coton et le (pause)	*cotton and* (pause)
76	*Male*		
	student:	le lin	*linen*
77	*Aline:*	rayon	*rayon*
78	*Male*		
	student:	(xx)	*(xx)*
79	*Aline:*	le (xx) quoi?	*the (xx) what?*
80	*Marcel:*	naturel	*natural*
81	*Aline:*	c'est ça	*that's right*
82	*Marcel?:*		
	Kevin?:	et synthétique	*and synthetic*
83	*Aline:*	(xx) naturel et	*(xx) natural and*
84		synthétique (pause) si je	*synthetic* (pause) *if I*
85		commence avec les	*start with natural*
86		fibres naturels (pause)	*fibres* (pause) *okay*
87		okay la laine (pause)	*wool* (pause) *what*
88		quelles autres sortes de	*other kinds of fibres*
89		fibres qu'on connaît qui	*that we know that are*
90		sont relativement	*relatively common*
91		communs là	
92	*Male*		
	student:	le coton	*cotton*
93	*Aline:*	le coton	*cotton*
94	*Male*		
	student:	(xx)	*(xx)*
95	*Male*		
	student:	la soie	*silk*
96	*Maria:*	wool sheep	wool sheep
97	*Several*		
	students:	wool wool	wool wool
98	*Aline:*	ouais puis un dernier	*yeah and a last one*
99	*Female*		
	student:	(xx)	*(xx)*
100	*Aline:*	oui?	*yes?*
101	*Jean-*		
	Paul:	(Jean-Paul has just	
102		moved to Toronto from	
103		an asbestos-producing	
104		area in Quebec)	
105		l'amiante	*asbestos*
106	*Aline:*	quoi?	*what?*
107	*Jean-*		
	Paul:	l'amiante	*asbestos*

108	*Aline:*	non	*no*
109	*Michel?:*	l'amiante non	*asbestos no*
110	*Female*		
	student:	oh yes	<u>*oh yes*</u>
111	*Male*		
	student:	c'est naturel	*it's natural*
112		(Many students talk at	(Many students talk at
113		once)	once)
114	*Jean-*		
	Paul:	(xx) il y a des vêtements	*(xx) there are clothes*
115		en amiante	*made of asbestos*
116	*Aline:*	disons que c'est comme	*let's say it's like*
117		de la cellulose, ce sont	*cellulose, they're long*
118		des fibres longues euh	*uh thin fibres but it isn't*
119		fines mais c'est pas	*let's say we don't make*
120		disons qu'on fait pas le	*clothing with it*
121		linge avec ça	
122	*Jean-*		
	Paul:	ben un manteau	*well a coat*
123	*Justin:*	oui fait disons du linge	*yes make let's say*
124			*clothing*
125	*Jean-*		
	Paul:	y a des pompiers des	*there are firemen*
126		pompiers oui	*firemen do*
127		(Many students talk at	
128		once)	
129	*Aline:*	ouais	*yeah*
130	*Male*		
	student:	le cuir Madame on fait	*leather Madame we*
131		des habits en cuir	*make leather clothes*
132	*Aline:*	ben okay peut-être	*well okay maybe*
133		(Many students talk at	(Many students talk at
134		once)	once)
135	*Aline:*	okay mon Dieu okay ce	*okay my God okay*
136		que vous allez faire chut	*what you are going to*
137		(students are still	*do shh (students are*
138		talking) chut	*still talking) sh*
139	*Student:*	le *suede*	<u>*suede*</u>
140	*Aline:*	on continue okay chut	*we continue okay shh*
141		(Here there is a long	
142		episode in which the	
143		class watches a film	
144		about natural fibres.	
145		After the film, Aline	

146		asks the students to	
147		open their textbooks,	
148		and she reads sections	
149		which she then	
150		comments on or	
151		synthesizes, and about	
152		which the students ask	
153		a few brief questions.	
154		After having read a	
155		section on monomers	
156		and polymers, she adds:)	
157	*Aline:*	(...) à côté de coton	*(...) next to cotton*
158		et lin on a pas du tout	*and linen we haven't*
159		(discuté du?) lin le	*at all (discussed?)*
160		quatrième produit	*linen the fourth natural*
161		naturel, le lin 'linen' en	*product linen <u>linen</u> in*
162		anglais okay donc	*English okay so add*
163		ajouter le lin dans votre	*linen to your list of*
164		liste de fibres naturels	*natural fibres or of*
165		ou de polymers naturels	*natural polymers (noise*
166		(noise of chairs) le lin	*of chairs) linen <u>linen</u> in*
167		'linen' en anglais	*English*
168		(There follows a	
169		discussion about the	
170		properties of materials	
171		made from natural	
172		fibres, in which the	
173		students' real world	
174		knowledge of cloth	
175		comes into play. Having	
176		discussed linen and	
177		cotton, they go on to	
178		wool:)	
179	*Aline:*	(...) quels sont les	*(...) what advantages*
180		avantages à porter de la	*are there to wearing*
181		laine, pourquoi est-ce	*wool, why do we like*
182		qu'on aime ça? Parce	*it? because it*
183		que ça	
184	*Maria:*	ça donne chaud	*it gives [makes you] hot*
185	*Aline:*	c'est chaud avantage	*it's hot advantage it's a*
186		c'est un bon isolant	*good insulator*
187	*Justin?:*	désavantage ça pique	*disadvantage it scratches*
188	*Aline:*	ça pique désavantage	*it scratches disadvantage*
189		okay avantage un bon	*ok advantage a good*

190		isolant désavantage	*insulator disadvantage*
191		est-ce que ça se lave	*is it easy to wash?*
192		facilement ça?	
193	*All*		
	students:	non	*no*
194	*Aline:*	pas vraiment	*not really*
195	*Amanda:*	ça (se?) rétrécit aussi	*it also shrinks*
196	*Female*		
	student:	(you have to?)	<u>*(you have to?)*</u>
197		handwash (it?)	<u>*handwash (it?)*</u>
198	*Aline:*	(xx) donc désavantage	*(xx) so disadvantage is*
199		se lave difficilement	*hard to wash*
200		(After a few more turns	
201		on the subject of wool,	
202		they turn to silk:)	
203	*Aline:*	c'est très confortable	*it's very comfortable*
204	*Marcel:*	les *honeymooners* (xx)	<u>*honeymooners* (xx) *silk*</u>
205		la soie (xx) le	*(xx)* <u>*honeymoon*</u>
206		*honeymoon*	
207		(Female students laugh)	(Female students laugh)
208	*Aline:*	les quoi? qu'est-ce que	*the what? what are you*
209		tu dis là?	*saying?*
210	*Marcel:*	*when two people*	<u>*when two people*</u>
211		*honeymoon* (xx) la soie	<u>*honeymoon* (xx) *silk*</u>
212		(xx) lune de miel	*(xx)* <u>*honeymoon*</u>

There are many things to be said about this extract. The first point I want to make about it is that Aline uses the I-R-E format, and a unified floor, without much challenge, despite the fact that the interaction calls on students' experiences, not just school-based knowledge. When the students get out of hand, that is, when they break up the unified floor and all talk at once, Aline brings them back in line with a few '*chut*'s, '*okay*'s and '*on continue*'s (see lines 136, 138, 140).

Second, Aline explicitly calls on students' real-world knowledge in order to teach them something relatively abstract about the structure and functioning of acids and bases, monomers and polymers, as well as to demystify scientifically the nature of the everyday world. By using this strategy she does get herself into a bit of trouble, since the common-sense criteria she gives students to allow them to brainstorm (these fibres occur naturally and we make clothes out of them) unfortunately lead them to some materials (leather, asbestos) which lie outside the category she is aiming at (see lines 105–39). Most of the time, though, the students are on track, and provide, in French, the information Aline is seeking. Here, the pedagogical objective seems primary; on the few occasions when students provide information in English (and it is not surprising that their knowledge of materials and clothing might be mediated by English-language experience in the community), Aline accepts it, sometimes translating it into French (just as she translates everyday language, like '*ça donne chaud*' ('it makes you warm'), into scientific language, '*c'est un bon isolant*' ('it's a good insulator'); see lines 184–6). In lines 159–67, Aline herself refers back to this English-mediated knowledge in dictating her notes: '*le lin* linen *en anglais*' (although linen was not one of the lexemes used in English by the students). (In a separate interaction, Lise once revealed how routine this practice is when one of her Somali-speaking students asked her the meaning of '*indice*'. Lise's response was to think of the English equivalent, until it became clear that the student did not, in fact, speak English, and Lise had to define it in French).

It is only when Marcel uses the occasion of discussing the advantages of silk to discuss honeymoons (not a subject on which he has first-hand information), does Aline directly challenge a student's contribution ('*les quoi? qu'est-ce que tu dis là?*' ('the what? what are you saying?'); see lines 208–9). Even here, it is not clear whether she is focusing on the fact that Marcel used English, or on the content of his contribution. After a few exchanges and much laughter, Aline closes the episode with a comment on the content, not on the form ('*Okay Marcel t'as de bonnes idées*' (Okay Marcel you have good ideas)). At other times, Aline has not reacted to Marcel using English; for example, close to exam time Marcel, a highly motivated, high-achieving (and almost always French-speaking) student was talking about how stressed he felt. Other classmates told Aline that Marcel tears his hair out, literally, when he suffers from exam stress. Aline said: '*Oh oui, le stress, mais t'es seulement en dixième année, qu'est-ce qui va arriver quand t'es rendu en troisième année d'université?*' (Oh, yes, stress, but you're only in the tenth grade, what will you do when you are in the third year of university?). Marcel replied: 'I'll be bald!' Aline did not react at all to this use of English. On another occasion, Aline reprimanded a student who used objectionable language, as it happened in English, with a '*chut, langage*', '*langage*' being a term more likely to refer to the content of what was said than the language choice. Despite all these indications that Aline copes with the contradiction between language norm and pedagogy by interactionally reinforcing French but tolerating marginal infringements of the norm, Marcel still recognizes Aline's action as potentially constituting a regulation of his language choice, and responds by switching to French.

Through the imposition of unified floors, and through controlling students' turns at talk, Champlain staff have at their disposal a means for regulating linguistic performances. Through this means they are able to build a front stage in which the public face of the school is constructed and which is monolingual, and a back stage where the contradictions of the concretely bilingual experiences of participants in school life can be managed. There is some leakage, of course, but the work gets done.

In the next section, I shall discuss the other major dimension of the school's public francophone image which requires daily facework, namely the management of the nature of the French used on stage. For Champlain staff and students, as for most of *la francophonie*, this is understood as a problem of linguistic quality, that is, of ensuring that the French spoken is as good as it can possibly be.

4 *La qualité de la langue*

The problem of language quality is a long-standing one, emerging out of nineteenth-century Romantic nationalism in a way similar to the ideology of monolingualism (Grillo 1989; Balibar 1985). And also, in a similar way, it has served to construct hegemonic relations among ethnocultural groups and social classes, as well as between men and women (Outram 1987; Gal 1988). Despite the widespread nature of the issue, it is well recognized that France has developed far more than most other countries an institutional basis for the regulation of the quality of language, and the ideology of language quality with regard to French is more pervasive and more public than perhaps for any other language (Éloy 1995). When it comes to language quality, Franco-Ontarians are particularly beset. For one thing, they are in daily contact with English, the dominant world language (being in contact with just about any other language would arguably be easier). For another, Franco-Ontarians must cope with the highly charged nature of the social significance of varieties of French (Heller 1996; see Cajolet-Laganière and Martel 1995 and Laforest 1997 with regard to debates in Quebec).

However, the public discourse on this issue in francophone Ontario (a discourse which occurs mainly in the arena of education) does not include a focus on relations of power and social reproduction. Rather, the focus is on upholding existing values through appeals to universal criteria. Recall, for example, Champlain's insistence on mastering each language perfectly in order to possess the best possible tool of thought and communication (Example 3.10). We saw another expression of this idea in the text cited as Example 3.8, the Ministry of Education and Training of Ontario's proposed mandate for its French-language schools. In this text, care was taken to recognize the fact that there are frequently differences between the French spoken by students when they come to school, and that which the school values. For convenience, I shall reproduce the relevant section of that text here:

20	– Élargir le répertoire	– *Widen students' linguistic*
21	linguistique des élèves et	*repertoires and develop their*
22	développer leurs	*knowledge of and*
23	connaissances et leurs	*competence in French, while*
24	compétences en français, en	*accepting their spoken French*
25	acceptant et prenant comme	*and using it as a point of*
26	point de départ leur français	*departure. This acquired*
27	parlé. Cette compétence	*competence in the*
28	acquise dans l'usage	*decontextualized use of*
29	décontextualisé du français	*French will allow them to*
30	leur permettra de poursuivre	*successfully pursue learning*
31	avec succès leur apprentissage	*all their lives in whatever*
32	toute la vie durant, quel que	*field of study they may*
33	soit le domaine d'études	*choose.*
34	choisi.	

In this section, the Ministry characterizes the difference by saying that the school variety is decontextualized; students are seemingly not expected to arrive at school already possessing knowledge of this variety (although they *are* seemingly expected to master what is called here a 'spoken' variety); rather, it is the school's job to help them acquire it.

However, in the document on Perfecting French, a somewhat different picture of this gap emerges:

Example 3.15   From: Programme-cadre: Actualisation linguistique en français et Perfectionnement du Français *(Ministry of Education and Training of Ontario, 1994, p. 25)*

1 *Le perfectionnement du*	Perfecting French. (PDF)
2 *Français (PDF)* Raison d'être:	*Rationale: the PDF*
3 Le programme de PDF	*programme is for students*
4 s'adresse à des élèves qui	*who express themselves with*
5 s'expriment avec une certaine	*relative ease in a regional*
6 aisance dans une variété du	*variety of French distant from*
7 français régionale éloignée de	*the language of*
8 la langue d'enseignement et	*instruction and who have*
9 qui éprouvent des difficultés	*academic difficulties as a*
10 sur le plan scolaire en raison	*result of their lack of*
11 de leur manque de familiarité	*familiarity with the language*
12 avec la langue d'enseignement.	*of instruction.*

Here, the gap between the French already mastered by students when they arrive at school and that valued by the school is characterized not as a difference between 'spoken' and 'decontextualized' French, but rather as a difference between 'a regional variety' and 'the language of instruction'. Already, the slippage has begun. The slippage as revealed in Ministry documents is echoed in life at Champlain.

What is it that characterizes the 'distant' or 'spoken' or 'regional' variety that the school does not privilege? The school clearly rejects what it considers insulting or aggressive language (swearing and obscenities, for the most part), and this is relevant to the set of general cultural values the school supports. However, here I shall focus on other major dimensions of the value attributed to the quality of French.

The question of what teaching French (and teaching in French) was all about was included in most interviews we conducted with school personnel. Example 3.16 is from an interview I conducted with Liliane, an elected school trustee.

Example 3.16   Interview with Liliane, 1991

Monica:	en Français t'as mentionné	*in French you mentioned*
	l'importance d'avoir euh la	*the importance of having*
	représentation de différents	*uh the representation of*
	(xx) est-ce qu'il y a d'autres	*different (xx) are there*

	éléments euh directives générales?	*other elements uh general directives?*
Liliane:	oui euh une des choses qui nous est aussi importante c'est l'utilisation du français euh dans euh son euh dans sa forme écrite et parlée (. . .) qu'on soit sûr que la qualité soit là et euh avec l'aisance que l'on veut qu'ils obtiennent en même temps	*yes uh one of the things which is also important to us is the use of French uh in uh its uh in its written and spoken form (. . .) that we be sure that the quality is there and uh with the facility that we want them to get at the same time*
Monica:	par qualité qu'est-ce que tu entends?	*by quality what do you understand?*
Liliane:	qualité du français euh je pense que ça c'est dans notre volonté d'avoir une éducation excellente euh qu'ils s'expriment mais qu'ils s'expriment en français puis là je vais utiliser quelque chose qui qui va être peut-être interpreté comme racisme comme on disait autrefois en chinois il faut que ça soit un français normal il faut que ça soit un français point	*quality of French uh I think that it is part of our desire for excellent education uh that they express themselves but that they express themselves in French and here I will use something which which will be perhaps interpreted as racism as we used to say in the old days not in Chinese it has to be a normal French it has to be a French period*
Monica:	est-ce que	*is*
Liliane:	ce qui ne veut pas dire un français sans accent euh y a y a le français correct qui est le français normal mais qui peut être utilisé avec x nombre d'accents ou même x nombre de variations entre un vocabulaire qui est aussi riche et aussi important	*which does not mean a French with no accent uh there there is correct French which is normal French but which can be used with x number of accents or even x number of variations between a vocabulary which is as rich and as important*

Here, Liliane shows how powerful the notion of an abstract, ideal 'normal' French is. At the same time, she must struggle with the evident contradictions between this universalist notion and the values of democratic pluralism to which she also subscribes.

Not surprisingly, the teachers of *Français* had the most to say about this issue. In the following interview extracts we can see that, on the one hand, they recognize diversity and contact conditions as being part of reality, but, on the other, they do subscribe to some notion of standard monolingual French as being central to the school's teaching objectives. They focus on traces of contact with English as the least desirable dimension of minority French, but struggle with a recognition of the bilingual reality which underlies them. They value the ability to communicate across contexts as a function of a uniformizing standard language, while rejecting the potential for exclusion and stigmatisation inherent in hegemonic practices.

Example 3.17   Interviews with Alain, Martine and Lise (1992)

1	*Alain:*	soyons très honnête,	*let's be very honest,*
2		le français est	*French is probably the*
3		probablement la matière	*subject which interests*
4		qui les intéresse le moins	*them the least in most*
5		dans la plupart des cas.	*cases. A generalization,*
6		Généralisation,	*obviously, but a*
7		évidemment, mais	*generalization*
8		généralisation qui	*which could be made*
9		pourrait être concrétisée	*real if we look at the*
10		si on regarde l'emploi	*use of French in the*
11		du français en salle de	*classroom, and even in*
12		classe, et même dans des	*Français classes where*
13		cours de Français où les	*students necessarily tend*
14		élèves ont forcément	*to use the English*
15		tendance à utiliser la	*language in the*
16		langue anglaise dans les	*corridors, you rarely*
17		couloirs, on entend	*hear students express*
18		rarement les les élèves	*themselves in French,*
19		s'exprimer en français,	*outside obviously they*
20		à l'extérieur	*have few occasions to*
21		évidemment, ils ont peu	*use French, the media*
22		d'occasions de	*they listen to, that they*
23		s'exprimer en français,	*use are rarely in French.*
24		les médias qu'ils	*So French is a language*
25		écoutent, qu'ils utilisent	*which can die easily if*

26 sont rarement en
27 français. Donc le
28 français est une langue
29 qui peut facilement
30 mourir si on ne fait pas
31 attention. (...)
32 [j'espère qu'un jour les
33 élèves auront] pris
34 conscience que demain,
35 si je ne maîtrise pas bien
36 la langue française, je
37 vais me faire taper
38 sur les doigts, je vais
39 perdre des emplois, à
40 cause de carences dans
41 ma langue. (...) on ne
42 peut pas imposer à
43 quelqu'un des
44 connaissances. Et c'est
45 peut-être le malheur de
46 l'état du français dans
47 cette école, dans
48 certaines régions de
49 l'Ontario, c'est qu'on
50 essaie par tous les
51 moyens d'imposer. Si
52 seulement l'élève venait
53 à l'école désireux
54 d'apprendre, je pense
55 qu'on n'aurait plus
56 besoin de tous ces
57 manuels, de toutes ces
58 techniques, ces
59 méthodes pédagogiques,
60 ces ressources, que l'on
61 utilise toujours afin de
62 convaincre la personne
63 que le français, c'est
64 utile. (...) il y a eu des
65 changements majeurs
66 en ce sens que la
67 francophonie connue
68 dans les années 75 a

we are not careful.
(...) I hope one day
the students will have
become aware that
tomorrow, if I don't
have a good command
of the French language,
I'll get rapped on the
knuckles, I'll lose jobs,
because of weaknesses
in my language. (...)
You can't impose
knowledge on someone.
And maybe it is the
misfortune of the state
of French in this school,
in some areas of
Ontario, that we try by
all means to impose. If
only students came to
school with the desire
to learn, I think we
would no longer need
all those manuals, all
those techniques, those
teaching methods,
those resources, that
we always use in order
to convince the person
that French is useful.
(...) There have been
major changes in the
sense that the
francophone community
as it was around 1975
has more or less
disappeared, has been
buried by a whole
range of new
francophones, people
with rights [to French
schools], francophones
from around the world,

69	plus ou moins disparu,
70	a été ensevelie par toute
71	une gamme de nouveaux
72	francophones, des
73	ayants droit, des
74	francophones de partout
75	dans le monde, qui nous
76	permettent d'élargir
77	notre esprit, qui nous
78	permettent de
79	comprendre qu'il n'y a
80	pas une littérature
81	franco-ontarienne, ou
82	québécoise, ou
83	canadienne-française,
84	qui nous permettent en
85	tant que professeurs de
86	se renouveler, de se
87	ressourcer, et de
88	respecter l'apprentissage
89	et d'apprendre (. . .)
90	Qui dit qu'une classe
91	devrait être homogène,
92	qui dit que tout le
93	monde devrait connaître
94	ses pronoms relatifs, et
95	devrait écrire de la
96	même façon, qui dit
97	que on devrait tous lire
98	les mêmes auteurs,
99	Molière, Racine, etc.?
100	Ça change, ça a
101	beaucoup changé, ça
102	changera encore
103	beaucoup, et espérons
104	que ce changement va
105	se faire à l'intérieur d'un
106	cadre français, espérons
107	que ce changement va
108	nous amener à
109	comprendre ce que c'est
110	que la globalisation de
111	la langue (. . .)

who help us broaden our minds, who help us understand that there is not one Franco-Ontarian, or Québécois, or French Canadian literature, who help us as teachers to renew ourselves, to acquire new resources, to respect learning, and to learn (. . .) Who says that a class should be homogeneous, who says that everyone should know their relative pronouns, and should write the same way, who says we should all read the same authors, Molière, Racine, etc.? It's changing, it has changed a lot, it will change still more, and let's hope that this change will take place within a French framework, let's hope that this change will lead us to understand the nature of the globalization of language (. . .) today, through all these accents, all this sentence structures which differ each from the others, all this knowledge of how to be, all these values lived by language, I am aware that my French isn't The French, and

112		aujourd'hui, par	*that there is not a soul*
113		l'entremise de tous ces	*on this earth who can*
114		accents, de toute cette	*really say, look, this is*
115		structures de phrase	*The French that should*
116		différentes les uns des	*be spoken.*
117		autres, de tout ce savoir-	*Extraordinary challenge,*
118		être, de toutes ces	*challenge I adore.*
119		valeurs vécues par la	
120		langue, je suis conscient	
121		que mon français n'est	
122		pas Le Français, et qu'il	
123		n'y a personne sur cette	
124		terre qui peut vraiment	
125		dire, eh bien, voici Le	
126		Français qui devrait être	
127		parlé. Défi	
128		extraordinaire, défi que	
129		j'adore.	
130	*Martine:*	[enseigner en milieu	*[teaching in a minority*
131		minoritaire] oh c'est	*context] oh it's difficult,*
132		difficile, je pense que	*I think it's more difficult,*
133		c'est plus difficile, bon,	*well, and it's normal,*
134		puis c'est normal, les	*the students make*
135		élèves font des erreurs	*mistakes that you*
136		que l'on trouverait pas	*wouldn't find in a*
137		dans un milieu	*really francophone*
138		francophone	*milieu. They think in*
139		francophone. Ils pensent	*English, it's difficult, you*
140		en anglais, c'est difficile,	*can't stop them, and*
141		on ne peut pas les	*not only those whose*
142		empêcher, et non	*mother tongue is*
143		seulement ceux dont la	*English, not only,*
144		langue maternelle est	*francophones, there are*
145		l'anglais, non seulement,	*also francophones who*
146		des francophones ça y	*do not speak French*
147		a des francophones	*at home they always*
148		aussi qui ne parlent pas	*think in English, uh they*
149		français à la maison, ils	*constantly live in*
150		pensent toujours en	*English, so that results*
151		anglais, euh ils vivent	*in sentence structure*
152		constamment en anglais,	*that is completely*
153		alors ça donne des	*English. (. . .) [in my*
154		structures de phrase qui	*evaluation] the general*

155		sont tout à fait	grade takes all of that
156		anglaises. (. . .) [dans	into account, the
157		mon évaluation] la note	vocabulary, anglicisms,
158		globale tient compte de	things like that.
159		tout ça, le vocabulaire,	
160		les anglicismes, les	
161		choses comme ça.	
162	Lise:	(. . .) ce que j'aimerais	(. . .) what I'd like to
163		faire avec les élèves c'est	do with the students is
164		en fin de compte de leur	in the end to give them
165		donner les outils (. . .)	the tools (. . .) to
166		pour bien écrire, pour	write well, also to speak
167		bien parler aussi sans	well maybe without
168		peut-être utiliser trop	using too many
169		d'anglicismes, quoique	anglicisms, although I
170		je les comprends, parce	understand them,
171		qu'on reste dans un	because we live in an
172		monde anglophone,	anglophone world, it
173		c'est pas facile de tout	isn't easy to cut all that
174		couper ça, je peux pas	off, I can't ask them to
175		leur demander de me	speak to me in French
176		parler en français	like a French person
177		comme un Français le	would in Paris or like
178		ferait à Paris ou comme	a Québécois would in
179		un Québécois le ferait à	Montreal, it's
180		Montréal, c'est	impossible, it's
181		impossible, c'est pas	unthinkable, anyway
182		pensable, de toute façon	there are too many
183		y a trop y a trop de	there are too many
184		différentes nationalités	different nationalities
185		dans la classe pour	in the class to ask
186		leur demander d'être	them to also be very
187		aussi très uniforme avec	uniform with that, uh,
188		ça, euh, mais qu'i soient	but for them to be
189		capables de s'exprimer	able to express
190		assez bien en français	themselves well enough
191		pour que je puisse les	in French so that I can
192		comprendre sans avoir	understand without
193		toujours à poser des	always having to ask
194		questions (. . .)	questions (. . .)

The counterpart of what constitutes good French is an identification of what does not fit. As we have seen, everyone can name

anglicisms, that is, the extent to which French in contact with English bears traces of that contact, or has managed to maintain its purity. This concern emerges both in interviews and in language practices, as well as in some course texts (such as Clas and Horguelin (1979)), the 1993 course text for *Français des affaires* (Business French); this text contains a section on anglicisms, explicitly identified as forms to be avoided). In addition, there is also a question related to the value attributed to different ethnocultural, regional or social-class varieties of French, which may differ from the standard in lexicon, syntax, morphology or phonology. Of course, these overlap, to the extent that traces of contact are more likely to be characteristic of marginal ethnocultural or hierarchically lower social-class groups, at least in places like Canada where linguistic purism and monolingualism (in the ideological sense of the term) are elements of the mechanism of reproduction of social standing and power of the existing élite. The concern about traces of contact with English is much more evident than concern over other non-standard features. In part, I believe this is due to the political salience of language contact in this situation. In part it is probably also due to the nature of the students' linguistic repertoires, since so many of them learn French under conditions which expose them more to the standard than to other varieties, and which simultaneously have contact with English as their most salient feature. It may also be due to the recognition of the fact of diversity in Franco-Ontarian classrooms, and a societal emphasis on combating racism in educational institutions. Finally, the issue of regionalisms is at the heart of one of the paradoxes of francophone mobilization: a simultaneous valuing of authenticity and authority, of the local and the global.

La chasse aux anglicismes has a long and glorious history in francophone Canada. L'École Champlain is carrying on a tradition, although the degree of commitment to that particular cause varies, in the same way as does the degree of commitment to the school's ideology of monolingualism. As a result, we see teachers of *Français avancé* avoiding them on stage, or heavily flagging them on the rare occasions when they seem either unavoidable (lexical gaps) or advisable (for example, for building solidarity with students). Teachers of other subjects, again also depending on their own linguistic repertoire and degree of personal and professional investment in the norm, may be less careful.

Lise is an interesting example in this regard, as a teacher of
Français who shares the bilingual experience of many of Champlain's students, and who has no professional investment in the
subject area. Nonetheless, she does seem conscious of the norm
required of her at least in her guise as a *Français* teacher (and, of
course, our presence in the class may have had something to do
with it too). On several occasions, she self-corrected her uses of
anglicisms. During one class, she explained to students how to use
a checklist, and told them to '*checker*' the boxes. Then she paused,
looked at one of the students, and said '*cocher*'. Here are two
more examples from other occasions (see lines 6–8 in Example
3.18, and lines 6–10 in Example 3.19):

Example 3.18   10th grade Français général, *1991*

1	*Lise:*	(. . .) euh ce que j'aimerais	*(. . .) uh what I'd like us*
2		qu'on fasse vendredi, c'est	*to do Friday, is for us to*
3		qu'on se rencontre à la	*meet in room 155 and then*
4		salle 155 et puis qu'on	*for us to have what they*
5		fasse ce qu'ils appellent à	*call 'by the luck of the*
6		la fortune du pot ou un	*pot' or a potluck in*
7		*potluck* en anglais, la	*English,* 'la fortune du pot'
8		fortune du pot	

Example 3.19   10th grade Français général, *1991*

1	*Lise:*	(. . .) alors ce qu'on va	*(. . .) so what we're going*
2		faire aujourd'hui, on va	*to do today, we're going*
3		sortir les textes que vous	*to take out the texts which*
4		avez eus hier sur le futur	*you got yesterday on the*
5		dépasse souvent la	*future often overtakes*
6		technologie [. . .] ça va	*technology [. . .] it will*
7		être uh *timé*, moi je pense	*be uh timed, I think it's*
8		c'est vraiment le le (pause)	*really the the (pause)*
9		chronométré je devrais	'chronométré' *I should say,*
10		dire, mot anglais, okay	*English word, okay you*
11		t'as ton texte . . .	*have your text . . .*

In the following example, Louis, a teacher of a 10th grade class
on the geography of Canada, does a similar flagging (lines 2–9)
followed by a self-correction (lines 23–4).

Example 3.20   10th grade Géographie avancé, *1992*

1	*Louis:*	c'est ça et ce sont des	*that's it and they are*
2		(tuyaux?) qu'on appelle	*(pipes?) what they call*
3		des *pipelines* hein, ce	*pipelines eh, they are*
4		sont des (xx) des tuyaux	*(xx) pipes which*
5		qui transportent le	*transport oil and*
6		pétrole et le gaz naturel	*natural gas from Alberta,*
7		de l'Alberta, ce sont ce	*they are what they call*
8		qu'on appelle des	*pipelines (. . .)* 'oléoducs'
9		*pipelines* (. . .) les	*are pipes which transport*
10		oléoducs ce sont des	*oil while* 'gazoducs'
11		tuyaux qui transportent	*transport what?*
12		le pétrole alors que les	
13		gazoducs transportent	
14		quoi?	
15	*Male student:*	le gaz	*gas*
16	*Louis:*	(. . .) nous transportons	*(. . .) we transport (xx)*
17		des (xx) pour la	*to use, for example,*
18		consommation, par	*for our cars and all that,*
19		exemple, pour nos	*we need oil, so here in*
20		voitures et tout ça, on a	*Toronto they have (xx)*
21		besoin de pétrole, donc	*pipelines I should*
22		ici à Toronto i ont des	*say* 'oléoducs' *for the*
23		(xx) des *pipelines* je	*oil (. . .)*
24		devrais dire des oléoducs	
25		pour le pétrole (. . .)	

Example 3.20 includes both self-correction and translation as an explicit strategy for coping with having used English-mediated real-world knowledge as a pedagogical strategy. In this and the following two examples, it is likely that Lise and Louis are respond-ing to normative pressures both from above and from below, insofar as many of the students in both classes are non-English speakers from Africa who have attended French-language schools in their country of origin.

Example 3.21   10th grade Français avancé, *1991. Lise is conducting a review session.*

1	*Lise:*	okay on passe à la partie	*okay we go to part D.*
2		D. Derrière le masque	*Behind the mask* (pause)
3		(pause) problème,	*Problem, each of the*

4		chacune des phrases	*following sentences*
5		suivantes contient un	*contains an acronym an*
6		sigle un sigle c'est par	*acronym is for example*
7		exemple PUMA c'est un	*PUMA is an acronym*
8		sigle ou euh *IRA* c'est	*or uh IRA what is*
9		quoi *IRA? Ireland Irish*	*IRA? Ireland Irish*
10	*Male*		
	student:	Republican Army	*Republican Army*
11	*Lise:*	army le IRA en français	*army IRA in French that*
12		ce serait quoi?	*would be what?*
13	*Male*		
	student:	l'armée républicaine de	l'armée républicaine de
14		l'Irlande	l'Irlande

Example 3.22   10th grade Géographie avancé, 1992. Louis has asked students to look up the names of steel companies across Canada.

1	*Louis:*	Dofasco, okay, Dofasco.	*Dofasco, okay, Dofasco.*
2		Dofasco est un nom de	*Dofasco is a company*
3		compagnie, le nom d'une	*name, the name of a*
4		compagnie qui ben c'est	*company which well it's*
5		une compagnie le nom de	*a company the name of*
6		la compagnie à	*the company in*
7		(Hamilton?) s'appelle euh	*(Hamilton?) is called uh*
8		parce que vous savez qu'en	*because you know in*
9		anglais le mot acier veut	*English the word* acier
10		dire *steel*, donc le nom	*means steel, so the name*
11		(xx) Stelco. (. . .)	*(xx) Stelco. (. . .)*

Teachers are thus quite conscious of the importance of impression management. Their own linguistic performance has to correspond to the performance they demand from their students. In Example 3.23, in the course of providing a sample dictation as part of an exam-readiness exercise, Lise is caught in the embarrassing position of being questioned on her use of an English word by one of her students. Her difficulty reveals how complicated it is to try to maintain a sharp distinction between French and English under current conditions of global as well as local language contact.

Example 3.23   10th grade, Français général, 1991

| 1 | *Lise:* | la réponse (pause) | *the answer (pause)* |
| 2 | | recevèrent la réponse | *received the answer* |

3		quelques heures plus tard	*several hours later*
4		quelques heures plus tard	*several hours later by*
5		par l'intermédiaire du fax	*means of the fax*
6	*Saïd:*	par l'intermédiaire du du	*by means of the the*
7	*Lise:*	du fax du fax oui	*of the fax of the fax*
8	*Saïd:*	comment on écrit 'le	*yes how do you write*
9		fax'?	*'the fax'?*
10	*Lise:*	f-a-x	*f-a-x*
11	*Saïd:*	quoi?	*what?*
12	*Abdillahi:*	f-a-x	*f-a-x*
13	*Lise:*	f-a-x pas de 'e'	*f-a-x no 'e'*
14	*Saïd:*	non pas de 'e'	*no no 'e'*
15	*Lise:*	c'est un mot anglais	*it's an English word*
16	*Saïd:*	alors c'est pas en vrai	*so it's not in real*
17		français ça (laughs)	*French (laughs)*
18	*Lise:*	ben c'est un mot c'est	*well it's a [word] it's*
19		un mot emprunté	*a borrowed word*

Louis encountered a similar problem, only with respect to varieties of French, when, in response to a question about paper products, his European-trained African students used a European French term for brown wrapping paper with which most Canadians are unfamiliar:

Example 3.24　10th grade Géographie avancé, *1992*

1	*Male*		
	student:	papier Kraft	*Kraft paper*
2	*Louis:*	papier (a?)grafé?	*(stapled? 'grafé') paper?*
3	*Male*		
	student:	papier Kraft	*Kraft paper*
4		(Many students talk at	
5		once)	
6	*Male*		
	student:	monsieur, c'est très	*Sir, it's very <u>sharp</u>*
7		*sharp* faites attention	*be careful*
8	*Louis:*	du papier brun	*brown paper*
9	*Male*		
	student:	ça c'est du papier Kraft	*that's Kraft paper*
10		(Sounds of laughter and	
		applause)	
11	*Louis:*	ça s'appelle comme ça?	*that's what it's called?*
12	*Female*		
	student:	c'est la marque	*it's the brand name*

The above examples point to some ways in which teachers encountered contradictions in constructing 'good French' in the classroom, whether because their own knowledge of French was based in the Canadian vernacular (or even the Canadian standard), because their students' knowledge of standard French was judged insufficient, or because their students' exposure to English was constant. Despite this, it is also possible to document efforts to nonetheless sustain the notion of good French. Elsewhere I have documented organized campaigns to support French-language quality, campaigns which generally involve identifying anglicisms or vernacular items or structures, and replacing them with standard forms (Heller 1994a, 1995). The majority of these campaigns focus on the lexicon, although some syntactic shibboleths also receive attention (these include, notably, the use of the post-verbal question particle '-tu', as opposed to subject–verb inversion, for interrogative phrases; and use of the relativizers 'qu'est-ce que' instead of 'ce que' and 'que' instead of 'dont' and 'où'). The only institutional campaigns Champlain engaged in were the literary activities cited above, which were designed both to promote the use of French and to encourage valuing standard French through literary production.

In *Français* classes, and in other classes as well, students' written French was always corrected, and the use of anglicisms and other inappropriate vocabulary and structures usually explicitly signalled. There was some debate about whether teachers of other subjects should also correct students' spoken French, but on the whole, most teachers did so to greater or lesser degrees. Here is an example from a class in Accounting, in which a student, Julien, is making a presentation. I provide below the excerpt of the presentation (which is on the financial crisis of Julien's favourite hockey team) to which the teacher, Thérèse, later refers in her comments:

Example 3.25   11th grade, Comptabilité, 1994

Julien:	Ça veut dire que, lui	*That means that for*
	s'embarquer là-dedans c'est	*him to get involved in*
	vraiment un risque pour lui.	*that, it's really a risk*
	Perdre son poste puis trouver	*for him. To lose his job*
	une somme d'argent aussi	*and find such a large*
	énorme, ça ça sera le euh	*sum of money, it it will*
	très le c'est comme un peu	*the uh very the it's a bit*

	irréalistique pour la ville de Québec	*unrealistic for the city of Québec*
Thérèse:	(. . .) Les mots en -ic hein? c'est des mots souvent anglais, *realistic,* (xx) il y a plusieurs qui l'utilisent comme ça. C'est réaliste, euh réaliste, idéaliste, et cetera, mais il y a beaucoup d'élèves qui utilisent ces mots-là avec la la terminaison -ic, ça n'existe pas en français, ça c'est de l'anglais (. . .)	*(. . .) Words ending in -ic eh? they are often English words, realistic (xx) there are many who use it like that. It's* réaliste *uh* réaliste, idéaliste, *et cetera, but there are many students who use those words with the the ending -ic, it doesn't exist in French, that is English (. . .)*

Notwithstanding the attention paid to these issues by teachers of other subjects like Thérèse, in daily interaction in the classroom, the quality of language received most attention in *Français* classes. This was most obvious in the *Français avancé* classes, in which students frequently made oral presentations on which they received immediate critical evaluation from the teacher (and sometimes from their peers), orally and in public. Comments were usually made according to a wide variety of criteria (interest of the topic, organization of the presentation, physical stance, loudness and so on) but always included evaluations of the quality of the language used. Again, this included, for example, use of a broad range of vocabulary, but also included anglicisms, and, in one instance, a comment on the too regional nature of the student's accent (although teachers generally agreed that they were more concerned about vocabulary and grammar than about accent).

In addition, it was possible to exploit the conversational order to monitor students' linguistic production. In Example 3.26, the 10th grade *Français avancé* teacher, Martine, is trying to introduce a reading activity by leading a discussion on the importance of reading. This is how the activity begins:

Example 3.26   10th grade Français avancé, *1991*

1	*Martine:*	pourquoi lit-on?	*why do we read?*
2	*Michel:*	pour relaxer	*to relax*
3	*Martine:*	pour se détendre, 'relaxer'	*to 'se détendre' (relax),*
4		c'est anglais	*'relaxer' is English*

On other occasions, Martine used the same kind of conversational structure to supply the standard '*soixante-dix*' for the Belgian and Swiss variant '*septante*' (seventy), and the standard '*se disputer*' for the Canadian variant '*chicaner*' (argue). (It is interesting to note, however, that Martine subsequently attenuated her suppression of *septante*, noting that the student was from Belgium.)

In Example 3.27, Lise is conducting an activity related to the unit on fantasy stories as a narrative genre. She introduces a character, Petrouschka, and a situation. The students are then asked to provide candidate pieces of narrative to jointly construct the story. Even here, Lise retains control over that joint construction, accepting some ideas and not others, and correcting the form as well as commenting on the content. The story has reached a point where Petrouschka is fleeing danger in a car, when:

Example 3.27   10th grade Français général, *1991*

1	*Stéphane:*	elle a un *flat*	*she has a flat*
2	*Lise:*	elle a une crevaison	*she has a flat*

In Example 3.28, Lise uses an I-R-E format to polish up another student's utterance. Here, Lise is conducting a comprehension check after the students have just finished watching a film of *L'Avare*, a classical 17th century play by the classical French playwright Molière (a play she is having the students read as a way of resisting the curricular differences institutionalized in streaming).

Example 3.28   10th grade Français général, *1991*

1	*Lise:*	okay, qu'est-ce que vous	*okay, what did you*
2		avez compris de l'histoire?	*understand of the story?*
3		Comment s'est terminée	*How did the story end?*
4		l'histoire?	
5	*Ginette:*	Harpagon a retrouvé sa	*Harpagon found his*
6		cassette *whatever*	*purse whatever*
7	*Lise:*	Harpagon a retrouvé sa	*Harpagon found his*
8		cassette	*purse*

Ginette provides an accurate answer, mitigated through the attachment of 'whatever'. One can read this use of 'whatever' in three ways: it can signal Ginette's insecurity about the content of the answer; it can signal her insecurity over her French; it can signal her uncertainty about the word '*cassette*'; and possibly all three. Certainly, Ginette, as we shall see in a subsequent chapter, was not a confident student academically, nor was she secure about her French. In addition, '*cassette*' is used here in an archaic sense ('purse'), rather than in its more contemporary sense of 'audiotape'. Finally, the item in question, 'whatever', itself has ambiguous status;

while everyone knows it comes from English, it is widespread in Canadian vernacular French, and can be used even by people who otherwise speak little English. In any case, Lise drops the 'whatever' in her ratification of Ginette's answer, thereby removing the uncertainty on all four counts, and providing the model for an answer which is adequate both semantically and linguistically.

Ginette's dilemma encapsulates the two fronts on which struggles for language quality are conducted: the struggle against English and the struggle against stigmatized variants within French (however fuzzy the boundaries of that language may be). In this section we have seen a variety of ways in which the preference for standard monolingual French at school manifests itself in a concern for the quality of language. This concern is evident both in concerted and institutionalized public efforts, and in the exploitation of the school's preferred mode of social organization of interaction, both with respect to the linguistic production of students, and with respect to the linguistic production of teachers. This is most evident with respect to *anglicismes*, those traces of the contact with English which the school exists to minimize. But we also have seen it manifested with respect to variants within French, with, in all cases, standard variants preferred to Canadian vernacular or other regional or social-class forms.

5   Normativity and strategic ambiguity

In this chapter, I have demonstrated the school's attachment to the norm of standard monolingual French, some of the ways in which it is manifested, and some of the strategies used to create ambiguity which permits contradictions to be managed without threatening the school's linguistic investments.

First, the degree of pressure towards normativity varies according to the symbolic load of school activities and the extent to which these activities are part of constructing the school's public face. Second, activities vary as to the extent to which they are likely to encounter contradictions arising from their necessity for dealing with non-normative linguistic forms, whether because of contact with the world outside school, or because of the nature of the participants' linguistic repertoires (and this includes both students and teachers). Given these two dimensions of variability, we can construct a range of behaviours which range from extreme monitoring of one's own and others' linguistic production, to tolerance of non-normative forms.

This range is constructed actively through the social organization of specific activities. The school has a preference for activities to take place on a unified floor and through sequential turn-taking. This normative order is supported by spatial organization affecting participant structures, and is legitimized through the ideology of respect. It constitutes the official, public floor. In some cases, that is, those where there are the most extreme forms of normative pressure, it is necessary to suppress any other kind of social organization. In others, where contradictions must be confronted, it is possible to create backstage areas where non-normative linguistic forms can be tolerated. Alternatively, when there is no way around such a confrontation, it is possible to exploit the normative form of social organization of talk to monitor and correct linguistic production, or to discursively signal a distancing from the very non-normative forms one is in the process of using.

The result of the processes presented here is to allow the school to construct its norms, and to minimize the threat to its public image which is represented by the contradictions inherent in the conditions of its existence. While the contradictions do give rise to a discourse of crisis, this in turn only serves to strengthen the legitimacy of the school as an institution which is needed to avert the much worse crisis francophone Ontario would be facing if the school did not exist.

In the chapters which follow, I shall discuss in turn a variety of ways in which students respond to the school's efforts to invest itself and them in the standard monolingual norm, and to cope with the contradictions inherent in such an investment. As we shall see, students' linguistic practices vary according to a number of dimensions, the most important being the linguistic resources they possess and their interest in collaborating with the school's agenda. Their actions and stances also have an effect on what the school can be and do, and will likely force the school to confront some of the contradictions its strategies of ambiguity have so far so successfully allowed it to avoid.

PART II

4 Being bilingual

1 Playing the game

The bell rings. It is time for *Français avancé*. The students in Martine's class come downstairs from their other advanced-level courses, laughing and chatting in English, for the most part. The occasional new arrival from Quebec or France tags along, slightly mystified by all this talk in English. The students arrive on time and take their places in their assigned seats. They sit in rows facing the blackboard, where Martine stands, ready to begin class. When class begins, students raise their hands when they want to answer one of Martine's questions. When they take the public floor, they only speak in French. While Martine, or other students, are speaking for public consumption, the other students usually listen. Of course, they aren't perfect gems, so sometimes they do other things. They might work on homework for this or for another class. Occasionally, they rest their heads on their arms on the desk and briefly close their eyes. The girls do up and undo their long hair into ponytails and chignons, with elasticized bands known as 'scrunchies'. Sometimes the students pass messages to friends, messages that are written almost always in English. Or they pass materials, such as liquid correcting fluid, or a pen. If Martine's back is turned, or her attention engaged in another direction, they might whisper to each other in English, asking each other how they did on tests, or how they are addressing the task at hand.

The same bell announces the beginning of *Français général*. Students straggle out to the portable classroom where class will be held. Lise is almost always the first to arrive. Several students are late, and some never show up. Students gravitate to their friends, and continue conversations in English or Somali begun earlier in the day. The volume of their talk is not lowered once they pass through the classroom door. Some are listening to rock music or African music on portable cassette players. Sometimes they listen alone, absorbed in the world of the music; sometimes they share earphones with a friend or a curious classmate. When class begins they speak to Lise sometimes in French (especially if they are non English-speaking Somalis), sometimes in English, sometimes both at once. They continue their other interactions while class goes on. They talk about music, sports, weekend activities. Some students work on assignments alone, or help each other. One or two students regularly interrupt Lise to ask for an explanation of the activity she wishes them to engage in, asking her to explain why they should do it at all.

The *Français avancé* students are playing the game. They keep the public face of the school French, they relegate their seemingly contradictory use of English to backstage, and they otherwise mainly do what the school asks them to do: show up on time, be orderly, take a turn to talk when the teacher says they can, do the work assigned. The *Français général* students resist this social order, in the way they organize themselves in the physical space of the classroom, in the organization, form and content of their talk, in their failure to do their work regularly in the way they are supposed to do it. In this chapter, I shall consider first the ways in which some students, notably those in the advanced level, collaborate with the school's norms and sociolinguistic practices, as well as the ways in which their interests converge with those of the school. Here we shall see that these are students who have invested in the acquisition and maintenance of bilingualism as defined by the school. This is largely a result of the ways in which their families' social position in the community affects their access to standard French and English, and influences their chances of participating in social networks and institutions, especially post-secondary education and professions, where those linguistic varieties are valued.

Ironically, this investment in normative bilingualism provokes a stance on the part of these students which is at variance with the ideal promoted by the school. For these students, it is important to display bilingualism in the only arena available to them where their displays of bilingualism will be appreciated, namely, among the audience of their peers at school. While they collaborate with the construction of a French monolingual public face, they act out their bilingual experience of life, their bilingual identities and the value they place on bilingualism by performing bilingualism. This means using English, or occasionally both French and English, in the spheres which they consider to be private, under their control rather than that of the school. They therefore daily attack the integrity of the monolingual '*oasis culturel*' that Champlain is supposed to be, while at the same time they need it in order to become the kind of bilinguals they want to be, and the school also wishes for them. They resolve this problem by positing a distinction between public and private space, a distinction which holds no meaning in terms of the official institutional ideology of the school.

The investment on the part of these students in normative bilingualism is paralleled by their investment in standard French. Many of them have no access to any other kind of French in any case, either because their own families are standard speakers or because their only access to French is through school. Certainly, their investment in the standard is consonant with their investment in parallel monolingualisms, the two being the complementary faces of the linguistic practices associated with social mobility. The students display this investment not only in their preference for standard French in their own practices, but also in their active rejection of Canadian vernacular French, and vernacular French-Canadian culture. We shall examine some of these constructions of the French Canadian as contemptible as they were performed in public displays of French Canadian language and identity. Just as the school used public performances to define a certain image of the school (see, for example, the discussion of Champlain's twenty-fifth anniversary celebrations in Chapter 2), so too did the students, who had control over some important performance situations, such as plays, student council-run school assemblies performed as a series of skits, student council elections, and fashion shows.

The domination of this student vision of the school, and of these student practices, is also highlighted by practices which do not conform to this model. In the subsequent sections of this chapter I shall consider practices which at least attempt to challenge the norm. First, there is the contradictory position in which monolingual francophone students find themselves. Their expectations of school life are close to those of the school, and yet they are confronted with peer practices which both affirm and undermine the school's ideology of monolingualism. French-Canadian students are, in addition, faced with the contradictory value placed on their own language variety and cultural heritage by the school, which recognizes the authenticating value of these linguistic and cultural resources, but does not really treat them as important for educational success; they must also contend with being rejected by their peers. Reactions vary, but tend to cluster in the range from accommodation to bilingual practices to isolation or flight into monolingualism, whether English or French. Occasionally a student will challenge the school to recognize Canadian French as a variety worthy of consideration in the context of educational success; occasionally a group of students will hoist the *fleur-de-lys* of Quebec or the banner of a Quebec hockey team on stage (see below); but these are fleeting expressions of a confrontation that never really takes place.

Second, there are challenges posed by students who speak neither French nor English as a first language, but who expect the school to offer them a place to continue to perfect their French. They rely on their English as a Second Language (ESL) classes at school, and their experience of life in their neighbourhoods, to help them learn English. School is for French. Furthermore, school is for learning standard French in a directed, explicit, focused way, despite the ambivalence many students from former French colonies may feel towards the language. For them, French is both a symbol of colonial oppression and a means of social advancement. The practices of teachers who take into account the bilingual nature of students' experience, and who focus on French less as an object of instruction than as a medium of cultural development, are baffling to many of these students, who do not share the French-Canadian experience of French as an oppressed language. While, to a certain extent, they share the bilinguals' notion that talk among peers is private space where any language can be spoken, they also expect the common language, among students who do not share a first language, to be French. When they discover that the peer culture has implanted English as this common language, the reactions vary from bewilderment to strong feelings of exclusion and rejection.

What these students all have in common is that they are trying at least to play the game according to the rules defined by the school. Or at least, they are trying to profit from the access to bilingualism the school provides. The problem is that not everyone interprets the rules in quite the same way. In addition, the contradictions inherent in the school's ideology, and reflected in practices meant to contain those contradictions, place the students themselves in a variety of contradictory positions which they themselves must attempt to resolve one way or another. But sometimes the resolution involves either challenging the school, challenging peers or renouncing one's chances of succeeding on the school's terms.

2   Luc/Luke and Sandra

Luc steps up to the microphone on stage, in front of his assembled schoolmates and teachers. In period costume, he provides a rendering of a passage from a classical French play. He speaks in flawless actors' French, his accent not quite identifiable, but perhaps influenced by Paris. He is a good-looking boy, the object of numerous crushes, and at one point the acclaimed 'stud' (sic) of the school. A few minutes later, he returns, *sans* costume, to cries of 'Luke! Luke!'. He takes the microphone again, to make an appeal on behalf of the student council. This time he speaks in a different style, still not quite identifiable, but influenced perhaps more by Toronto than Paris.

The two guises of Luc/Luke are the two guises of Champlain's bilingual students. On the floor, or stage, under school control, they act like francophone monolinguals, and standard-speakers to boot. Where other students dominate the frame of reference (and this can happen, as we have just seen, in precisely the same physical space), bilingual practices prevail. Luc speaks standard French, follows sequential turn-taking conventions, does his homework and participates actively in school life. Luke speaks English, or English-influenced French, or codeswitches with his friends in the corridors, in front of the school, or in the cafeteria. Luke makes jokes, acts up a bit, throws the occasional girl into the snow, or maybe smokes a cigarette every now and then.

The Lukes of the school tend to have certain things in common. One of the most important is a fairly long experience of life in a setting like Champlain; indeed, many of them have been in school together from kindergarten at Rouillé, Champlain's main feeder school (Rouillé is named after the French fort established in the

Toronto area in the seventeenth century). They grew up in an English-dominated community, going to a French school. The other thing they have in common is a deep desire for academic success. They all want to go to university, and are all concerned about getting the grades they will need to ensure that that happens.

In this section, I shall describe some of the ways that these students define what it means to be a Champlain student, in terms of how they define themselves and their feelings about Champlain, and in terms of the images of others they construct in that public space. Most importantly, they link their possession of bilingual skills to academic and career success. They require the school to be monolingual in order to be the kind of bilingual they think it is important to be, but that does not mean that they themselves should be the kind of monolingual-type speaker of French the school imagines its students should be. On the contrary, being bilingual means acting bilingual. It means being able to be Luke and Luc, sometimes at the same time. In addition, I shall show how these students have been able to dominate the public discursive space of the school, and thereby not only gain privileged access to the resources of the school, but also to construct the parameters of school social life with which others must cope. In playing the school's game, these students in turn are able to define the rules for those domains under student control; incoming students find an established social reality which they can enter, avoid or resist.

As I mentioned earlier, the most important part of playing the school's game is speaking French, and only French, and, to the extent possible, standard French, on the public floor. For some of these students this is not a problem; they are sure and confident in their French, they seek occasions to answer questions or to engage the teachers in public or private discussion, they volunteer information, they speak loudly and with assurance. In Chapter 3, we saw examples of such behaviour in *Sciences avancé*, in which class Marcel took a disproportionate number of turns. Marcel is fairly typical of these students; he is of North African origin, and lived for several years in France. Others like him may have been born in Toronto, but maintain the kind of ties with francophone milieux that Marcel has enjoyed, and often speak French at home. Others are less confident of their French; nonetheless, during an oral presentation, or while trying to answer a teacher's question, if such a student cannot find a word or phrase to convey his or her meaning, he or she will hesitate and shift uneasily, rather than say what he or she has to say in English. Often, these students will remain relatively quiet in class, although some have mastered the art of placing questions in just the right conversational slot to be heard, and maximize their chances of being heard by sitting close to the teacher. They participate considerably more, however, in classes such as *Sciences* where there is not so much of an emphasis on speaking French, only French, and 'proper' French. Whatever their background (and many have at least one francophone parent), these students' principal link to French is through school.

Sandra is a good example. She has one francophone grandparent, and still feels ties to the francophone community in which her mother was born and raised. And while those ties are important to her, as well as to her mother, they rarely spoke French at home when Sandra was small, and never do any more. Sandra's parents put it like this:

Example 4.1   Interview between Monica, Laurette and Sandra's parents, 1992

Mother: (...) I think I probably put more emphasis on the French, I think, with Sandra. Being the eldest I think you just push it a little bit more
Monica: do you speak French to her usually?
Mother: no, not much
Monica: why was that important to you with her, why is it important?
Mother: that she speaks French? I guess because of my French roots, number one
Father: it's a bilingual country too
Mother: I think it's such an asset to have another language, I mean I probably didn't realize that until I moved to Toronto, I probably think that even more now that when I see people speak three or four languages
Father: yeah maybe what should be now that your French is there good for because we are a two language country, so that was good, for me it is worthwhile to have that, and I think that from that now we say, here how about Spanish, because of the North-South free trade (*a reference to the North American Free Trade Agreement, signed in 1990, facilitating links among Canada, Mexico and the USA*), how about Chinese or something like that because there's going to be big markets, you

know, it would be nice to have this go on to a third or
fourth language

Mother: I just think of it as being another thing that a person
has, I mean, you could take another subject, so why
not know another language, I just think it is an asset

This is a clear statement of the view that knowledge of French
is a kind of resource, the value of which is at least in part determined by its exchange value in economic marketplaces, although
there may be other sources (unspecified here beyond a reference to
'roots') of its value as an 'asset'.

Sandra sees it like this:

Example 4.2   Interview, Monica and Sandra, 1993

Sandra: (. . .) I like having a small school, and I want to keep
on to my French, because I don't speak it anywhere
else, so I mean

Monica: what is it, I guess, needs you to have that French?

Sandra: well, when I was younger, you know, people used to
ask, you know, 'What school do you go to?', and I'd
always be like, 'oh, no', you know, 'Champlain', you
know, 'it's a French school', you know, like all
embarrassed. And now it's like, I say it and I'm proud
of it, because I know two languages, and I have an
advantage over everyone else. And it's also I guess
because my Mom knows French. So I mean like people
on my Mom's side and my Dad's side, like they know
French sort of thing, so it's kind of like that's kind of
not the background, but a lot of (*pause*) they always
knew French, so I also want my kids to speak French
as well. It's like it's my background, you know. They
spoke French, so I think I should keep it up as well

Monica: are they, I don't know, proud of the fact or happy that
you speak French? Does it matter to your family?

Sandra: I think that they just think it's useful for me to have
more than like one language. That it's useful to be able
to communicate with other people. I think that's
basically why they (*pause*) Because my Dad's always
talking about, 'you should learn Spanish or Chinese',
all these other ones

Sandra's view represents well the views of both her mother and
her father, in her foregrounding of the notion of bilingualism, or

even better multilingualism, as an 'advantage', and in her some-what ambivalent appeals to her 'background' (note the hedges ('kind of', 'sort of'), hesitations ('like', pauses) and reformulations in her discussion of this topic).

The second dimension of Sandra's orientation to school that needs to be stressed is her focus on academic success. Sandra's mother says, 'Well, we always stress that that school is the number one, you know'. Neither of Sandra's parents went to university (apart from some night courses her mother once attended); Sandra's father has worked his way up the hierarchy in a bank, and Sandra's mother recently went back to work in a clerical position. Perhaps because they are both aware of what else they might have accomplished had they had university degrees, and perhaps because they feel that there are fewer interesting entry-level work opportunities now available to high-school graduates of the kind that Sandra's father was able to enjoy, both firmly believe in the importance of university studies, and expect both their children to attend university. They have begun saving towards that end, because they are concerned about what they can afford; Sandra expects to contribute financially through savings from her current part-time job as a lifeguard, and through part-time work throughout her studies. She does this despite the fact that her parents think she should spend more time studying rather than working, in part because she feels that this way she will feel more invested in and focused on her studies. At one point she planned to become a veterinarian, and had already done volunteer work in a local veterinary clinic. Later, she became less sure of her specific career aims, although planned to remain in science, since she seemed to be doing especially well in those courses. She plans to study at an English-language university in Ontario, because they have more programmes of the kind that appeal to her, and because in the end she feels more comfortable expressing herself in English:

> I know I'm going to an English university because, first of all, they offer more programmes, like the programmes that I want, and it will be easier for me to like explain myself in English, you know, especially when I'm going to have to do like a lot of essays and stuff. English is my first language and I can write better and stuff.

Sandra belongs to a group of friends at school who all share her orientation to school success. Most of them have known each other since elementary school at Rouillé. They tend to take many of the same courses, and in class they sit together. Their lockers are located on a corridor allocated to all students in their grade, but they occupy the central ones. At lunch-time they sit in the corridor directly in front of their lockers, leaving only enough space for one person to pass. Other students in their grade level eat elsewhere. Some of the lunch-time conversation is devoted to talking about friends, about magazines, restaurants and movies, or other things related to leisure. However, often they share impressions of a test to come or just completed, frequently expressing nervousness or despair about not doing well, despite the fact that most of them consistently get high grades. They ask each other for help with homework or test preparation, either in the hallway after lunch, or in the library, or even over the telephone in the evenings. They check each other's grades, and look over their friends' corrected papers and tests. Sandra says:

> We often call each other, like usually for a test especially like we'll have like a whole bunch of questions, and 'Did you get this one?' and you know. And if we can't get it then we'll just like, we'll figure it out together sort of thing. (...) I don't know, I find that our school, maybe it's just because we don't have as many people, but, or maybe it's just the friends I hang around with, but like all my friends want to do well in school. It's not like ah, who cares, you know, whatever. And I know a friend that used to be a bit like that but she changed to an English school, and (pause) see, I don't know, maybe it's just the group of friends, but from the way she talks about it, like, people skip all the time, and they don't get caught and stuff like that. It's a lot more, I guess, I don't know, I find that our school is pretty good, like there are a lot of people that try to do well, you know (...) all my friends are going to university (...) generally (going to college) is looked down upon compared to going to university, you know.

Sandra makes a distinction between doing well in French and doing well academically. For her, the ability to express oneself well in French is not a good reflection of how smart you are, or of how much you know. She feels this keenly, since she is often aware of what she would like to say or to write, but can't. This is something of a problem, given the emphasis Champlain places on the ability to use French.

(. . .) for me the biggest problem is that like even in Biology and stuff like that, when you have *questions de développement* (essay questions) I have all the answers up here in English. So when I'm trying to explain them in French, it doesn't make as clear a sense. So I mean sure the teacher can pick out things like that, but I'd really be able to explain it a lot better in English (. . .) like I was complaining about how like everything (*pause*) in my Ancient History class my project, I got docked a whole bunch of marks because I had so many French mistakes. And I was really upset because it's not a French, this is not a French class. And on the other hand the teacher was saying, 'well, if you're at a French school you should know how to', you know, 'speak French', and stuff like that. So I was really angry about that.

This means that she has less interest in the work she does that requires her to produce text in French:

(. . .) for me like the struggle is like just like trying to write properly in French, you know. That's one thing, it's like when I write in English it's like my ideas really count, and the structure and everything counts, and it's like the ideas I put into it, because I can already write well in English. In French, I don't really care about the ideas. I took the simplest thing I can just so I can word it properly, so that I'm not doing *anglicismes* and that, and et cetera et cetera, so (. . .) it makes it very boring for me because I want to use certain words but they might be *des anglicismes*, so I just like to keep it simple, you know.

This surely accounts in part for her increasing interest in Science and Mathematics, and her greater level of participation in those classes. However, she has ways of coping with this problem, notably through the exchange of help and information with her friends. She can help others in Mathematics and Science; she feels comfortable asking them for help in French: 'I just call the people who speak it at home.'

So Sandra has made some compromises in her academic life, in order to gain the advantages of bilingualism. The compromises she makes have little effect, however, on her academic standing. Most of the time she is evaluated on terms other than her ability to sound like a native speaker of French, and she has learned how to get information and provide convincing academic performances in ways that do not expose her vulnerability. And when it comes to the crunch, her social network helps her get by.

3   Bilinguals rule

For bilinguals like Luc and Sandra, playing the school's game does not mean accepting the premises of the game. They have their own interests, which lead to practices different from those which the school would predict. The school's investment in monolingualism and the standard would have students (and teachers) practising French in those ways in all interactions on school grounds (if not also beyond). As we saw in Chapter 3, school representatives cope with contradictions which make that dream difficult to realize by creating a distinction between official, public, front stage space, where the ideal image of the school can be constructed, and private, back stage space, where contradictions can be managed and contained (although they can easily openly acknowledge neither the contradiction nor the strategies used to contain it).

Among those contradictions is the fact that, while bilinguals need the school to maintain its ideological position in order for them to be seen as having acquired an authentic bilingualism, they do not need to perform consistently in the monolingual way the school desires. Instead, it makes more sense to them to perform their bilingualism in the one arena of their social lives where others can understand what their bilingualism is about: the school. It is with Luc and Marcel, and others like them, that Sandra shares the experience of living in a mainly English world, and gaining access to French through education. The front stage/back stage distinction which permeates their experience of school life is also, then, available to them as a way to manage their own version of the contradictions and concerns of Champlain bilingualism. Specifically, it allows them to be seen to be playing the game through monolingual standard practices on the public floor, while they can construct their shared experience of that bilingualism with other students back stage. Hence the whispered conversations in English in class, and the open use of English, or English that contains some school-related French vocabulary, in what they consider to be their private space outside class. For these students, school is about bilingualism.

In addition, as healthy teenagers, Sandra and her friends are interested both in creating their own world, and in obeying school and parental authority only up to a certain limit. Since French symbolizes that authority, as well as the control over public space that the school exercises, students like Sandra's group would in any case need to develop alternative linguistic practices that would help them demarcate their territory. The obvious thing to do is to speak English, in part because that is a linguistic resource to which everyone has access, in part because it is the language of popular culture, and in part because it is precisely the language the school wishes to banish from school-dominated discursive space.

Most of the time, Sandra and her friends manage to carve out distinctive discursive spaces for themselves, which they define as 'back stage' through the use of practices like whispering or passing notes, or through defining non-classroom territory as theirs. While at school, they spend most of their time outside of class in their corridor, or, if the weather is good, outside right in front of the school, the best space for talking and playing. They sometimes work in the library, where they aren't supposed to talk above a whisper anyway. They never eat in the cafeteria, which is supervised by teachers who occasionally remind students that they should be speaking French. The space over which they have exerted control is the most prominent and most comfortable of the public spaces available to students. By colonizing the corridor at lunch, they force other students to walk the halls or eat in the cafeteria. By dominating the space in front of the school, they force other students into the parking lots, the smoking area behind the school, or into staying inside on a nice day.

For most of the time we worked at Champlain, this group of students also controlled most of the extra-curricular activities of the school. Volleyball – the only sport at which Champlain tended to be successful, and therefore its most prestigious sports activity – attracted many students with bilingual practices and interests (Sandra was one of them). The student council was dominated by them, and therefore so were student council-sponsored activities, such as the general meetings in which the student council addressed the school, or the activities of groups supporting the student council, such as dances, or fund-raising through pizza sales, or the organization of the school prom. The annual fashion show was a showcase for many of them. They were less prominent in talent shows, and left other spaces, such as the media club or the yearbook, to others. (These other spaces tended to be activities

which supported their own and highlighted their importance; the media club filmed their activities, for example, and the yearbook prominently featured their group as well.)

The ways in which the bilinguals used the discursive space they controlled is revealing of the image they had of themselves and of others. We have seen how they manage different guises (as Luc and Luke) to turn in creditable performances as both French speakers and English speakers. Mostly, as we have seen, they keep these languages relatively separate (this is, of course, completely consonant with staff strategies for containing the sociolinguistic contradictions of the school, and with the school's underlying ideology of bilingualism as parallel monolingualisms). In some circumstances the frames of reference associated with each language collapse, usually when students have to perform verbally in school-sanctioned (and maybe even evaluated) situations in front of an audience of their peers. This happens, for example, in oral presentations in class, or in public, student council run *réunions générales*. These are the situations in which students might codeswitch (although the English is confined to meta-commentary or discourse markers set off from the main message), or more frequently adopt an accent which is recognizable neither as French nor as English. These public situations are occasions where these students define themselves as bilinguals, and set themselves off from the image the school would like to portray. Here is one example from a written form of public discursive space: the yearbook. The yearbook is put together by a student committee under the supervision of a teacher. It is one of those situations in which the students have to comply somewhat with school regulations, but the basic point of the text is for students to send messages to each other. Here is what Jason, a graduating senior, wrote as a text to accompany his photograph:

Example 4.3   From the 1992–93 Champlain yearbook

> *Je m'exkuze pour leuh kalité de lengue, mès kum vous savé tousse, la frensaix ne fue jammait une çujais dent lakel je sui d'ouwer.*

This is a difficult text to translate, but a translation might go something like this:

> I apolajize for thuh kwalitee ov thuh langwij, but as you all no, Frentch wuz never a subjik in witch I am giftid.

The standard French version would read something like this:

> Je m'excuse pour la qualité de langue, mais comme vous savez tous, le Français ne fut jamais un sujet pour lequel j'étais doué.

The point is that Jason knows enough about French to carry off this satire of Champlain's language norms: he deliberately makes gender errors (*la frensaix* instead of *le français, une çujais* instead of *un sujet*, and so on); he knows about the somewhat esoteric tense of the *passé simple* (*la frensaix ne* fue *jammait*...), although his tense concordance perhaps leaves something to be desired; he knows enough about spelling conventions to substitute plausible letters to produce the same sounds. He *can* produce the desired performance; he *chooses* not to.

At the same time as these students send up the school's focus on language norms, they also construct a devastating image of authentic, working-class Canadian French. The student council regularly used the occasion of a *réunion générale* (of which there were typically three or four a year) to present their message through a series of dramatic skits (rather than, say, speeches, which would likely have been more boring). The messages were complex, but tended to focus on the planned activities, or occasionally the motivational philosophy, of the student council committees. As a whole, they were designed to contribute to 'school spirit', that is, to convince all students to participate in extra-curricular activities, and to see those activities as both fun and important.

Three skits stand out as revealing of the bilingual students' image of Canadian French. In one, two boys played stereotypical French-Canadian lumberjacks, dressed in plaid shirts, tuques and construction boots. Seating themselves on cases of beer, they introduced themselves as representing the *Fédération québécoise de la bonne poutine* (The Québec Federation of Bonne Poutine). *Poutine* is a mixture of french fries, melted cheese curds and gravy, invented, so the story goes, in a Quebec diner in 1957. It was not well known until about 1980, when it became very popular in Quebec. It has since become a symbol of Quebec francophone culture, albeit one about which many feel highly ambivalent. In this skit, the two FQBP 'representatives' proceeded to complain, in exaggerated but excellent Quebec French, about the terrible quality of the poutine sold in Champlain's cafeteria.

In another, two students played a working-class couple, he with a pot belly, she in rollers, housecoat and fluffy pink slippers, both sitting on the couch and watching television. Again, their dialogue is produced in exaggerated Quebec French, although with some tell-tale signs of overgeneralization. For example, the diphthongization of certain vowels is characteristic of the variety, but does not occur in all linguistic environments; the housewife in this skit (whose own usual French bears traces of her mother's European origins) says not only *moé* and *toé*, but also *quoé* (*quoi* = what).

In a third, a row of young students, trying to convey the notion that students should not pollute their environment, interrogated an old vernacular-speaking granny on the evils of irresponsible garbage disposal. They ask her in turn whether certain items, which they show her, should be thrown into the garbage; of course, the correct answer is that the item should be recycled, and each one is tossed into a large mock recycling bin on stage. At the end, the 'kids' ask whether old grannies (speaking old-fashioned dialects) like her should be thrown out, and decide to toss her as well into the recycling bin. A male member of the council then tells the audience that if you throw out old worn-out objects you get back, as your reward, beauty. To underscore his point, he reaches into the bin and out comes a beautiful long-haired (and silent) girl.

In all of these skits, vernacular French is associated with something alien and ridiculous. The characters are set up as objects of mockery. The traits of vernacular French are exaggerated, sometimes to the point of error. The vernacular is clearly something that is not part of the ordinary practice of these students (although some master it better than others), but it is meaningful to them, meaningful but dangerous. It is something to be mocked, made alien, removed from serious consideration in the public discursive space of the school.

This is clearly a challenge to the legitimating ideology of the school. While the school has clearly invested in some form of standard French, it still pays homage to the vernacular as a symbol of authenticity, if only through its literature programme. The school's stand with respect to its use in school is, as we have seen, somewhat ambivalent, because of the tensions between the authenticity which legitimizes the school's existence and the authority of the standard which opens the doors which francophones seek to pass through. The bilinguals' position carries no such ambivalence.

This position is also clearly a challenge to those students who consider themselves speakers of that vernacular, and for whom that vernacular has a significance that it cannot have for the bilinguals. In the next section, I shall discuss how these students respond to the speech economy which the school and the bilinguals have manged to define, and attempt to impose on others.

4   *Les Québécois*[1]

In 1991, I interviewed Jean-Paul, a 10th grade student who had just arrived in September from a small city in Quebec (see Chapter 3, Example 3.14). Although he had taken English classes since Grade 4, as do all students in Quebec, he did not really speak English. This is how he described his first day at Champlain:

moi quand j'étais arrivé ici je pensais que je me suis trompé d'école. Ici, c'est l'école française et y a l'école anglaise à côté, je suis rentré ici, il fallait aller à la cafétéria, j'ai demandé à quelqu'un où est-ce qu'elle était la cafétéria en français, et elle m'a répondu qu'elle parlait pas en français, puis je me suis dit, qu'est-ce qu'elle fait ici d'abord? Puis là je m'en vais demander à une autre personne, puis j'i demande ça, puis là elle me répond, mais avec un gros gros accent, puis les mots elle les cherchait toujours, je me suis dit, pour moi, je me suis trompé d'école, puis aprés ça j'ai vu qu'ils faisaient plus pas mal parler en anglais qu'en français	*when I arrived here I thought I'd got the wrong school. This is a French school, and there's an English school next door, I came in here, we had to go to the cafeteria, I asked someone where the cafeteria was in French and she answered that she didn't speak French, so I said to myself, so what's she doing here then? And then I went to ask another person, and so I ask her that, and she answers, but with a heavy heavy accent and she kept searching for her words, I said to myself seems to me I've got the wrong school, and after that I saw that they pretty much speak more English than French*

Jean-Paul's reaction is fairly typical. Many monolingual francophone students are told by their parents when they move to Toronto that they should not worry, they will be going to a French-language school. Unfortunately, it turns out that the image they have of a French-language school, formed in Quebec, or France, or Haiti, or Djibouti, turns out to be somewhat different from Champlain. They expect the other students to be similar to them, and in particular they expect them to prefer to use French at all times, whether or not they speak any other languages. The first encounter with the prevalence of English in the corridors of Champlain is therefore unsettling.

---

[1] This section was written in collaboration with Donna Patrick.

These students react in a number of different ways. Some eventually learn English and start to act like Luc, especially if they arrive young enough to feel that they have some long-term future in the school, and in Toronto, to warrant making such an investment in learning to act and think differently. Clearly, this is all the stronger in cases where a return home is impossible or difficult to achieve. But students from monolingual parts of French Canada, and from Quebec in particular, have a more complex position with respect to Toronto life and to Champlain, for a number of reasons.

One is that most of these students are in Toronto against their will. Sometimes, the family has been obliged to move in order for a parent to keep or to find a job; sometimes family problems accompany economic motivations. Toronto is seen by the parents as a good place to start over, or else is the only place readily available where survival is likely. And the decision to move can be made and executed rapidly, without time for a reluctant teenager to get used to the idea. In other cases, the move is temporary (typically, a parent has a one- to three-year assignment at the Toronto office of the company he or she works for, or a student decides to substitute a year of studies in Toronto for the equivalent in Quebec as a way to learn English), and there is little motivation to invest in local practices. Students coming from farther away (with the exception of refugees) tend to be more likely to suppose their move might be permanent, and to have had a longer time to get used to the idea. Refugees are more likely to recognize the impossibility of staying where they were, because conditions at home were more clearly intolerable.

Another is that the political consciousness concerning language is particularly well developed in Quebec, for historical reasons connected to the nationalist mobilization of Quebec francophones, and its continuous salience in Quebec life since the 1960s. Even high school students have an opinion about independence and nationalism, and tend to take for granted the importance of the struggle for francophone rights. In this, they are ideologically closer to the generation of Champlain's founders, and to its current adult supporters, than to most of their age-mates at Champlain. However, they also associate that struggle specifically with Quebec state nationalism, not with the Franco-Ontarian cause, and it is difficult for them to give up their strong affiliation with Quebec. In the occasional instance when functionally monolingual French-Canadian students may be from Ontario or New Brunswick, they have often been influenced by the ideology of the neighbouring province (perhaps through their parents or other family members, perhaps through geographical and cultural proximity), and if they weren't before, they become so once at Champlain. All these students become symbolically cast as 'Québécois', whether or not they were born in Quebec.

One example of this strong tie is the use of Quebec symbols by these students, especially in the way they dress. Hockey sweaters have long been a fashion item of choice for boys (and even at times for girls) – a way of signalling shared values, and of making local social distinctions based on the identity of the team whose sweater you wear. While the expansion of the National Hockey League has multiplied the possibilities recently, for many years the salient social distinction for Canadian children was based on a rivalry between the Montreal Canadiens (symbolic representatives of French Canada) and the Toronto Maple Leafs (symbolic representatives of English Canada). Intra-mural hockey at Champlain is no stranger to this trope, as the Lucs of the school parade around in Maple Leafs sweaters, while the Québécois wear those of the Canadiens (or briefly, those of the short-lived Québec Nordiques). One student council-run *réunion générale* exploited this rivalry to set up a skit advertising the beginning of the intra-mural hockey season: most of the student council were on stage in their Maple Leafs sweaters, and were then followed on stage by seven or eight boys in Canadiens sweaters, waving the Quebec flag.

One of these Québécois students is Étienne. Here are some of the things he had to say:

Example 4.4   Interview, Monica and Étienne, 1993

Monica:	dans les questions que je vais te poser, c'est un peu pour savoir comment c'était l'expérience pour toi en venant ici, comment t'as réagi, à Toronto, à l'école, euh un peu tout ça	*in the questions that I'm going to ask you, it's kind of to see how it was for you coming here, how you reacted to Toronto, to the school, uh kind of all that*
Étienne:	okay, ben la façon que j'ai réagi, a été la première	*okay, well, the way I reacted was, the first*

	journée j'ai été très très choqué
Monica:	c'était quand que t'es arrivé?
Étienne:	c'était euh le 12 septembre 91, ça fera deux ans au mois de septembre (. . .) ben j'étais arrivé à l'école, l'école avait l'air normal, comme l'école que j'avais au Québec, pas mal plus petit, pis et j'ai trouvé qu'y avait beaucoup de monde qui venait euh beaucoup d'immigrants tout ça, ça c'était pas un problème, pis euh quand j'étais arrivé dans l'école, première journée, ils disent dans l'intercom 'levez-vous pour l'hymne national', alors là là je pouvais pas, je me suis dit 'dans quel bateau je m'embarque, c'est quoi, c'est un zoo ou quoi', je me suis même pas levé, j'étais assis pis je riais, je disais 'ça se peut pas', le prof il disait 'lève-toi', 'ah non, je suis pas capable'
Monica:	pourquoi?
Étienne:	euh chez moi, je viens du Québec, pis je suis séparatiste pis euh
Monica:	ah okay oui
Étienne:	s'i: fallait que je dise ça à mes amis que je me lève le matin pour l'hymne national du Canada là (. . .)

day I was very very negatively surprised
when was it you arrived?
it was uh September 12th 91, it'll be two years in September
(. . .)
well I had arrived at the school, the school looked normal, like the school I had in Quebec, much smaller and and I found there were lots of people who came uh lots of immigrants all that, that wasn't a problem, and uh when I had arrived at school, first day, they say on the intercom 'Stand for the national anthem', so then I couldn't, I said to myself 'what boat have I gotten on, what is this, it's a zoo or what', I didn't even stand, I was sitting and laughing, I was saying 'this can't be', the teacher said 'stand up', 'oh no, I can't'
why?
uh at home, I come from Quebec. and I'm a separatist and uh
oh okay yes
if I had to say that to my friends that I stand up every morning for the national anthem of Canada (. . .)

Étienne's reaction is perhaps somewhat stronger than that of others in his position, but conveys nonetheless something of what they all experience. Also, like many of them, Étienne never really gave up his ties to Quebec. He returned every chance he got, which was often, given that he was old enough to travel alone, the distances are not great (for Canada), and he had many relatives and friends with whom he could stay. He began almost immediately to make plans to attend a post-secondary institution in Quebec, and indeed that is where he went upon graduation. During the remainder of his time at Champlain, he was often alone, or with one or two of the other Québécois. He insisted that others speak to him in French: '*ils savent quand qu'ils viennent de parler anglais, s'i: me parlent anglais ils ont pas de réponse, quand qu'ils viennent me parler ils parlent français à moi*' (they know that when they come to speak English, if they speak to me in English they get no reply, when they come to speak to me they speak French to me). As a result, his exchanges with students whose linguistic practices differed from his were extremely limited. Most of his free time was spent as a member of the Audio-Visual Club, a group responsible for technical support (filming, sound systems, etc.) for school activities (concerts, dances, the fashion show, and so on). This club was staffed entirely by male students marginal to the main stream of school social life, most of them recent arrivals from francophone milieux. Whenever Étienne saw me, he kept me posted on how many months or weeks remained until he could, finally, leave Toronto: '*Je retourne à Montréal, t'sais, je m'en vas de la jungle*' (I'm going back to Montreal, y'know, I'm leaving the jungle).

François, another Québécois student in shoes similar to Étienne's, experienced his four years at Champlain in much the same way. Like Étienne, he came because his mother found work in Toronto. His father, now remarried, remained in Quebec, and François went often to visit him and other friends and relatives in the small town that was his birthplace. François felt comfortable immediately with the staff at Champlain, especially those who were from Quebec themselves (and there were many). In a 1993 interview with Florian, he said:

Puis les profs, t'sais, plus d'amitié. Je suis arrivé en même temps qu'un autre prof, Louis, à l'école. Il vient de Valcourt, puis Valcourt ben c'est la place où Bombardier a commencé ses	*And the teachers, y'know, more friendship. I arrived at the same time as another teacher, Louis, at school. He comes from Valcourt, and Valcourt well that's the place where*

motoneiges, fait quand j'ai su ça ben tu sais ben que je l'avais dans l'oeil le prof, fait qu'on parlait de motoneiges, puis il me racontait tout ça de Valcourt, comment ça fonctionnait, pis comment ça se représentait, tu sais. Ça crée des liens comme ça. Puis l'autre prof ben l'autre c'est d'autres choses, puis c'était chaleureux.

Bombardier started their snowmobiles, so when I learned that you can guess that I had my eye on him, that teacher, so we talked about snowmobiles, and he told me all that about Valcourt, how it worked, and how it was, you know. That creates links, like that. And the other teacher, well the other it's other things, and it was warm.

However, François, like Étienne, never made friends with students other than fellow Québécois.

Ce que j'ai remarqué c'est que les Québécois qui veulent parler français vont se tenir ensemble (. . .) Au début surtout, même tout le long, ç'a peut-être été plus avec les profs qu'avec les élèves. J'ai pas eu beaucoup de fréquentation à l'école, dans le sens qu'avec des vrais chums. Tout ceux-là ils sont tous partis. J'ai eu comme des Québécois, comme je te dis, tu sais. On vient qu'on se ramasse à un moment donné tu sais pis on se tient en gang, pis t'en spottes deux trois qui ont de l'air à être corrects puis tu te tiens avec, mais là ils sont tous partis, ils sont tous retournés au Québec. Après ça ben, les Anglais, bien moi je parlais pas beaucoup anglais au début, fait que tu oses pas leur parler non plus en anglais, parce que je parle tout croche (. . .) Les profs me disaient ou les orienteurs même avaient dit au début, tout le monde parle français ici, même s'ils parlent

What I noticed is that the Québécois who want to speak French will stick together (. . .) At first, even all the way through, it was maybe more with the teachers than the students (that I spoke). I didn't have many contacts at school, in the sense of real pals. All of those are all gone. I had like some Québécois (friends), like I say, you know. We get to be that we get together at some point you know, and we hang together as a gang, and you spot two three who seem all right and you hang out with (them), but now they've all left, they've all gone back to Quebec. After that well, the English, well I didn't speak much English at first, so you don't dare speak to them in English either, because I speak all wrong (. . .) The teachers said to me or even the guidance counsellors had said at first, everyone speaks French here, even if they speak in English,

en anglais, tu peux parler en français. Le gars parle tout le temps en anglais même dans la classe. Tu dis, parles-tu français? T'oses pas lui parler. Il parle-tu vraiment français là? Je connais pas ça ce monde-là. C'est un peu délicat là.	*you can speak to them in French. The guy speaks English all the time, even in class. You say, do you speak French? You don't dare speak to him. Does he really speak French? I don't know those people. It's a bit delicate.*

So for François, as for Étienne, Jean-Paul and so many others, the world of the Champlain peer group is foreign and strange, peopled by '*les Anglais*' (the English), whose practices make no sense, or worse, threaten some very fundamental values about French and a strong sense of identity. At best you might hope to find one or two others like you, and if you aren't put off by differences in pedagogical content and style, you might get along with the teachers. Mostly, you feel like François: '(...) *il y avait ben des moments donnés là que j'étais dans les nuages puis je pensais à mon Québec (...)*' ((...) there were plenty of moments when I was in the clouds, thinking of my Quebec (...)). When Florian said to him, '*Alors toi t'es pas un Franco-Ontarien, t'es pas devenu un Franco-Ontarien, t'es encore un Québécois?*' (So you you aren't a Franco-Ontarian, you haven't become a Franco-Ontarian, you're still a Québécois?), François laughed and added '*En éxil*' (in exile). As soon as he graduated, he too left for Quebec.

The feeling of alienation is compounded by difficulties over the value accorded to their language practices in the school setting. While the teachers tend to be thrilled by the Québécois students' preference for speaking French all the time (even when they can get by in English), they aren't always so thrilled by the nature of the French they speak:

Example 4.5   Interview, Florian and Michel, 1993

Florian:	okay, tu parlais t'es fier de ta langue, okay, euh si on parlait par exemple parce que je me souviens qu'une fois tu m'avais mentionné que dans des cours de Français des fois euh t'avais pas été bien noté parce que ta langue	*okay, you were saying you're proud of your language, okay, if we talked for example because I remember once you had mentioned to me that in French classes sometimes you hadn't been graded well because your language*

correspondait pas à ce qu'on
attendait probablement
de toi, pourrais-tu me
parler un petit peu de
toute la question des
bonnes langues ou des
mauvaises langues,
qu'est-ce que tu penses de

Michel: moi je crois pas à ça
t'sais, euh y a des
professeurs à l'école ici je
vais pas mentionner des
noms   qui euh qui
Florian: okay
Michel: croivent que le français
ça devrait être de telle
façon, tout autre là, ben
disons, toute autre forme
de français c'est pas bon,
parce que moi j'avais fait
un exposé oral euh deux
deux ans je pense et puis
c'était une belle présentation,
un bon contenu, j'ai ma
tante est professeure (. . .)
pis ma tante elle m'avait
dit c'est bien, là j'ai fait
mon exposé devant mon
prof, mon prof me dit
bon contenu, sauf la
langue, euh c'est pas un
bon français, donc faudra
améliorer ton niveau de
langue, puis euh moi je
suis un peu déçu
(. . .)
parce que c'est pas juste,
parce qu'on veut tous
garder notre, tu sais à
l'école ils disent tous (tUt)
ah parlez français parlez
le français, mais si ils
nous critiquent, s'i: disent
ah ta langue, ton français

*didn't correspond to what
they probably expected of
you, could you talk to me a
bit about the whole
question of good languages
or bad languages, what do
you think of*

*I don't believe in that,
y'know, uh there are
teachers at the school here
I won't mention any
names   who uh
    okay
who think that French
should be in such and such
a way, any other, well let's
say, any other form of
French is not good, because
I had done an oral
presentation uh two two
years (ago) I think, and it
was a nice presentation,
good content, I have my
aunt is a teacher (. . .) and
my aunt said it's good, then
I did my presentation in
front of my teacher, my
teacher says good content,
except the language, uh it's
not a good French, so
you'll have to improve your
level of language, and uh I
was a bit disappointed*

*(. . .)
because it isn't fair, because
we all want to keep our,
you know at school they all
say ah speak French speak
French, but if they criticize
us, if they say ah your
language, your French from
Quebec or from Ontario,*

du Québec ou de l'Ontario, c'est pas bien ça, moi je veux que tu parles le français de France, et c'est un peu hypocrite, s'i: nous encouragent à parler français à l'école, pis ils vont venir nous dire 'On parle pas de même, tu devrais parler comme un Français de France'	*that's no good, I want you to speak French from France, and it's a bit hypocritical, if they encourage us to speak French at school, and then they come and tell us, 'We don't speak like that, you should speak like a French person from France'*

Michel seems to have been caught off guard by his teacher's reaction to his French; everything should have been fine, and suddenly, his French isn't right. And here he had always thought of himself as a native speaker of that language, and a serious student (*'comme je l'ai dit je prends l'école au sérieux'* (like I said, I take school seriously). Michel is in school to get to university; both he and his parents agree on that goal. His father says, for example: *'(. . .) mais y a jamais été question est-ce que SI ils allaient à l'université, c'est dans quoi pis quand est-ce que, t'sais'* ((. . .) but it was never a question of will IF they would go to university, it's in what and when will they, y'know).

On top of that, Michel characterizes himself as a bilingual francophone with respect for his first language: *'c'est une richesse là que t'as été élevé avec le français, tu devrais le garder'* (it's valuable, to have been brought up with French, you should keep it). He shares the school's orientation to monolingualism:

moi, j'aimerais ça là que l'école soit complètement français, pas l'anglais là, on entend de l'anglais dehors là moi j'aimerais (. . .) au Québec (. . .) t'entendais le monde parler français, j'aimerais ça que ça soit de même ici. Y en a qui disent 'oh c'est pas *cool* de parler en français, c'est *cool* de parler en anglais', moi, j'aimerais ça une école juste le français	*I'd like it if the school were completely French, not English, you hear English outside I'd like (. . .) in Quebec (. . .) you heard people speaking French, I'd like it to be the same here. Some say, 'oh it's not cool to speak in French, it's cool to speak English', I'd like a school just French, myself*

So Michel's expectations and behaviour are exactly in line with what the school wants, and yet somehow his French is not good enough, and he is subject to public correction. The experience sours his feelings about the school; it makes him feel that such teachers are 'hypocritical'.

This kind of judgement can come not just from teachers, but also from other students. We have seen how the Lucs and Sandras of the school can, quite innocently in many cases, construct stereotypes of the French Canadian as bumbling and stupid. In Michel's class, the day of his oral presentation, it was not just the teacher who made comments about his French; a fellow student (from Europe) commented that his accent had been *'trop québécois'* (too Québécois). Lorraine, a student who spoke English well, but who nonetheless retained her Quebec variety of French, reported this incident from one of her History classes in 1993: *'C'est comme, "hé, Lorraine, comment qu'on dit* sixteen *en français?" Moi je suis là, "Seize". "Ah, t'es Québécoise. C'est pas /sajz/, c'est /sɛz/"'* (It's like 'hey, Lorraine, how do you say *sixteen* in French?' I'm there *'Seize'*. 'Ah, you're Québécoise. It isn't /sajz/, it's /sɛz/.). Even Sandra fell into this trap: one day in *Sciences*, as part of a discussion of the digestive system, she volunteered a comment about how her esophagus sometimes feels like she is swallowing a potato. The word she used for 'potato', likely from her experiences in her mother's home village in Manitoba, was *patate*; a fellow student, and good friend, immediately turned around and told her she should have said *pomme de terre*.

Usually, students like Michel adapt, or continue to do what they do and suffer the consequences, dreaming of the day when they can return to a place where no one makes fun of their French. One or two, like Étienne, try to stand up for their French. Here is one of the rare testimonies we have of such resistance (from an interview with Mark, and hence in English, in 1994): Claudia is of South American background, and moved to Ontario from Quebec when she was in elementary school. Simone is also from Quebec, of francophone background; she has been in Ontario for about five years. Diane is a Québécoise who arrived in Toronto in late 1993.

Example 4.6   Interview, Mark, Diane, Simone and Claudia, June 1994

Mark:	what happens when you use French in the classroom? do you get respect for your type of French or do they

All three:	nooooo, no
Claudia:	The French they're teaching us, is instead of saying *toi* I'll say *toé, moi-moé* okay, and that's Quebec French, that's how we were taught that French and now they're trying to change it to be French from France, un vélo, une bicyclette (laughter, xx) okay they're changing it. It's like she did this, where you put a lemon in your mouth and you're talking (xx)
Mark:	so they don't respect your type of French?
Simone:	no, they say that that's not real French
Diane:	yeah, like in French we gotta say *oui* and us Québécois say like *ouais ouais ouais*, you know you're not on their couch, you're not at their house, in your house and you say *oui* at school
Mark:	okay, let me ask you whether you agree with this or don't agree with this or would like to change something. Look, the school doesn't respect the type of French that you speak, so what you do often is that you'll use English, that's kind of a way of saying 'to hell with you'
Claudia and Simone:	no no no
Claudia:	because even if they tell me not to talk my French, I'll do it. 'Cause it's my language. The English we're talking right now, it's not the proper English, the real English is from England. The proper French for them is from France. So we're like the English ones right now (xx simultaneous talk) Because most of the black people (xx) they're always transferred in France, and then they come here. So of course they have a better French, like, okay I have this problem with Isaak (xx) he was in my class, but my teacher was Monsieur Dumont at that time and he was from Quebec and everything, and then we started talking about the French language. I go (xx) I'm sorry you're not going to tell me what's the right French (xx simultaneous talk)
Simone:	and also last time it was Madame Martin, it was in geography class, and I started speaking French, and then she goes, 'you know, you really have a bad French'. I'm like 'excuse me Madame, my Mom taught me how to speak that way'. You're not gonna start dissin' my mother, because she kind of

Claudia: dissed my mother, because my Mom taught me how to speak that way, and I'm proud to be bilingual

Claudia: (xx) it's not an insult for you (xx) it's an insult for your parents 'cause that's how they raised you. They think they did good. Screw the French we're talking about

Mark: okay would you ever sometimes use your type of French in a classroom just to drive home the point?

Simone: I'm not gonna change my French for anybody

Claudia: we'll write a composition in French, we write it in our French, and then you get it back and you see all these red circles

(. . .)

Look, I left Quebec when I was in Grade 3, when I just learned out how to write like tied together, you know? But when I moved to Ontario, I went to a French school, okay, French elementary school. But they would tell me I'm not allowed to write compositions with your Quebec words, so I would get angry, and I would write it anyway, you know. So I'm not gonna change my French, I understand some of it don't make sense, and I'll let them correct it right, but I don't agree with it sometimes, just change the mistakes, or tell me this would sound better, but you can't change my composition, because it won't be called my composition, it would be called hers (xx). Me, English and French, I write it the way I speak. Instead of writing 'toi' t-o-i, I'll write 'toé' t-o-e and the accent, with the accent, and that's the way I'll write, I'll write like I speak, and like for me that's the way (xx) that's the way that I speak and then they go and change it on you. I'm like listen, that's the way I speak

However, especially in written work, teachers just as insistently correct her 'Quebec words'. While 'Quebec words' might be fine for private conversations, and are valued as a part of Champlain's heritage (and even appreciated in the literary works which made an important political statement by dealing with the everyday life of francophone Quebec), they are not fine for public performances, whether oral (as in Michel's case) or written (as in Claudia's and Simone's).

The result for the Michels and the Étiennes is not so bad, to the extent that these are middle-class students with academic aspirations, with access to standard French outside school, whose own goals regarding bilingualism resemble those the school has for them, and whose French is not so far from the standard. Even Diane is prepared to make the shift, attributing her ability to do so to the fact that she went to a good boarding school in Quebec up until that autumn. For Claudia and others whose academic situation is already in danger, who have no access to standard French outside school, whose bilingualism is of a variety which is stigmatized by the school and by other students, or, to put it differently, whose vernacular is farther from the standard, the problem is greater. While Claudia fights, others drop out, or struggle. Boys in particular resist by simply speaking English all the time (since nobody judges them in that language), and, since they frequently have access to ways of making money outside school, they often come to school less and less often, and may drop out altogether. Girls seem to have fewer opportunities for making money outside school (although one did drop out to work as a salesgirl in a mall, and another to work as a hairdresser); some of them transfer to English schools (as did Claudia, in the end), and some try to hang on, half-heartedly and full of linguistic insecurity (Simone, a Québécoise friend of Claudia's, explained her decision to drop out of a course because of this: *'Je parle mal, j'utilise beaucoup d'anglais, et il y a beaucoup d'anglais dans mon français'* ('I speak badly, I use English a lot, and there is a lot of English in my French'). Students like Claudia and Simone say that they come to school to be with their friends (in contrast to students like Michel, Sandra or Luke, who are there to make sure they get into university). The solidarity of their peer group is much more important, in the end, than anything else (this shows up in their behaviour through intense exchanges and sharing of objects, like make-up, or cigarettes, or portable CD players, or money; and through the exclusion of former friends who are thought to have betrayed the group one way or another). This concern with peer solidarity is not surprising, given that these students get the support they need from their friends, not from the school.

Ginette is fairly typical of such girls. In 1991–92, Laurette and I spent time in the *Français général* and *Sciences général* classes she was taking. *Sciences* worked out fairly well for Ginette, since the linguistic demands it made on her were minimal. Most of the work she had to do in French involved reading materials and listening to the teacher's instructions. The rest of the time was spent doing lab work in small groups, where she could function in English, except for the occasions when she had to interact with a Somali group member who spoke no English. She kept those interactions very short, limiting them for the most part to directions on how to do part of the lab, what materials to get, or similar brief instructions. Tests were often multiple choice, or required short answers. Labs did need to be written up, but even those texts were fairly simple.

Français was more difficult. Ginette tried hard in that class, but found it difficult. In an interview in 1991, Ginette told Laurette that she felt unprepared when she arrived at Champlain in Grade 7, from a Catholic French-language elementary school in a working-class suburb (note that Ginette chose to do the interview in English):

> I went to Notre-Dame, it's a French school (. . .) I didn't learn a lot at that school, I wasn't prepared to come here, like grammar and all that stuff, so when I came here it was really hard (. . .) I didn't know how to spell and that was no good (. . .).

At one point, she sat in front of her papers in the middle of the class, saying 'I can't do this, I can't do this'. She flatly refused to give an oral presentation in front of the class; in the end, Lise convinced her to do it privately, with just the two of them in the room. Her participation in class was full of switches back and forth between French and English; this is a mode of communication perfectly normal for most of the Franco-Ontarian working class, and in Ginette's case it may also have represented a way for her to participate in class and still somehow keep her feet on English territory, where she may have felt safer. Certainly, the hedges in her contributions ('like', 'whatever') accentuate her academic and linguistic insecurity. Here are some examples of Ginette in Lise's class:

Example 4.7   The class is jointly constructing a narrative. Others have suggested that the protagonist wanders into an abandoned house, opens a door, and finds syringes and knives on the floor

Lise:	qu'est-ce qui peut se passer avec tous ces seringues, couteaux?	*what could happen with all these syringes, knives?*
Ginette:	il peut y avoir des *psychos*	*there could be* <u>*psychos*</u>

Example 4.8   Mohamud is making a presentation about arranged marriages

Ginette:	moi je trouve que c'est pas juste pour les filles comme, les femmes (xx) rien qu'à choisir, comme quand tu te maries, c'est parce que *like like you love each other* comme (xx) mais ça c'est juste comme payer *you know* pour une femme, c'est pas vraiment	*I think it isn't fair for girls like, women (xx) just to choose, like when you marry it's because <u>like like you love each other</u> like (xx) but that's just like paying <u>you know</u> for a wife (woman?), it's not really*
Mohamud:	non non tu choisis jamais un homme	*no no you never choose a man*
Ginette:	oui toi tu me *instead of* tu me choisis *like* (xx) on s'aime pas comme deux personnes, c'est quoi?	*yes you you (choose) me <u>instead of</u> you choose me <u>like</u> (xx) we don't love each other like two people, what's that?*

Example 4.9   Lise is asking the class comprehension questions concerning the play L'Avare

Lise:	(. . .) okay qu'est-ce que vous avez compris de l'histoire, comment s'est terminé l'histoire?	*(. . .) okay what did you understand of the story, how did the story end?*
Student:	d'une bonne façon	*in a good way*
Lise:	Ginette	*Ginette*
Ginette:	Harpagon a retrouvé sa cassette *whatever*	*Harpagon found his purse <u>whatever</u>*
Lise:	Harpagon a retrouvé sa cassette	*Harpagon found his purse*

Michel and Ginette represent two poles of the experience of speakers of Canadian French. The differences in their experiences and in their strategies stems largely from the position with respect to languages and academic success which they brought to school. While they both feel alienated by the lack of value placed on the kind of French they speak, Michel is oriented towards the school's monolingual ideology, while Ginette is most comfortable in a bilingual milieu. Michel, and others like him, manage by establishing a

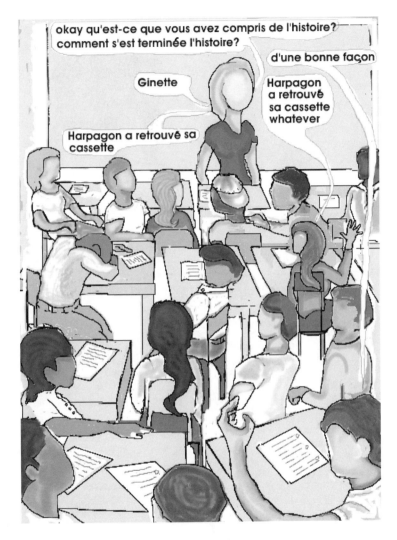

closed 'Québécois' monolingual French space, where they do not
have to speak English, and where their French will not be judged
negatively. They manage their relations with others, to the extent
that they have them, by working on the standardization of their
French (for class), and by learning English (for students). Alternatively, they isolate themselves, and flee to Quebec early and often.
Students like Ginette manage less well; they tend to also carve out

private marginalized spaces (in the smoking area, in the parking lot, off to the side in classrooms) where they can speak what they want, when they want, without being judged, although they recognize the value the school attaches to these spaces, and by extension to them. For example, Simone and Diane said the following in a discussion with Mark:

Example 4.10   Interview, Mark, Diane, Simone (and Claudia), 1994

Simone: they're ashamed of smokers, that's why they put the
smokers out in back. Before it was in front (. . .) (The
school) is ashamed of smokers, people that don't dress
perfectly, and stuff like that. So they all try to hide us
away from Northtown (the school next door). The
school beside us is a rich school. So they're trying to
make this school perfect by hiding everyone.

Diane: And it's like (they're) afraid of troubles or problems.
You know, we're teenagers, okay. It's like natural for us
to have problems and it's like okay you're gonna have
problems, we'll just have to hide it or keep it secret.

On the rare occasions when these students have to give a public
performance, they find a way around the problem if they can.
For example, Diane, Claudia and Simone were in a class in which
all students were expected to provide a performance at the *café
littéraire*; rather than provide individual, spoken performances,
the three girls got together and sang a song from the current
Québécois pop charts. If no such strategy presents itself, they
avoid doing the work altogether (such as Ginette's refusal to do
her oral presentation). The Michels mainly end up doing rather
well in school, at least well enough to think about post-secondary
education, and even university. The Ginettes are hanging on by the
skin of their teeth.

5   'Je ne comprenais rien'

Students from other parts of the francophone world have quite a
different position with respect to French, especially in cases where
French has been for them primarily a language of instruction,
learned in homelands which are former French colonies, and which
still lie under the influence of France. They also may be as mystified as the 'Québécois' by the prevalence of English in interaction
among students at Champlain when they first arrive, but their
position with respect to that practice is not quite the same. While
this is the case for students from a wide variety of places, it is
expressed most clearly by Somali students, and to a certain extent
by Haitians. Two factors contribute to the salience of these issues
for these two groups of students: the fact that there are enough of
them sharing the same experience to be able to articulate both the

experience and a strategy for dealing with it, and the fact that linguistic differences are heightened by fairly deep cultural differences, and by the divisive nature of racial distinctions.

In this section, I shall first discuss some positions taken with respect to French, positions which tended fairly (but not completely) uniformly to support the value of the standard 'international' French with which most of these students arrived in Canada, and to devalue the Canadian French which was part of the school's legitimizing authenticity. Second, I shall discuss ways in which some of these students made sense of the prevalence of English in peer group life at school. As we shall see, some reacted by drawing further away from others at Champlain; the problem of the use of English became a contributing factor to the sharpening of racial and cultural lines. Others came to feel that English was important for them too, and tried hard to learn it, although their motivation was less the ability to get along at school than it was to get along in Canadian society, whether in terms of jobs and daily survival, or in terms of participation in popular culture, especially that influenced by African Americans.

Example 4.11   Interview, Monica and Aïcha, 1992

Aïcha:	(. . .) ici, tu vois, les langues québécoises sont plus faibles que les langues françaises	(. . .) here, you see, the Québécois languages are weaker than the French languages
Monica:	dans quel sens?	in what sense?
Aïcha:	si on voit la qualité, et puis les Français ils parlent le pur français, et ici ils sont mélangés, comme si, c'est mélangé, j'ai compris du 'là, là, là', mais on veut pas de répétitions en France. Le français, il faut pas qu'il y ait de répétitions, oui, mais ici alors là!	if you look at the quality, and the French they speak pure French, and here they're mixed, as if, it's mixed, I understood 'là, là, là,' but they don't want any repetitions in France. In French, there should be no repetitions, yes, but here, honestly!
Monica:	est-ce que tu trouves que c'est difficile à comprendre, le français d'ici?	do you find it difficult to understand the French here?
Aïcha:	oui, ah moi, j'avais du mal à comprendre, parce qu'il y	yes, oh I had difficulty understanding, because

avait beaucoup de 'là', je comprenais rien	*there were many 'là's, I understood nothing*

'*Je ne comprenais rien*' – 'I understood nothing'. This is the first reaction of many students from outside Canada to the French they hear upon arrival. They react to many things; Aïcha feels it is not 'pure', it's 'mixed' (by which she presumably means it is mixed with English). She thinks Canadians repeat the discourse marker '*là*' too much. And not only is it hard to understand, it is not at all clear that it is worth understanding; its 'quality' is not high enough. This causes major problems with Canadian-French-speaking students, with teachers, and with some teaching material, such as French-Canadian novels:

Example 4.12 Interview, Monica and Aïcha, 1994

Monica:	le matériel écrit, tu trouves ça intéressant, les livres, les manuels de cours?	*the written material, you find that interesting, the books, the course manuals?*
Aïcha:	les livres?	*the books?*
Monica:	les livres qu'on utilise, les textes écrits qu'on utilise dans les cours, comment tu trouves ça?	*the books you use, the written texts you use in class, how do you find that?*
Aïcha:	c'est pas intéressant. Non.	*it's not interesting. No.*
Monica:	pourquoi, c'est trop, le contenu est pas	*why, it's too, the content is*
Aïcha:	c'est un peu banal. Oui, même les livres dans les bibliothèques, c'est pas des livres écrits par la France, ce sont des Québécois. Je comprends pas. Il y avait un livre qui avait beaucoup de 'là', au lieu de dire 'Bon Dieu', ils disaient 'Bon yeu', comme si, c'est un peu, je comprenais rien	*it's a bit ordinary. Yes, even the library books, they aren't books written by France, they're Québécois. I don't understand. There was a book which had a lot of 'là's, instead of saying 'Bon Dieu' (Good God) they said 'Bon yeu', as if, it's a bit, I understood nothing*

This feeling of mystification, sometimes accompanied by contempt, was a first reaction, and one which in some cases led to deep disaffection, either short- or long-term. In some cases, it led students to put little effort into reading novels assigned in class, or doing the work associated with them. Sometimes, students despaired of being able to follow what was going on in class, and thought about dropping courses, or did drop them.

Example 4.13   Interview, Awad and Hodan, 1994

Hodan:	(. . .) la façon dont les gens parlaient, au début je n'arrivais pas à comprendre le professeur, il parlait québécois, alors . . . Il y a une fois que j'ai même pensé de quitter le cours parce que je ne comprenais pas ce que le prof disait, mais quand-même	*(. . .) the way people talked, at first I couldn't understand the teacher, he spoke Québécois, so . . . One time I even considered dropping the course because I didn't understand what the teacher was saying, but all the same*
Awad:	c'est-à-dire est-ce qu'il était parlait c'était l'accent ou c'était la	*that is was he was he speaking it was the accent or it was the*
Hodan:	c'est l'accent québécois, oui	*it's the québécois accent, yes*
Awad:	puis tous les mots	*and all the words*
Hodan:	oui mais il parlait vite, okay, il parlait vite, mais quand-même il avait un accent que j'ai jamais entendu, des fois je me disais je me demandais s'il parlait français ou pas, je t'assure, c'est (rires)	*yes but he spoke fast, okay, he spoke fast, but all the same he had an accent I had never heard, sometimes I said to myself I wondered if he was speaking French or not, I assure you, it's (laughs)*

Example 4.14   Interview, Laurette and Amina, 1993

| Laurette: | et qu'est-ce que (xx) le français qui est ici est-ce que c'est différent de ce que tu connais? | *and what (xx) the French here is it different from what you know?* |
| Amina: | mm mm le français ici est québécois, puis c'est pas du tout pareil avec le français que j'ai appris en Somalie, au début je trouvais, euh avec Monsieur Boudreau, j'étais comme, | *mm mm the French here is Québécois, and it isn't at all the same as the French I learned in Somalia, in the beginning I found, uh, with Mister Boudreau, I was like, I* |

j'étais sur le point de quitter la classe parce que je comprenais rien du tout dans son cours, puis euh d'autres professeurs aussi, mais maintenant je suis habituée	*was about to drop his course because I understood nothing at all in class, and uh other teachers too, but now I'm used to it*

Examples 3.22 and 3.23 in the previous chapter have already introduced us to the disdain many European-trained students have for the influence of English on French in Canada (Example 3.22), or for Canadian ignorance of European lexicon (Example 3.23).

Those feelings are part of a position taken up which locates them outside of Canadian French; as we see below, for Marie-Paule (a student from Haiti), and others like her, Canadian French (which they characterize sometimes as *le québécois* and sometimes as *joual*) is different from what they recognize as being French. It is alien to them. While Marie-Paule dismisses the differences as not being very deep (*c'est juste l'accent qu'ils mettent sur les voyelles* – it's just the accent they put on the vowels), she certainly considers that it is others (they) who do that; she is not particularly interested in learning how to do that herself.

Example 4.15   Interview, Laurette and Marie-Paule, 1993

Laurette:	qu'est-ce que tu penses du créole, qu'est-ce que tu penses du français, ou du français canadien, du français?	*what do you think of Creole, what do you think of French, or of Canadian French, of French?*
Marie-Paule:	qu'est-ce que je pense du français?	*what do I think of French?*
Laurette:	oui	*yes*
Marie-Paule:	eh le créole moi je trouve que c'est la même chose. Si quelqu'un parle français il peut comprendre le créole. Si quelqu'un parle le créole il peut très facilement comprendre le français, vice versa. Alors c'est presque pratiquement la	*eh Creole I think it's the same thing. If someone speaks French he can understand Creole. If someone speaks Creole, he can very easily understand French, vice versa. So it's almost practically*

	même chose. Mais le français canadien, comme pas le pas celui mais le joual quoi, comme moi je suis, j'ai pas l'habitude de l'entendre trop trop souvent, quand je l'entends c'est pas (xx) l'intonation, c'est pas que ça m'énerve non plus *but* ça sonne bizarre	*the same thing. But Canadian French, like not not this one but* joual, *like I'm I don't usually hear it very very often, when I hear it it's not (xx) the intonation it's not that it bothers me either* __but__ *it sounds weird*
Laurette:	quand tu es arrivée au début à Toronto, est-ce que c'était difficile pour toi de comprendre les gens?	*when you first arrived in Toronto, was it hard for you to understand people?*
Marie-Paule:	c'était très difficile de s'assimiler	*it was very hard to assimilate*
Laurette:	ah oui	*ah yes*
Marie-Paule:	surtout les accents sur les voyelles, comme 'ben là toué', c'est juste l'accent qu'ils mettent sur les voyelles	*especially the accents on the vowels, like* 'ben là toué' *it's just the accent they put on the vowels*

This notion that Canadian French is at worst bad, or at best simply alien, is connected to students' expectations about the kind of French that should be taught, and how it should be taught. Many students expect to be taught French formally and explicitly, partly along the model of the way they were taught before, partly taking into account the fact that they do not consider themselves to be native speakers of French, nor do they see why they should consider themselves to be such. This raises two problems. The first has to do with the politically motivated idea that Champlain and her sister schools are schools for students whose first language is French. No one would disagree that students like Marie-Paule and Aïcha, for whom French is a second language, belong at Champlain. It is simply that the school has not found any comfortable way of thinking about their place there, and about the consequences of their presence for things like curriculum content and language pedagogy. The second has to do with prevailing notions about language pedagogy in North America. Whether for first or for second languages, the idea of structuralist-functionalist methods has come under attack. While there is no consensus about how best to teach French in Canada, in Ontario at least *Français* programmes have been heavily influenced by communicative language teaching theories and practices, which have generally become well entrenched in both English (first-language) and French (second-language) pedagogy. Below, Saïda expresses a frustration with the way French is taught at Champlain, with its emphasis on literature over language structure, and its expectation that French is something you should already know.

Example 4.16   Interview, Awad and Saïda, 1994

(. . .) la matière française n'était pas vraiment la même, là-bas on nous apprenait tout ce que le français voulait dire, ce c'était en plusieurs catégories, on apprenait plusieurs catégories, on apprenait le vocabulaire, la conjugaison, la grammaire, la, ici c'est c'est la littérature à chaque fois à chaque fois, on lit un livre pendant toute l'année, on évalue, ninani ninana, mais c'est il y a pas ces catégories qui sortent dans le système, et c'est vraiment dangereux parce que c'est pour ça je je je blâme pas les élèves qui ne peuvent pas différencier le tu le la le la off c'est tellement difficile lorsque tu n'as qu'un livre à apprendre, c'est tellement difficile

(. . .) *the French subject wasn't really the same, over there they taught us everything that French meant, it it was in many categories, we learned many categories, we learned vocabulary, conjugation, grammar, the, here it's it's literature every time every time, we read one book during the whole year, we evaluate, ninani ninana, but it's there aren't those categories which come out in the system, and it's really dangerous, because that's why I I I don't blame the students who can't tell the difference between the* tu le la le la *off it's so hard when you only have one book to learn, it's so hard*

Below, Mohamud once again disrupts a *Français général* class. He is frustrated because he, like Saïda, expects explicit structural teaching. He expects a focus on form, an orientation to mastery of *le bon français*. During the semester, he frequently asked Lise to give the students *dictées*, a method sometimes considered too traditional, too oriented towards memorization and transmission, and not enough towards students' active participation in the communicative processes of the classroom. In any case, it was certainly not part of the course programme. (Lise did finally break down, but told Mohamud that if he wanted *dictées*, he would have to organize them, which he happily did.) In the following example, Lise is trying to organize a writing activity, asking students to answer questions about a text they have read and discussed. Mohamud challenges the legitimacy of this activity.

Example 4.17   Français général, *1991*

Lise:	ouais, je vais les écrire au tableau (xx) vous pouvez commencer avec ça, ça doit pas vous prendre plus qu'une demi-heure, si il y a des trucs que vous ne comprenez pas, venez me voir, je vais l'expliquer (xx) majorité parce que c'est (xx) de la révision pour vous autres	*yeah, I'll write them on the board (xx) you can start with that, it shouldn't take you more than half and hour, if there are things you don't understand, come see me, I'll explain it (xx) the majority because it's (xx) revision for all of you*
Mohamud:	non mais quel rapport il y a avec le le	*no but what does it have to do with the*
Lise:	l'examen, ça va être les questions	*the exam, that'll be the questions*
Mohamud:	le français, non, avec le français, Madame	*French, no, with French, Madame*
Lise:	ça	*that*
Mohamud:	le français ça	*French, that*

What we see in these examples is an orientation to standard French, and to traditional pedagogy oriented towards mastery of the standard language. We also see an alienation from ways of using language which are tied to the school's authenticity, and which can serve to render problematic the development of ties with teachers and other students who consider themselves to be francophones.

At the same time, these students, like the 'Québécois', are taken aback by the preference so many students have for English. While they may not necessarily share the school's ideological commitment to making the school an island of French monolingualism, they at least expected to be able to communicate with everyone else in French. Not only do they find much of the French they encounter difficult to understand, but frequently what they encounter isn't even French.

Example 4.18   Interview, Monica and Mohamud, 1993

Monica:	c'est important pour toi de venir dans une école française?	*it's important for you to come to a French school?*
Mohamud:	oui parce que je parle pas très bien anglais	*yes, because I don't speak English very well*
Monica:	mm	*mm*
Mohamud:	je pratique maintenant, mais je parle toujours en français, alors quand les élèves parlent en anglais je me sens à part des élèves, je suis étonné de voir ce genre de chose, ce phénomène	*I'm practising now, but I still always speak in French, so when the students speak in English, I feel left out, I'm surprised to see this kind of thing, this phenomenon*

Like Mohamud, Saïda, Amran and Hodan are put off by this widespread use of English. And the consequences for all three are similar: they can talk to others in French, or perhaps after a while in a bit of English, but the walls are up, and interactions are limited.

Example 4.19   Interview, Laurette, Amran et Saïda, 1992

Laurette:	et avec les élèves, comment ça se passe?	*and with the students, how do things go?*
Saïda:	non les élèves ça va	*no, the students, it's fine*
Amran:	les élèves leur grand problème c'est si tu connais pas l'anglais tu es tu vois c'est comme hm tu es comme euh	*the students, their big problem is if you don't know English you are you see it's like hm you are like uh*
Saïda:	un ami tu vois comme	*a friend you see like*
Amran:	tu vas juste être une amie, mais tu vas pas être vraiment, tu vas pas vraiment causer avec elle mais si tu	*you will be just a friend, but you won't be really, you won't really talk with her*

Laurette:	mhm mhm	*mhm mhm*
Amran:	connais vraiment l'anglais, tout ce qui l'intéresse c'est parler avec eux juste en anglais	*but if you really know English, all that interests her is talking with them only in English*
Saïda:	oui, la première fois que je suis venue ici ils m'ont dit 'est-ce que tu parles en anglais?', tu vois, tout le monde était comme, j'ai dit 'non', après, tu vois, ils me disent toujours aujourd'hui 'bonjour', ils parlent avec moi, mais tu vois, j'ai pas trop de communication, je peux pas dire que cette personne elle est raciste, c'est parce que juste on se on se parle mais (...)	*yes, the first time I came here they said to me 'do you speak in English?', you see, everyone was like, I said 'no', afterwards, you see, today they always say 'hello' to me, they speak with me, but you see, I don't have much communication, I can't say that this person is racist, it's because we only we speak to each other but (...)*

Example 4.20   Interview, Laurette and Hodan, 1993

Laurette:	et qu'est-ce que tu penses de de en tout cas quand tu es arrivée dans l'école, parce qu'y a certains élèves qui m'ont dit que c'était bizarre qu'ils entendaient parler les élèves en anglais, comment t'as trouvé ça, toi?	*and what do you think of of anyway when you arrived at school, because there're some students who told me it was weird that they heard the students speaking in English, how did you find that?*
Hodan:	moi aussi j'ai trouvé bizarre, parce qu'on savait pas parler en anglais, y avait dans les classes c'était pas vraiment difficile parce que la plupart des élèves parlaient en français, mais dans les couloirs tout ça les élèves parlent en anglais, c'est différent	*I also found it weird, because we didn't know how to speak in English, there were in classes it wasn't really difficult because most of the students spoke in French, but in the corridors all that the students speak in English, it's different*
Laurette:	comment tu as fait alors toi?	*so what did you do?*

| Hodan: | euh je leur parlais juste lorsque j'avais besoin d'eux, je leur parlais en français, c'est tout (. . .) | *uh I spoke to them only when I needed them, I spoke to them in French, that's all (. . .)* |

Not only did differences in language practices get perceived as exclusionary, they contributed to active rivalries. In the following example, Omar and Hussein reveal the resentment they felt that students who patently were violating not only basic politeness conventions, but also the most fundamental expectation about school language practices, were nonetheless not suffering any negative consequences. Yet they themselves were playing the game by the rules, and this was not reflected in their marks.

Example 4.21   Discussion in a restaurant, Awad, Omar and Hussein, 1994

Awad:	l'intégration linguistique pour toi qu'est-ce que t'as représenté, parce que j'imagine les élèves il y en a pas mal d'élèves quand même ou la majorité parle le français, parle plutôt anglais que français	*linguistic integration, for you, what did you represent, because I imagine there are many students all the same or the majority speak French, speak English rather than French*
Omar:	oui ça aussi	*yes that too*
Awad:	alors comment vous avez réagi vis-à-vis ça? est-ce que vous êtes intégrés tout de suite? ah vers vers l'anglais ou ah?	*so how did you react to that? did you integrate right away? ah to to English or ah?*
Omar:	non non on s'est pas intégré	*no no we didn't integrate*
Hussein:	d'abord ça nous a pris	*first it took us*
Omar:	ça nous a pris je dirais un bon moment, beaucoup de temps de comprendre ah l'anglais premièrement, et puis c'est que nous étions surpris, c'était dans notre pays là, lorsqu'on était en Somalie ou bien en Djibouti à Djibouti ce qui nous avait surpris le plus là on on si	*it took us I'd say a good while, lots of time to understand English, first, and then it was that we were surprised, it was in our country, when we were in Somalia or at Djibouti, in Djibouti what surprised us the most we we if we have projects to do for*

on a des projets à faire par exemple, si on a des présentations qu'on doit faire là, notre présentation se fait dans une langue où tout le monde peut comprendre, que ce soit langue française, et puisque notres écoles c'était une langue dans école française là, donc on avait communiqué en français pour que tous les élèves comprennent. Il y avait il y a pas eu il y a eu jamais une école qu'on a utilisé le somali et le français, et puis il y a certains élèves canadiens qui sont dans notre école là qui faisaient leurs conversations en anglais et puis en français, et puis ça c'était pas permis, et qui recevaient une meilleure note une plus (haute?) note que nous, qu'on parlait nous qui exprimaient bien le français, qui parlaient bien notre français et qui ne mélangeiaent pas le français entre somalien

example, if we have presentations to do, our presentation is done in a language where everyone can understand, that is the French language, and since our schools it was a language in a French school, so we communicated in French so that all the students could understand. There were there isn't there was never a school that we used Somali and French, and there are Canadian students who are in our school who did their conversations in English and then in French, and that was not allowed, and who received a better grade, a (higher?) grade than us, that spoke we who express French well, who speak our French well and who never mixed between French and Somalian

Some students reacted by retreating into what they felt comfortable with, French and Somali, and by refusing to learn English.

Example 4.22   Interview, Monica and Aïcha, 1993

Monica: est-ce que t'as appris l'anglais depuis que t'es ici?
Aïcha: non, je m'intéresse pas. Je m'intéresse pas. Il y a de

have you learned English since you've been here?
no, I'm not interested. I'm not interested. There's

	l'anglais que je le connais,	*English that I understand*
	tu vois, je comprends, mais	*it, you see, I understand,*
	je veux pas répondre.	*but I don't want to answer.*
Monica:	est-ce que tu fais des choses	*do you do things in your*
	dans ton quartier?	*neighbourhood?*
Aïcha:	non, je m'intéresse pas à	*no, I'm not interested in*
	l'anglais. À vrai dire, je	*English. To tell the truth,*
	m'intéresse pas.	*I'm not interested.*

Others began to feel that English would be important for them, along with French. Both are languages you need in order to get by in the world, although that does not have to mean changing your cultural practices or your sense of identity. Other languages could be important too; and school is crucial to gaining access to all of them. This was illustrated powerfully by a conversation I was privy to among a group of five Somali-speaking girls, all close friends who spent most of their free time together in school, took classes together, and frequently saw each other outside school. A Canadian-born student of French-Canadian and Polish background had become interested in the situation of the Somali-speaking students, and worked hard to help them. One of her efforts involved getting approval for a Somali-language course to be included in the curriculum; through successful circulation of petitions, she was able to prove to the administration that student interest was sufficiently high to justify running such a course the following year (subject, of course, to sufficient enrolment). On the day that the following year's course schedule was published, these five girls repaired to the library to discuss their course selections. (Significantly, they undertook this as a collective discussion and decision.) One girl suggested that they take the Somali course. Another ridiculed this idea, saying that they already spoke Somali, and anyway, where was Somali going to get them in the world? No one was interested in their Somali. She counter-proposed that they take Spanish, a language with some value on the world market. A second girl took her side in this discussion. After a few attempts to say how nice it would be to take Somali, and how this would help get them good grades, the girl who proposed taking the Somali class backed down. Most of the girls decided to take Spanish.

The following examples all show aspects of the importance French and English have for many of these students, an importance which derives from a fairly cynical calculation of what it will take for them to survive in a world still dominated by the languages of former colonial powers.

Example 4.23   Interview, Laurette and Amran, 1993

Laurette:	et maintenant, comment tu dirais que tu te débrouilles en anglais?	*and now, how would you say you're getting along in English?*
Amran:	je me débrouille beaucoup par rapport à avant, parce qu'avant je savais pas l'anglais, là, maintenant ça fait quatre ans et en quatre ans j'ai appris	*I'm getting along much more than before, because before I didn't know English, now it's been four years and in four years I've learned*
Laurette:	ben j'imagine. Est-ce que tu vas tu veux travailler en anglais plutôt que français, qu'est-ce que tu penses?	*well, I imagine so. Will you do you want to work in English rather than French, what do you think?*
Amran:	je voudrais être bilingue là, travailler en anglais et en français, mais je dois améliorer mon français, je crois que je vais le faire là	*I'd like to be bilingual, to work in English and in French, but I have to improve my French, I think I'll do that*
Laurette:	ah oui	*ah yes*
Amran:	oui, parce que je sais j'ai plus le vocabulaire que j'avais avant, pis je commence à perdre, et je voudrais aussi améliorer mon français	*yes because I know I no longer have the vocabulary I used to have, and I'm starting to lose, and I would also like to improve my French*

Example 4.24   Interview, Laurette and Hodan, 1993

Laurette:	apprendre, est-ce que tu trouves ça difficile?	*learning, do you find that difficult?*
Hodan:	anglais, je pense que l'anglais est plus facile que le français, mais je (xx) mais je l'apprendrai	*English, I think English is easier than French, but I (xx) but I'll learn it*
Laurette:	c'est important pour toi d'apprendre l'anglais?	*it's important for you to learn English?*
Hodan:	pour vivre à Toronto, il faut apprendre l'anglais	*to live in Toronto, you have to learn English*

Example 4.25   Interview, Awad and Abdi, 1994

Awad:	euh alors euh qu'est-ce que tu dis par rapport à l'anglais, qu'est-ce qu'il te représente?
Abdi:	pour moi, l'anglais et le français pour moi, ça représente pas une grande différence, tous les deux pour nous Éthiopiens ou presque tous les Africains ce sont des langues qui nous ont été imposées, ce sont des langues qui nous viennent des colonisateurs qui nous ont colonisés, mais dans un sens pratique quand même on apprend dans presque tous les pays africains, on réclame d'apprendre le le français et l'anglais par rapport aux autres langues, de notre propre langue, l'anglais pour moi ça représente un moyen, c'est juste un moyen pour pouvoir trouver un travail correct, pour pouvoir accéder au reste du monde, ça représente pas, c'est pour moi une langue comme les autres

uh so uh what do you say about English, what does it represent to you? for me, English and French for me, it doesn't represent a big difference, both for us Ethiopians or almost all Africans they are languages which were imposed on us, they are languages which come to us from the colonizers who colonized us, but in a practical sense just the same we learn in almost all the African countries, we ask to learn French and English rather than other languages, our own language, English for me represents a means, it's just a means to find decent work, to have access to the rest of the world, it doesn't represent, it's for me a language like the others

Example 4.26   Interview, Awad and Saïd, 1994

Awad:	qu'est-ce qui tu représente l'anglais?
Saïd:	l'anglais? c'est une langue de business (rit) c'est une langue qui te ouvre les portes, tu connais l'anglais le français tu es bien parti dans la vie
Awad:	oui c'est vrai c'est vrai euh c'est plus que ça, je pense surtout à l'école par exemple

what does English represent to you? English? it's a language of business (laughs) it's a language which opens doors for you, you know English French you've got a good start in life yes that's true that's true uh it's more than that, I'm thinking mainly of school for example

Saïd:	à l'école	*of school*
Awad:	même même si si tu veux faire des amis et tout ça tu dois parler anglais	*even even if if you want to make friends and all that you have to speak English*
Saïd:	oui pour vivre dans la société il faut que tu saves l'anglais, parce que si tu ne sais l'anglais comment tu vas aller dans comment tu vas aller dans la société ça va être vraiment dur, et c'est à cause de ça que j'ai appris vraiment le français c'est à cause que la société, parce que je boff, avoir seulement des amis qui parlent français, mais il faut que je m'entend à l'extérieur aussi alors	*yes to live in society you have to know English, because if you don't know English, how are you going to go, how are you going to go into society, it will be really hard, and it's because of that that I really learned French it's because of society, because I boff, only to have friends who speak French, but I have to get along outside too so*

The result of this process is a group of students who speak to each other in French, Somali or Creole, and who rarely, if ever, use English to speak to their peers, and who rarely, if ever, get English used by others to address them. Language practices may even be divergent; Amran's account below seems to imply that students use more Somali at school than elsewhere, perhaps in an attempt to close ranks after having suffered what felt like an active exclusion on the part of those who were there when they arrived.

Example 4.27   Interview, Laurette and Amran, 1993

Laurette:	avec qui tu utilises le français en dehors de l'école, est-ce que tu utilises le français?	*with whom do you use French outside school, do you use French?*
Amran:	oui, souvent avec les amis, comme entre Somaliens, on préfère parler français plutôt que parler en somalien	*yes, often with friends, like among Somalis, we prefer to speak French rather than speaking in Somali*
Laurette:	ah oui, c'est vrai?	*oh yes, is that so?*
Amran:	oui, les élèves, c'est juste on parle à l'école en somalien, des fois les personnes ne comprennent pas ce qu'on dit, mais on préfère (. . .)	*yes, the students, it's just we speak Somali at school, sometimes the people don't understand what we're saying, but we prefer (. . .)*

What that means, of course, is minimal communication. In addition, ties to francophone Canadians are rendered problematic by the differing values placed on Canadian French by the two groups, and by different stances with respect to the importance of the authenticity of the school as a basis for its legitimacy. Affiliation with the school is rendered problematic by the ambiguity of the school's stance with respect to the use of Canadian French and English. Nonetheless, these students insist on the validity of their values, and the legitimacy of their presence, and of their interests, in the school context.

It is clear that many of these students were bewildered by the contradictions they faced; sure of the value of the knowledge they possessed, knowledge systematically devalued in classroom and corridor, they ended up deciding that the only sensible explanation for what was happening to them was racism, whether overt or systemic. As we shall see in Chapter 6, this consciousness was an important factor contributing to the development of an ethic, even an ideology of inclusiveness in the school, one that was to have major consequences for public discourse and the construction of identity at Champlain.

6 Conclusion

Being bilingual at Champlain is a constant process of taking perspective and of adopting social and linguistic strategies that allow a student to exploit, maximally, the linguistic resources they have available to them, trying to get around obstacles, and taking advantage of opportunities. There are students who are in a position to see the kind of bilingualism Champlain has to offer as an 'advantage', as Sandra would say, and who are motivated to collaborate with the necessary compromises the school has to make in order to maintain its public, monolingual, standard-speaking face. If they do that, they end up with a diploma from an authentically French school, a credential that should help them either as a sign of distinctiveness, in Bourdieu's sense, or in more practical ways as an emblem of a form of linguistic capital they might some day actually be expected to deploy. It is expected to help them both get into university, and later, on the job market. Their practices allow the school to continue its *sub rosa* separation of public and private, although its official position that all zones of the school should be monolingual does entail an official monitoring of the private zone. At the same time, the continuous monitoring does serve to legitimize the school further, proving as it does that the situation is drastic, and requires constant resources. Students like Sandra do not actually suffer greatly from this surveillance, although it may channel their energies into areas more protected from it than they might otherwise have chosen, and does obligate them to find strategies for coping. Nonetheless, these strategies (notably peer help) also serve the broader purpose of achieving academic success. The bundle of strategies they adopt allows them to occupy the front and centre of school discursive space; it is they who define the terms of how things will go at school, terms which all other students have to deal with one way or another.

The way other students react depends on their own positioning, both with respect to language, and with respect to school. There are many who come from places where French is the language of instruction, and students arrive expecting to use their monolingual French strategies at school to help them both make friends and do well academically. It is a shock to find they need English to make friends, and that the variety of French they speak may or may not be well received. Along some dimensions, then, there are students whose interests converge with those of the school, and sometimes with those of the discursively dominant group, at least in terms of a value attached to 'international' French, or to bilingualism as parallel monolingualisms. The problem is that, for most of these students, convergence along one dimension is matched with divergence along others. The Somali speakers, for instance, as well as many of the Haitians, consider 'international' French to be the most valuable, and share with the dominant group a disdain for '*joual*'. On the other hand, they expect to be able to make friends in French, but this turns out to be impossible. Canadian vernacular speakers share with the Somali speakers an expectation that peer group life should function in French, but suffer from the stigmatization of their linguistic variety.

These processes lead to a struggle over the peer group controlled discursive space at Champlain. The dominant group has staked out one position, which by its force serves to marginalize everyone else. What we have seen in this chapter is a process of marginalization which operates along the lines of linguistic repertoires – repertoires which have everything to do with the social positioning and life experience of Champlain students. In the next chapter, we shall examine some other ways in which students struggle over the definition of self and other, this time through categorization based on gender. As we shall see, gender too is bound up with how students are positioned with respect to the most valuable things school has to offer, namely school success and bilingualism. In the subsequent chapter, we shall see how these different positionings led to a more active struggle, with consequences for how the discursive space of Champlain was to be reshaped, entailing greater advantages for some, and fewer for others.

5 Girls and boys[1]

1 Gender and public space

As we have seen, the major issue confronting Champlain as a social institution is the question of what it means to be a French-language school. In previous chapters, we have examined ways in which the school constructs its views and copes with contradictions between the ideal and the real, and we have looked at ways in which the social positions of students help to explain why they take up the public discourse of the school in the ways that they do. In particular, we have looked at how students with a long experience of language contact, and who aspire to university studies, collaborate with the school's vision, without sharing its practices. Most importantly, this group dominates the discursive space of the school, forcing others to react to its particular view of bilingualism. In the next chapter, we shall see how some marginalized groups were able to gain some ground, challenging the prevailing view of the school in an attempt to paint it in the hues of a broader, inclusive, pluralist vision of francophone Ontario. First, however, we want to take a closer look at the workings of peer discursive space, and in particular at ways in which the construction of and reactions to the dominant bilingual view of the school were profoundly gendered.

In this chapter we shall look at the ways in which the girls and boys of Champlain worked together to produce a public discourse on bilingualism which was gendered in two, sometimes contradictory,

---

[1] This chapter was written with the collaboration of Phyllis Dalley.

ways. Most of the public discourse produced by the students while we were there was produced by males, and significant portions of this discourse was either specifically devoted to the reproduction of gender stereotypes, or included such themes. At the same time, the school, as an institution of socialization, does have a history of linking its mission of maintaining language and culture to the traditional female role of cultural transmission and socialization. This notion finds an echo in the minds of many students, including girls who talk about the importance of speaking French to their own children as a way of transmitting their cultural heritage, and boys who talk about the language socialization of their future children as being primarily the responsibility of their future spouse. These two tendencies take shape in different ways for the boys and girls of the main social groups of the school. Nonetheless, the result is that males dominate public discourse, and include gendered stereotypes in their discourse in a way which serves to maintain their privileged position with respect to the definition of what the school is, or should be.

As we have seen, it is the bilinguals of the advanced level who produce much of the public discourse of the school. Here it is mainly the males who do this, and the central gendered theme is a specific vision of romantic love, in which the male is the pursuer and the female the object of desire. The one major event to be dominated by females is the fashion show, itself an event primarily devoted to the reproduction of this ideology of gender relations. The only other public role readily available to girls was as support to the central activities of the male-dominated student council. Within that context, girls can aspire to some degree of power within the school, but in ways that tend to be associated with nurturing school spirit. Thus girls at the same time could aspire to (and achieve) academic success, as well as social and political power as agents of school spirit, and collaborate in their own objectification as objects of sexual desire or romantic love, as well as in their political marginalization as supporters of, rather than primary producers of, public discourse.

In marginalized groups, alternative options were equally gendered. In particular, boys seemed to have many more options for making a life outside school than did girls. Girls tended to act more conservatively, less radically challenging the school and its vision and its rules; they also tended to feel keenly the tension between their own strong ties to language and culture (whether Somali, Creole, French, or anything else) and the competing values of the dominant views of bilingualism, or of English as the primary means of resisting the power and authority of the school. But here as well, there was little to challenge traditional gender roles.

The embedding of traditional gender roles into the public life of the school was clearly problematic for gay students, who tended to remain in the closet, and usually left the school rather quickly. It was also a problem for a small group of girls who shared the dominant group's views on bilingualism, for the most part, who shared their values regarding academic success, but who were unprepared to share in the gendered behaviour that participation in those networks entailed. Calling themselves the 'Nerds', they attempt to create an alternative space for themselves. This space entails rejecting the prevailing view of romantic love, by rejecting the notion of romantic love as an important part of female identity, through the construction of a (possibly fictive) lesbian identity, by separating their romantic life from life at school, or by focusing on sexuality and female sexual pleasure (in opposition to feminine stereotypes of passivity and focus on love rather than sexuality). While these strategies worked well for some of the Nerds, and less well for others, in either case they did little to directly challenge the gendered nature of public discourse at Champlain.

Two conclusions emerge from these images. The first is that, despite a strong public commitment to equity in education, the focus on issues of language and culture at Champlain serves effectively, if unintentionally, to obscure inequities based on socioeconomic position (as we saw in Chapter 4) and on gender (as we shall see here). The second is that the public discourse on language and culture at Champlain is gendered in some interesting ways. The school's mission depends on the reproduction of traditional gender roles, such that women continue to take on primary functions of cultural transmission through socialization. This function, however, contains two potentially contradictory elements: the work that girls do supports the public leadership of men, while at the same time the school offers girls avenues to positions of leadership, since power in the school is directly linked to the very arena in which girls are meant to specialize. While this might lead to gender-based conflicts over leadership positions, such conflicts never emerge, partly because the gendered dimension of the struggle is subordinated to language and culture, partly because boys always have other opportunities, and partly because girls can always support the roles of boys.

2   Studs and Juliettes

It is early February, near Valentine's Day. The student council has organized a dance and has decided to raise money by holding a sale of roses. To advertise these events the council has called a *réunion générale*. As usual, the meeting takes the form of a series of skits, performed by student council members and their friends on the school stage.

The skit is based loosely on a format known from television contests. The student council president, Marcel, acts as master of ceremonies. He announces that the school will now pick the school 'stud' (while he speaks in French, he uses the word 'stud' from English). Four boys from the senior grades are called up to sit in a row on the stage. Marcel passes from one boy to the next, asking each a question. He asks the first two boys where they will take their girlfriends for Valentine's Day. To the third, Ali, he poses the following question: '*Quel est le rôle de la femme dans la société?*' (What is the role of women in society?). Ali is visibly uneasy, and fails to answer. Luc says that he will answer the question, and eventually Marcel gives him the microphone. Luc answers: '*De servir et plaire aux hommes*' (to serve and please men). The audience responds loudly, with many boys cheering, and some girls (notably the Nerds) booing and giving the 'thumbs-down' sign of disapproval. Marcel returns to Ali, and asks him what would be the most eloquent thing he could say to his girlfriend on Valentine's Day. Ali still has a hard time finding an answer; several girls from the audience call out: 'I love you' and '*Je t'aime*'. Finally, Ali says, '*Je t'aime*'. Marcel then asks the audience to express which answer they liked the most by applauding for each boy. The volume and duration of the noise produced by the audience is a measure of their support for each boy. The one who receives the loudest and longest applause is Luc. Marcel tells him he has won a gift certificate worth 20 dollars at a local chocolate store (presumably so that he can buy a gift for his girlfriend, not for himself).

The boys descend from the stage, and Marcel announces that it is now time to greet the school's 'Juliettes' (interestingly the label for the male contest focuses on sexual desirability, while the label for the female contest focuses on romance). A procession of boys in drag takes the places of the would-be studs in the row of chairs on the stage. Now the event takes a different format. Instead of asking the audience to judge the 'girls', Marcel asks each 'girl' what 'she' would most like to receive from 'her' boyfriend for Valentine's Day: a diamond, a car, chocolate, money. Each 'Juliette' says no, none of these things. So, Marcel asks, what *would* they like? At this, the 'Juliettes' stand up and turn around, holding a piece of paper to their *derrières*. On each piece of paper is one letter; put together, they spell out R-O-S-E-S. With this, Marcel announces the rose sale, and encourages everyone (by which he presumably means the boys) to buy a rose for their girlfriends.

This Valentine's Day skit was probably the most extreme, but by no means the only, example of the gendered division of public discourse at Champlain. Not only does it reproduce traditional gender stereotypes, it so clearly takes the male perspective that females are not even allowed on the stage to play themselves. By the same token, here as in other skits produced by Champlain students, males in drag are seen frequently on stage and are considered funny, while the rare females seen in drag (two during the time we worked there) portray highly serious male characters.

During the time we were at Champlain, the student council was consistently dominated by males; only four or five females were even members over the course of those four years, and they usually took a back seat to the males in public displays such as the *réunions générales*. In fairness, at other times, girls have been student council presidents, and there have been female-dominated student councils. As we shall see in Chapter 6, girls took the lead in organizing activities related to the school's 25th anniversary, and put together a slate for the student council elections (which was, however, defeated). It is thus not impossible for girls to take on a leadership role at Champlain, it is just that that leadership is based on the opportunities provided by a school where women are associated with the school's linguistic and cultural mission, but where even that traditional association does not necessarily facilitate access to leadership roles. Thus, during the time we were at Champlain, most girls did not find paths to leadership.

While the student council was dominated by males, girls did play a supporting role. They were the ones most involved in fund-raising activities – for example, selling pastries and pizzas in the front hall. They also organized the graduation dance at the end of the year. Otherwise, their opportunities for taking the public stage were limited, and frequently involved displaying traditional images of female beauty. For example, in Chapter 4, I mentioned a skit about recycling in which a vernacular-speaking granny was thrown into the recycling bin. Clearly, here, the vernacular is associated not only with decrepit old age, but in particular garrulous, female old age. This is underscored by the skit's conclusion: one of the boys reaches into the recycling bin into which the granny was tossed, and pulls out a young, beautiful, long-haired blonde, who walks off the stage smiling silently on the young man's arm.

The annual fashion show was the most important single event contributing to the public construction of images of female beauty and their association with a particular, heterosexual vision of romantic love. The show was held each spring, with clothes donated by local merchants. The event was considered a prestigious one, and participating students rehearsed every day for months.

A small group of students (two girls, Nadine and Sylvie, and a boy, Patrick) were responsible for the organization of the show, under the supervision of a female teacher, and while female students vied to be accepted as part of the show (they were selected through auditions, and not everyone was accepted), male students had to be cajoled (although being approached could be seen as a sign of the girls' approval of them as romantic or sexual partners, and so few actually refused the invitation). However, boys controlled all technical activities for the school, and were not reluctant to turn those skills to the organization of the fashion show (as they did for all public events). Thus boys were responsible for the construction of the catwalk, and boys ran the sound system, the lighting and the videotaping.

While Patrick let Nadine and Sylvie take care of most of the daily, routine issues, his word was law when it came to discipline or conflict-resolution. For example, during one practice session, Sylvie had an argument with one of the boys in the show, who refused to do what she wanted him to do, and who ended up by asking why he should listen to her. Patrick, who had been sitting nearby, then got up and said, 'Because I have the last word'. That ended the argument. During another practice, someone turned out the lights, and Sylvie asked that they be turned on. The lights stayed off, and Nadine asked that they be turned on. They remained off until Patrick got up and shouted, 'Turn on the fucking lights!'.

Much of the time in practice was devoted to specific forms of self-presentation. Girls were told to come to practice in high-heeled shoes, and spent hours learning to walk like a runway model; this mainly meant moving one's hips from side to side while walking. For the boys, most of the attention was placed on how to walk and stand. This meant a certain square-shouldered stance, with specific things to do with one's hands while walking or standing (putting them in your pockets, folding one arm while holding your chin with the other hand). Boys were also taught how to look at the girls: 'check her out', Nadine told them. These movements turned out to be a difficult thing for most boys and girls; however, Nadine and Sylvie took the time to teach the boys and to give them models, whereas they tended to assume that the girls would know how to do this 'naturally'. This led to a certain amount of tension among the girls, many of whom did not feel comfortable acting this way. Nonetheless, by the evening of the show, they had all learned to do what they were supposed to do, albeit some more comfortably than others.

In keeping with the dominant mode of public discourse at the school, the fashion show was organized as a series of skits, or dramatic set pieces, each designed to tell a story built around thematically linked clothes (sports clothes, beach clothes, work clothes, evening clothes, and so on). In each one, students were paired off in heterosexual couples; Nadine explicitly ruled out any possibility of portraying homosexual couples, however fictive, although some of the boys playfully took a modelling stroll down the side of the stage together while the organizers' attention was somewhere else. The stories told in each skit were all scenes of courtship. In one such scene, a row of boys wait, sitting around a night-club set. One by one, four girls emerge, check out the boys, and each picks one as her escort. Only Luc (the acknowledged 'Stud' of the school) is left standing alone, although the spotlight is on him, and he doesn't look particularly sad. Then a fifth girl emerges, and the last boy is happily paired off. After taking a turn on the catwalk, each couple returns to a chair, the girl perched on her escort's knee. In unison, the boys feel the girls' legs, from ankle to knee. At this point, the girls pretend to slap the boys' faces, and they rise and walk off in a huff. Virtue is protected. The fashion show closes with a formal dress scene; at the end, each tuxedo-clad boy gives a red rose to his evening-gowned partner.

Interestingly, the fashion show became an avenue for access to mainstream prestige for students from marginalized groups; two Somali-speaking girls and one Somali-speaking boy in particular gained wide attention through participating in the fashion show, although no one outside their own circles had ever spoken to them before. They were permitted certain compromises; for example, the girls were not asked to parade in bathing suits, but were allowed to wear shorts instead for the beach scene. At about the same time, the two girls, along with others in their group, were starting to read romance novels in English, and to watch music videos on television. Later on, along with a third girl, they performed a contemporary, and very hip, dance at the annual talent show. The fashion show was thus part of their induction into Toronto bilingual society; learning English, learning locally fashionable dance and music, and learning how to act like a girl were all part of the same package.

It is important to note that despite being bound to traditional gender roles, girls at Champlain were as oriented to academic success as boys were, and as likely to do well. Nonetheless, it was necessary for them to accept the public domination of boys, or at least, not to challenge it openly. Thus not only do the girls accept supporting roles with respect to boys, and engage in public displays of ideal images of romantic love and beauty, they also accept boys' sexual domination. For example, a favourite winter-time activity of some of the boys was to pick a female victim, carry her outside, and throw her into the snow. The girls would struggle and cry out, but also laugh. No one would ever come to the rescue of a girl in this predicament. Of the 'popular' girls, only Sandra seemed exempt from this treatment. When asked why, she simply said that the boys knew that she would scream her head off if they tried that with her. She seemed to feel, however, that that was her private stance; in any case, she never attempted to intervene when some other girl was being hauled off into the snow. Being a 'popular' girl meant walking a fine line between assuming responsibility and credit for academic success, collaborating with the linguistic norms of the school, and accepting a degree of sexual objectification. The sexual objectification entailed keeping themselves to a supporting role with respect to the most important public discourse of the school; it meant not taking a public stand with respect to language and identity, but rather 'getting along' with everybody, while limiting one's actual activities in the public domain to (silently) supporting the activities of the boys, and hence letting them define the shape of the public floor and their vision of Champlain as a Franco-Ontarian school.

3   Ways in and ways out

Just as the mainstream discourse on bilingualism at Champlain is gendered, so are the reactions of students who are positioned outside the group that dominates that public discourse. In Chapter 4, we saw how two main groups of 'outsiders', the monolingual francophones and the Somali speakers, reacted to the dominance of the mainstream view of bilingualism at the school. But just as the mainstream view is construction in a gendered fashion, so are reactions to it.

For African students, reactions to mainstream bilingualism are connected to their relative access to activities inside and outside the school. Both boys and girls actively resist what they see as too narrow a vision of *la francophonie*, but it is the boys who speak the loudest on the public stage, while the girls, for the most part, organize and discuss more privately (although one girl in particular took an important leadership role). In Chapter 6, we shall take a closer look at some of the skits the African students organized to place their perspective on the public stage; for the moment, it is important to note that, in those skits, one of the central themes concerned the threat Canadian culture posed to students' traditional notions of gender roles, and in particular regarding the role of women. In one skit, a man ordered his wife to bring him coffee. She responded by throwing down her broom and stalking out of the room, saying that he could no longer tell her what to do. However, a few minutes later, she returned, holding her head in her hands, and lamenting, '*Qu'est-ce qui m'arrive? Je suis en train de perdre mes valeurs!*' (What is happening to me? I'm losing my values!). Similarly, African students felt uncomfortable with official positions on sexual harassment, saying that it seemed very strange to them that in Canadian society a woman in trouble would have to call a public phone number, and apparently could not count on her community to help her out.

At school, Somali-speaking female students, especially the older ones, tended to dress in conservative, elegant styles. Some wore veils, and sometimes wore Somali dresses. Many wore Somali dresses on the occasion of the annual multicultural lunch, which was also the major occasion for them to play a public role in the school: they took primary responsibility for organizing the event, and supplied a large proportion of the food. They formed close-knit friendship groups, mainly with other Somali-speaking girls, with whom they took classes, and spent time in the library and the cafeteria. Most of the males, as well as some of the younger females (such as the two who participated in the fashion show), oriented themselves quite differently to school and community. While sharing the girls' sense of the importance of French and Somali, and of their own cultural perspectives, the males (and younger females) also quickly discovered the powerful message of resistance to white authority embodied in African-American hip-hop culture. This was possible in large part simply because they have more opportunities to interact with the community outside home and school, but also because that community tends to construct all blacks as members of the same Afro-American cultural category, no matter where they are from. This is both an obstacle to self-definition, and an opportunity to take up a discourse of resistance to white domination. It was eventually reflected in these students' dress, in their musical preferences, and in their interest in basketball, which they played every day in the school gymnasium. This discovery also, ironically, laid the basis for a bridge between them and white students, who saw hip-hop culture as cool. In addition, through hip-hop, Somali speakers also learned English, thereby allowing them to communicate more easily with other students.

The oppositional stance of the Somali-speaking students seems to have served the interests of the boys better than it did the interests of the girls. It gave the boys a position of strength from which to argue for the inclusion of their concerns in the mainstream discourse of the school, as well as a place from which to begin to build the bridges which would ensure that they were not simply speaking into the wind. While the Somali-speaking girls gained the respect of many teachers, their practices tended to maintain their marginalisation. In addition, the boys' access to English gave them bridges and opportunities in which the girls, especially the older ones, could not greatly share.

The oppositional stances of monolingual francophones also differed along gender lines. Neither boys nor girls tended to be very vocal about the legitimacy of their perspective for the school's peer group culture, and many, both male and female, simply absorbed themselves into the bilingual mainstream. However, more boys than girls seemed to have options outside school. For many (like Étienne and François), those options involved simply going back to Quebec. For others, there was the option of obtaining work of some kind, usually in an English-speaking environment. Those boys often simply stopped speaking French at school, and then eventually stopped coming to school altogether. Girls, on the other hand, did not seem to have these options so readily available. Their social life focused on school-based friendship networks, or, occasionally, friendship networks involving outsiders. At school, they often spoke English, feeling very insecure about their French; or, like Ginette, attempted to participate in class through mixed, codeswitched, practices; or, like Diane, Simone and Claudia found ways to get around expectations for oral presentations, like singing. In all these cases, their practices were not highly valued by the school. At the same time, these girls tended to feel very strong attachments to their French identity, and would speak French in situations where they felt they would not be judged. The tension between French and English was much keener for them than for the boys. Interestingly, the only time these girls took the floor in public, coincided with a school-board wide campaign against sexual harassment. Some of them argued that they had been harassed by a teacher. They further felt that their attempts to bring this issue up in a legitimated public space (a kind of 'town hall' meeting of the entire school) had been curtailed, and so they organized a counter-meeting in the smoking section behind the school. Students seemed quite divided as to the legitimacy of the claim. In any case, the school followed common policy by removing the teacher from the school and allowing the charges to go forward to a hearing scheduled for the summer, when the school would in any case be closed. Here again, the oppositional stances of this group seem to work to the greater advantage of boys than of girls. The boys had choices open to them, choices they made; the girls were torn between the desire to resist their marginalization and the desire to conform to certain ideals of the school.

The final group that is clearly marginalized by the gender discourse of the school is that made up of homosexual students. Not only is the prevailing image of social life at school resoundingly heterosexual, homosexuality is seen as deviant; either repulsive or, paradoxically, cool, but in either case, definitely deviant. For many students, 'faggot' is one of the worst insults a student could hurl against a boy. The climate makes it difficult to be open about one's sexual orientation, to say the least. Here is what one gay student has to say about his experience after his orientation did become known:

> I got bashed, I don't mean physically, but I had some real bad comments (. . .) and then it was totally the opposite side of being abused, it was like almost a cool thing to hang around with a gay guy (. . .) at the beginning I thought it was quite funny somehow, but then it hurt me (. . .) you (the other students) just had to say 'I know someone who is gay' and it was a big deal (. . .) 'You know Bernard?' 'No.' 'Yeah, you know, the faggot, ah, that's Bernard.'

Bernard was one of the very few students at Champlain to attempt to be open about being gay. As an explicit attempt to challenge prevailing views, he decided to bring a male date to the graduation dance. When he announced this intention, a classmate became seriously concerned, arguing that Bernard simply could not do that: 'You can't, you're supposed to bring a girl!' For most homosexual students, there are only two viable options. One is to keep one's sexual orientation a secret, and the other is to leave Champlain for a school where the climate might be less hostile (this is what Bernard did before the end of his first year at Champlain). Obviously, neither strategy effectively challenges the discursive marginalization, indeed stigmatization, of homosexuality.

From the perspective of the dominance of the school's vision of bilingualism, and of that of the bilingual students, only the stance of the Somali-speaking boys could be seen as potentially posing a challenge. Their discourse is in part made audible by the existence of an institutionalized public discussion about anti-racist education. The other groups either manage to survive, or find themselves pushed out of school; either way, their perspectives remain marginalized. With the exception of the failed attempt on the part of a small group of girls to use a prevalent public discourse on sexual harassment to open discussions on their marginalization, none of these groups challenges the prevailing discourses of the school. And it is not even clear that that one moment of discussion of harassment challenged prevailing views on gender; instead, the gendered social positions of all students constrain the strategies available to them.

4   The 'Nerds'

In contrast, one group of girls did seriously resist the prevailing organization of gender at Champlain. This group of girls formed out of the common experience of rejection by the mainstream crowd. Most of them came to Champlain relatively late; four of them were graduates of French immersion programmes who passed Champlain's entrance exams (although one of them is actually from a francophone family), and the others moved to Toronto after having completed elementary school elsewhere. They all found it difficult to gain acceptance into the strongly solidary peer group they found upon their arrival, the Lucs and Sandras who had gone to Rouillé together. Their access to the mainstream, popular group, was further compromised by two things: for many of them, a relative lack of security in their French, and for almost all of them, a lack of fit with the valued image of the female body. Several of them recall at length having been made fun of by the others, because they were considered fat, or had acne. Some are also members of visible minority groups, while the popular group is principally made up of whites. The following is from a discussion session organized by Phyllis, and which took place on a fairly regular basis once a week for several months in the winter and spring of 1994:

Example 5.1   Discussion group 1, March 1994

Carmelle:	In grade 12 11 class, there's basically two types of people, well, three types. You have the Somalians, they speak Somalian
Chloé:	which tends to exclude those who don't
Lisa:	yeah
Carmelle:	a lot of them don't definitely exclude you but if you don't have a lot of confidence, you're not going to stay around and not (upset a thing?). You have

another group of people, most of them have been
together since I don't know when, and they'd come
from grade seven and eight into this school, and
they're all friends and they're all working toward the
same goal and they all have one idea in mind. Some
of them want to get married right out of high school
that their boyfriends will know their past history.
Then you have us, we're all weird in some way or
another, and if we weren't basically physically abused
like Lisa was, then we were emotionally abused,
isolated from that crowd for some reason or another

Most of these girls spent several years alone, or in small friendship groups on the margins of school life. They are conscious of
their marginality, and it hurts, although they try to see the posit-
ive side of things. Carmelle notes that she can sit quietly in the
corridor at lunchtime, and listen to the others talk: 'Because they
don't even notice me, I can just sit there and listen to them. That
way, I can know what is going on in the school.' Lisa says: 'That
is one advantage of being a reject, you know, people don't notice
you're there and you hear a lot of things.' In the same discussion
as that from which the first example was extracted, the Nerds say:

Example 5.2   Discussion group 1, March 1994

Carole:	there's something I want to mention here, most of us here were the losers to some extent, the ones that were picked on
Chloé:	oh yeah!
Carole:	and I think that really has given us a better insight
Debbie:	I think all of us (xx simultaneous talk)
Carole:	even human nature, like the way people really are
Carmelle:	not necessarily a better insight, but a different insight than
Carole:	no, it gives you a better insight
Carmelle:	no, a different insight
Chloé:	I think people who have everything served to them on a silver platter (are less?) sensitized to other people

In the end, whether their insight is 'better' or 'different', they
certainly feel that they know things that others do not, and can

take perspectives that the 'popular' girls cannot take. Of course, they are still somewhat angry about the way they were (and in many ways still are) treated, and may be somewhat jealous of the 'popular' girls' perfect bodies; they say that the popular girls' breasts are the right size, not too big or too small like theirs, and their hair stays in place. Debbie and Farah in particular are unsure of how they feel, sharing the experiences and perspectives, as well as many of the practices, of both the popular crowd and the 'rejects'. At the same time, all six argue that this lack of fit has made them more accepting of who they are, more honest, and better able to see beyond physical beauty.

Over time, individually and collectively, the Nerds began to resist the image of femininity that was at the source of their marginalization. They rejected the practices of the popular group. For example, Lisa commented after the Valentine's Day skit that the student council (who had organized the skit) was obliged to use boys in drag to play the part of the Juliettes because no woman in her right mind would take a rose over money or a car. They disdained the popular girls as being mindless and only interested in boys. They had nothing but contempt for what they saw as the popular girls' participation in their own sexual objectification: one of the Nerds wrote to Phyllis: 'They're nearly in their 20s and the "popular" girls are still getting molested (and they still love it. "Tee hee, stop, no! Don't take off my bra! Not in the hallway, tee hee!").' They reject the fuss made about the graduation dance:

Example 5.3   Discussion group 2, April 1994

Farah: (. . .) there's so many girls in our school that I mean for the prom okay our graduation is coming up in May, and these girls are flipping through the magazines, 'oh I want this dress, I want this dress, this is what I'm going to wear, don't you think this looks good', that's about it, it's basically brainwashing
Phyllis: but does that get supported in the school?
All: oh God yes
Chloé: look who are the ones that are on the student council, and all the ones that are in what do you call it, *Bureau de* (*xx*), it's all the cute little people (. . .)
Lisa: a perfect example of how different the thinking is in this school is like when you get into the people who would

be considered I don't know I guess (descended?) from
the popular crowd. I have been asked in the last two
weeks a total of fifteen times, three or four times by the
same person, what my prom dress looks like. I have not
asked one single person, not one, and it doesn't stop
there, okay. They want to know what kind of panty
hose you're wearing, what shade. Does it matter? Does
it matter whether I wear grey or taupe? Oh gee, I
wonder.

They had the following to say about gender relations among
the popular group, during a discussion about the student council:

Example 5.4   Discussion group 3, April 1994

Phyllis: do you think it's a coincidence that it's all guys in
             there?
Carole: no not at all, those guys have hung out with each other
Debbie: I think the girls are intimidated by them actually
Carole: oh they're a bunch of weak-willed spineless jellyfish,
             they're tee hee hee hee

Their rejection of the popular group's image of femininity is
accompanied by the development of alternative practices. One set
of practices involves being loud and sexually aggressive, rather
than quiet and sexually passive. Early on, two of these girls would
talk and sing loudly in the hallways, make jokes, and make verbal
sexual advances at boys (who would ignore them, or slink off
down hallways when they approached). Both girls transferred to
English-language high schools. Others who stayed began, however, to adopt a similar strategy. For example, they would loudly
insist on a turn at talk in class, although their remarks were not
always well-received. They also took to making high-volume remarks about sex in public; for example, the boyfriend of Denise,
one of the Nerds, came to her English class. After he left, another
student said, 'Look at her, she's so satisfied. She saw Tom'. Denise
replied, 'Oh yes! I just had an orgasm sitting here. Now I'm bask-
ing in my afterglow'.

Other strategies were designed principally to carve out an alternative sexual identity, or positioning, for themselves. Some of the
girls did this by presenting themselves to the outside world as
lesbian, and hence unavailable for sexual advances on the part of

males. The image of lesbianism also allows them to take an active sexual role; they each act out in turn making sexual advances on others in the group, some of them rather sadistic, in what is perhaps a parody of male objectification of women, for example, 'I'm going to stick a vacuum hose to your clit and drag you across the carpet'. Part of the purpose of this public discourse is to shock the popular students. Even Debbie and Farah, who were friends with both the popular group and with the Nerds, had a hard time with this kind of talk. For example, Debbie overheard the remark about the vacuum hose, and said, 'You guys! How can you talk about things like that? You're hurting me, look, I'm crossing my legs'. For the Nerds, this is a source of pleasure. One says that she 'enjoys corrupting unjaded minds'. Another writes to Phyllis, 'Have you ever wondered about your sexuality? I have and reached the conclusion that I am hopelessly straight as a board, although I do enjoy giving the opposite impression, part of my shock appeal I suppose.'

At the same time, while the construction of an image of lesbianism was largely a strategy for resisting dominant images of femininity, it was accompanied by a critical stance on the part of the Nerds towards the homophobic climate of the school. One of them accompanied Bernard and his male date to the graduation dance. Another befriended a lesbian student, and accompanied her on gay pride marches even after she had left Champlain. One day, Carole tells several classmates that she had kissed another girl in front of her boyfriend, and that he had enjoyed watching. She then turned to Debbie, and said, 'No, no, don't worry, I'm not a lesbian'. Melanie, one of the Nerds, said, 'Right, right, why do guys always think it's a turn on to see two girls make out? It's like gays should be shot and lesbians should be videotaped'. Debbie says that guys who kiss guys and girls who kiss girls are disgusting: 'If I saw that, I would puke right on them.' Carole replies, 'Oh right, don't you do that with your boyfriend? Walk down the street holding hands?'

Another element of the Nerds' strategy for carving out a different position on female sexuality was to adopt a discourse of Satanism, and indeed, to occasionally claim to be Satan. When a boy attempted to make an advance towards Lisa she rejected him, saying that she was Satan, and that since Satan was an asexual being, it would be impossible for her to respond to the boy's advances. Indeed, taking up that position cast the boy's advances in a distinctly unfavourable light: what was he doing coming on to the devil? To be Satan not only gave the girls grounds for refusing to participate in prevailing gender relations, but it gave them a position of strength from which to do so, a position which protected them from accusations of either being too virginal and pure, or else lesbian.

Two other members of the group protected themselves through religion. Carmelle adopted adherence to some aspects of Celtic religions, which she valued in particular for what she understood to be the central role of women in those religious beliefs and practices. Farah was Muslim, and despite some episodes of acting like a member of the 'popular' group, also had a commitment to more traditional Muslim gender roles, which made her relatively unavailable to non-Muslim boys. The final girl in the group was a member of a fundamentalist Christian group. She was somewhat marginal to the Nerds in several ways, among them her occasional flirtations with looking 'sexy' (that is, wearing clothes the 'popular' girls would approve of). However, she became pregnant; in and of itself, this would not have caused a problem for her relationship with the 'popular' students, except that she decided to keep the baby and put it up for adoption, rather than have an abortion. The rest of the Nerds rallied around her, and supported her in many ways. In addition, it was necessary for her to defend herself from disparaging remarks from classmates (such as the one who suggested that she alone was responsible for what had happened), thereby committing her further to a stance outside of, and critical of, prevailing views of sexual relations.

But perhaps the most important form of the Nerds' resistance to the prevailing models of success at Champlain took place on the terrain of academic achievement. Doing well at school was a value the Nerds shared with the popular students; to their great delight, they were able to achieve more in that domain than the popular students were able to achieve.

Example 5.5 Discussion group, March 1994

> *Chloé:* you'll see this later, but we were talking about this yesterday, about how the stereotype of the schools are like the bad kids are the ones that wear like the leather and they hang out together and they respond when

> teachers say something stupid or they kind of speak really loudly at *réunions générales* and all that stuff, and the other people, the ones that are the intelligent ones and the popular ones are the ones that look really nice and preppy
>
> *Lisa:*   but oddly enough
>
> *Chloé:*   it's the opposite
>
> *Lisa:*   out of the six people who are here, three of us got honour roll certificates today, and the other three of us maybe missed the honour roll by like point five per cent
>
> *Carole:* and most of us are fast-tracking too in some way or another

No victory was as sweet as the graduation ceremonies in which several of the Nerds received academic prizes; Lisa wrote to Phyllis: 'I deeply enjoyed going up to the podium five times as I watched their faces.'

The Nerds found a variety of creative and imaginative ways to turn their initial rejection by the 'popular' students into a position of strength. Their solidarity as a group also gave them a basis from which to develop a critique of their marginalization, and to cope with it. In addition, while their perspective allowed them to remain immune from the objectifying practices of their peers, it is only in the arena of academic achievement that they were able to set and achieve their own goals. As with most of the 'popular' girls at Champlain, they were left orienting themselves with respect to their identity without being able to contribute anything to the public debate on this matter. In their emotional lives, it is far from clear that they were able to invent anything more satisfying than what the prevailing discourse had to offer. They clearly occupied a position on the margins of life at Champlain, and the creativity and originality of their perspective and achievements went largely unnoticed in public discursive space.

5   Conclusion

It is in the end mainly the male students of Champlain who are able to use public fora to construct specific versions of ethnolinguistic identity: Québécois as tough, rugged, authentic francophones; bilinguals as hip, plugged-in to North American popular culture in music, dress and sports; Africans as privileged keepers of the

European standard and simultaneously anti-colonialist, anti-racist warriors, street-wise and cool. They have concomitant negative stereotypes of each other: the Québécois uncultured lumberjack, the bilingual sell-out to the Anglos, the African as both victimized and threatening. Language is key to all these images, as Canadian and European French, English and Somali all become emblematic of specific visions of the school and its identity.

Female students are left to position themselves with respect to these discourses. Some simply associate with them, cheering on the boys, helping them or playing their traditional roles within male-defined activities. Occasionally, they can exploit the window of opportunity presented by women's traditional role as primary agent of socialization to take control of events and committees such as the fashion show, the graduation dance, the multicultural lunch, the twenty-fifth anniversary celebrations, or even the student council. Others, notably the Nerds, resist, but in doing so they only marginalize themselves further from school life. Similarly, gay and lesbian students must position themselves with respect to prevailing norms, and find it impossible to participate in the main debates of life at school.

The struggle over the identity of the school is built on a gendered division of discursive labour. Male students have many more opportunities than do female students to say what they have to say about French and about *la francophonie* without having to be concerned with what that has to do with being a male. At the same time, the intense focus on ethnolinguistic and ethnocultural identity which dominates the school's discursive space serves to obscure the gendered nature of that space.

6 *Periphery to centre*[1]

1 Voices from the margins

In 1994, Mark Campbell, a member of the research team, spent a fair amount of time in the Grade 11/12 Drama class. A major mode of classroom organization for this course involved splitting the twenty or so students into small groups, each of which was responsible for writing and performing a skit. The students were allowed to choose their own groups. The result was five (more or less stable) groups: two groups of Somali students (all boys); two groups of white students, including the three girls in the class, and all of whom were linked in some way to the French Canadian heartland (they or one of their parents were from Quebec or another francophone majority area of Canada, or they had lived there for some time); and a small group of four boys, one of whom, Salim, described his group in this way: 'We are the multicultural group, we have one Nigger, one Chink and two Pakis.'

Through this group of boys (Salim, Jamie, Chris and Bill) we came to understand one of the major shifts experienced at Champlain. Initially somewhat marginal to school life, this group came to be associated with a redefinition of the school away from the old struggles between '*Franco-Ontariens*' inside and '*Anglos*' outside, or within the school, between '*franco-dominants*' and '*anglo-dominants*', between '*Canadiens français de souche*' and '*bilingues*', or even between Europe-oriented and Canada-oriented francophones. The new orientation that Salim and his friends came to

---

[1] This chapter was written in collaboration with Mark Campbell.

embrace, argue for, and even symbolize was an orientation towards the school as diverse and inclusive.

There were reasons for this, of course. We have argued already that built into the very logic of Champlain is the tension between a fictive homogeneous identity and a diverse reality, a tension augmented by the importance of an ideology of democracy and meritocracy in Western education. At the time of our fieldwork, Champlain was living through a period when the ambient educational discourse was focussed on inclusiveness, through the anti-racist/ anti-sexist education movement, and when the tension-neutralizing strategies of the school staff were beginning to lose effectiveness in the face of the combined pressures of this movement and of the burgeoning diversity of the school population. Salim and his friends thus found themselves situated at a convergence of several interests: the school's interest in integrating diversity into its legitimating ideology, the old guard's interest in access to the modern, globalizing world, and the refusal of the increasing numbers of new arrivals to accept a place on the periphery of school life. This new attitude was fuelled by the dynamic presence of the new cohort of Somali-speakers making a place for themselves at Champlain.

In this chapter, we shall track the development of the ideology of diversity. We shall first take a look at the story of Salim and his friends, beginning with their position in 1993, when Mark first met them: a small group of 'multiculturals', with their own take on the world, and their own strategies for getting the most out of Champlain. What this story tells us is that the structure of the social networks at Champlain at the beginning of our fieldwork made it difficult for relative newcomers to break into friendship groups. There are many points of difference that become high-lighted in this process of marginalization, as we have seen. Things like coming from an immersion programme, not conforming to dominant models of beauty, lack of experience of Toronto life, race, all become potentially salient. What is interesting about this particular story is how race and ethnicity became the salient issue; so salient, in fact, that it turned the school upside down.

It is this process of redefinition that will then be the focus of the rest of the chapter. We shall look at two major processes. The first is concerned with the way in which the music culture of the marginalized group began to move to the centre over the course of the fieldwork period. Largely due to the efforts of another small group of three male 'multiculturals', associated with Salim and his friends, the inclusive and resistant message of hip-hop provided a counter-point to the rock and techno music favoured by other groups in the school. The second has to do with the almost unintentional way in which a group of 'multiculturals' organized themselves as a slate in an alliance with the Somali students (and with the support of the hip-hop network) to run for student council on a platform of inclusiveness — and won. The two are connected, as we shall see, since specific music forms (rock/heavy metal, hip-hop and reggae) were associated by the students with participation in racially defined social networks, and with specific stances towards race and inclusiveness.

Thus, by the time we left the school in 1995, there was a new student council in place, a council with which the formerly marginalized 'multiculturals' were closely associated by kinship or friendship, and which was formed mainly of people like themselves. While we cannot say what the long-term impact of this shift might be, it is clear that a new way of thinking about Champlain had penetrated public space.

2   The phat boys

The first time Mark heard this, he thought, 'Fat?'. But, no, Jamie, Chris, Salim and Bill weren't actually fat. They were phat. The term is more widely used and better known now, designating a certain form of 'cool'. Chris defined it as 'good float, flow' (he said he learned it from watching rap videos on television). Among other things, it describes a way of using language, one of the central ways in which this group constitutes itself as a friendship group. The phat boys meet on the ground of shared values; these values are not particularly different from those of the school's dominant group, but the phat boys have to find a way to live them on the margins of that group, since they have been unable to penetrate the inner core of the school's social networks.

There are two major reasons why the phat boys had difficulty blending into the crowd. The most evident one is that they all came to the school from French immersion, Jamie and Chris from one school in Grade 9, Salim and Bill each from two other immersion schools, in Grade 7. They had therefore not been part of the long-standing friendship groups formed at Rouillé, Champlain's main feeder school, and had had no prior experience of Franco-Ontarian minority education elsewhere. They did not have the feeling of being comfortable in French that other students in the school possessed. Second, although the phat boys never say so, their race probably also played a role in their marginalization: Bill is of Korean origin, Jamie and Salim of Indian or mixed Indian-European origin (although their parents immigrated from quite different countries, their families having already participated in a generations-old immigration process out of India), and Chris of African-Caribbean origin (while Chris could have formed ties with other students of African origin, he did not have the affiliation with, and skills in, French that would have facilitated that relationship). While others with similar racial and cultural backgrounds were able to use shared experience of bilingualism and Franco-Ontarian schools to penetrate the bilingual crowd, this group of friends came too late to do so effectively. Their group is clearly not homogeneous in terms of background; what the phat boys have in common is their marginalization in an increasingly polarized system of social networks at Champlain, and the kind of shared social values which are reflective of class standing more than of ethnocultural affiliation.

In a discussion with Mark, Bill, Chris and Jamie had this to say:

Example 6.1   Discussion in a restaurant, Mark, Bill, Chris and Jamie, January 1995

Mark: okay, so what would you say, why is it that you guys became friends?
Bill: 'cause we're all anglophones
Chris: we can't speak French
Jamie: we play basketball um (pause) Jesus I don't know (. . .)
(. . .)
Mark: what else would you share in common?
Jamie: well, none of us have had our hair cut in a long time (all laugh) Um, well, we sort of share some of the similar views on things, I guess

The fact of having shared the experience of French immersion seems to result in all of them constructing themselves as 'anglophone', as 'unable' to speak French. Of course, they must speak French well enough to have gained admission to Champlain, and to follow along in class, since all of them are in advanced level courses, and are keen on academic success. Nonetheless, they clearly do not think of themselves as francophone, nor even bilingual, and so this places them on the margins of Champlain social life, at least its official version, and that constructed by the then-dominant bilinguals. Their marginality is underscored by their preference for basketball, rather than volleyball or hockey. The investment on the part of the phat boys in Champlain is therefore in the language, not in the cultural identification. At the same time, their own cultural identification is problematic for them, and serves both to marginalize them from sometimes polarized racially or ethnoculturally defined groups, while protecting them from the constraints of such categorization.

Above, Bill described the members of the group as 'anglophone'. Salim describes the group as 'Anglo-multicultural':

> We've got different backgrounds, but our culture is about the same, we all share a lot of things. The only thing we have different is religion (. . .) Jamie's background is Indian, but he's not really Indian, Bill is Korean, okay, but he's North American (. . .)

In the January 1995 restaurant discussion with Mark, Jamie, Chris and Bill discussed music preferences, skating around assertions they wanted to make for fear of being labelled racists. (Jamie: 'I have an explanation for this but I'm not gonna say that because it's racist' (laughs).) Mark pursues the issue:

Example 6.2   Discussion in a restaurant, Mark, Bill, Chris and Jamie, January 1995

Mark:	say it, don't worry
Chris:	this is open, don't worry
Mark:	no, in order to understand where group boundaries are, then go ahead and say it
Jamie:	well, the way we see it, like, I sort of, like, well, we actually well you (Chris) and I talked about this a few times, is that see white people can't dance, so they invented techno music, 'cause there is actually no way of dancing properly, and you get up there and you
Chris:	swing your arms and just swing around and just be just be loose you know

Jamie:	and that's sort of and that's how
	⌈we think
Chris:	⌊like it comes out
Jamie:	yeah
(. . .)	
Mark:	okay, so you said that hip-hop was
Jamie:	hip-hop is like black music
Mark:	yeah I think
	that's what you said. Okay, are you black?
Jamie:	no, definitely not
Mark:	okay, well could you or would you describe yourself as anything?
Jamie:	(laughs) that's a very difficult question
Chris:	that's what we've had trouble answering
Jamie:	see, like in a way it's perfect, 'cause like nobody can ever insult me like with a racist joke, because it's kind of like impossible, um, the way I see it like um well actually I have like white blood in me and whatever, and Indian blood and Portuguese blood, so Portuguese, British and Indian blood, basically what basically I guess it is, so whatever that makes me, you know, I don't know, but I don't see myself as white, and I don't see myself as black, I would say Indian 'cause it's the easiest thing to say, but I don't even know if I see myself as that necessarily
Mark (to Bill):	okay, how would you describe yourself then?
Bill:	ah, Oriental are an easy influence by both sides, say black and white, you see, you could have a group of Orientals who love rock, head-banging and everything, and you have other Orientals like dressing up like hip-hoppers and listen to music so
Mark:	okay then if you were to stick a label onto yourself, you'd call yourself Oriental or Korean or do you have a label or would you be comfortable with a label or no?
Bill:	actually, I wouldn't be comfortable with a label, I was born here in Canada uh I can say that I'm mostly Canadian, like all my family background, the rest of my family they're all in Korea, so I can't say that I'm not Korean, there so

Jamie: I can relate to that

Chris: (laughs) well I'm white (laughs) like I don't
know, like Bill said I'm Canadian first, though
really, so the rest of it is just secondary, it
doesn't really make a difference, or it shouldn't
anyhow, it comes out anyways, now I'm losing
my thought here, so I'm saying I'm Canadian
first, um I don't know if you want to get into a
colour thing, I'd just say black, because I don't
really like the term African-American

At the same time, the phat boys feel that they have little in
common with members of groups they identify as 'Somalian' and
'White and French'. However, they say that the lack of affiliation
is cultural and linguistic, not a question of race (or class). In the
1995 restaurant discussion, Jamie says the following of the
'Somalians':

(...) like you could never see relating with the Somalians and
stuff like that, like I'm friends with a lot of Somalians, like we all
are right, but never really could be part of that group, you know,
because, well, first of all, because we don't speak French that
well, so it's difficult to relate to them on a French basis, and they
don't speak French that well, so you have two bad Frenches
trying to speak to each other, it doesn't work that well (...)
I have an example (...) on the way home from one of the
basketball games we played (Jamie is on the Champlain boy's
basketball team) I ended up being in a taxi by myself, well, not
by myself, that's it right there, well, that's my point, being by
myself with the Somalians, see that's it, 'cause I never would
have said 'by myself' if it was like, anyways, all the same, it was
myself and three Somalians right, and uh it doesn't matter what
they're doing, but anyways so uh like the whole taxi ride home
I said like maybe a couple of words to them (...) if it was a
more complex comment I try to structure it in French, and I try
to convey my thoughts, but if it was English they'd understand
English like 'that was a good game', obviously they'd understand,
but like when I'm like unsure if they'd understand me in English
then I would say it in French (...)

With the 'White and French' group, the phat boys see both
differences and commonalities:

Example 6.3   Discussion in a restaurant, Mark, Bill, Chris and Jamie, January 1995

Mark:	okay, before we get too far, let me ask you an important an important question. Do you perceive the same way that you perceive the Somalians as a group, do you perceive there is such a thing as
Jamie:	a white group
Mark:	a white group, I've made reference to them, but we're assuming that there's, do you perceive there's such a thing as a white group, or maybe not
Jamie:	I'd say yeah, but not necessarily white, I'd say white and French
Mark:	can you please describe them?
Jamie:	white and French is definitely another group for me I ⌈think because
Chris:	⌊white and French?
Jamie:	white and French, that doesn't sound good, but well (laughs)
Mark:	no no no no
Chris:	(laughs) we'll just go with that for right now
Jamie:	yeah, like the Québécois people and Franco-Ontarians and they go off on their Québécois do that *joual*-type speak and like (xx) like what the hell are you speaking to me? (laughs)
Mark (to Chris):	okay, how do you feel about his his we'll use those terms just to work with
Chris:	it's interesting for me well I guess you know if you what to um I guess it's a language thing, and the fact that they have the same kind of French type of language I suppose, you know, they can relate to each other very well, I think better with themselves than with us, for example, because of course French is their first language and our second and you know we can't always talk about the same type of things
Jamie:	that's very true
Bill:	I think it's also music 'cause if you look at people like you know (. . .)
Jamie:	they listen to rock

Chris: listen to rock like eh during during lunch
              times you see them in the hallways well, some
              people are playing guitars, they're singing
              along, singing their own little rock songs, and
              like people like us we don't even know what
              the hell they're singing
Jamie: yeah like we listen to it, but we don't get
              into it like they do
Bill: and they know all these songs by heart
Jamie: and we just know
              (sings) that's all we know (laughs)
Mark: okay, so they don't play basketball
Jamie: not well (laughs)
Mark: there's a language barrier
Jamie: well, okay, that's not necessarily true because
              then again like Paul
Chris: well, it's not like barriers
Jamie: and like all, we're friends with them and all,
              well like I don't know, they're not really good
              friends with us, but like I can always hang out
              with them all day like 'cause when I go like
              when I'm going to go meet friends downtown I
              always go with them and stuff like that, so I
              can hang out with them, they just, that, I don't
              know how the hell it changes, it's just different
              somehow
Chris: It's hard to explain I think

The phat boys are thus conscious of themselves as a group, with things in common despite, or perhaps partly because of, their internal diversity. It is likely that Mark's line of questioning oriented their analysis of their own group and of others in ways that may have exaggerated the need to categorize; nonetheless, what they say in their discussions with Mark reveals both the availability of categorization practices in the discourse of the school and peer group, and the ambiguities and difficulties involved in those practices (note their frequent hesitations, hedges and circumlocutions when they try to talk about race). In any case, the phat boys' self-identification as anglophone (stemming from their family origins, and path through French immersion) cuts them off from the French-dominant or bilingual practices of other groups. Nonetheless, their command of English gives them access to the practising bilinguals (they can 'hang out' with them), despite the fact that their different social positions with respect to the school's resources leads to different cultural practices, especially as reflected in sports and music (basketball versus volleyball or hockey; hip-hop versus rock). Their consciousness of themselves as representing a certain critical stance on mainstream society, gives them a basis for an alliance with other marginalized groups, who also, as we shall see, express this stance through the same or similar sports and musical preferences, although for the time being, language, and perhaps culture or even race, act as a barrier to the activation of those common interests. In the end, the phat boys occupy some intermediate territory at the conjunction of social positions, practices and interests prevalent in the school.

Perhaps most important for the evolution of the phat boys' position in the school is the fact that they share with the school's dominant group and with the Somalis the values of hard work and educational success. First, it must be noted that, despite the boys' preference for and greater ease in English, they all choose to stay at Champlain. They have invested in French–English bilingualism as a strategy for socioeconomic success. However, within the curriculum, they prefer Science and English to other courses, especially French and Mathematics. Salim says that Science is 'real', while Mathematics is 'equations without meaning', and we must wonder if the parallel holds for the language courses. Salim's older sister, Farah, has this to say about Français and English:

> Oh, big difference, major difference. My favourite topic. The French classes are *extremely* boring, like, people dread French class. (. . .) they concentrate so much on like your grammar, and because the French language is so much harder to write than the English language, right. I think people like English class a lot more because in English class you can talk about anything (. . .) world issues, anything. (. . .) And, also, one thing that I noticed is that in French class you don't learn anything philosophical, but in English class you do. You learn, like, so much about the world and about life. I would consider English class more of a life class, like, lessons in life.

The investment in bilingualism is thus not without a certain degree of ambivalence. Nonetheless, the phat boys stick it out, for what credentialized bilingualism can do for them. In this respect, they are no different from the vast majority of students at Champlain. What dominates in their orientation to school, then, is educational success, and they have developed cultural practices which reproduce this orientation. Some of these practices have to do with investments in subject areas where their competence in French will not slow them down. Others are more general interactional patterns, which resemble the patterns of the culture of success of the practising bilinguals (see Chapter 4). These interactional strategies are meaningful and effective only within the bounds of the trust obtaining within the friendship group, and serve to reproduce both the value attached to doing well at school and the ties of friendship among the boys. Salim said:

> We're pretty competitive, it's competitive and it matters (. . .) it's more honour and respect. If you get like 70, and everyone else gets like 80, the day after, you're excluded, you're out of the group for a day. They joke about it, and the three of them put themselves in one group, and you're put outside.

So the boys have an arrangement, a ritual practice, which serves to remind them of the importance of good grades, without actually threatening the cohesion of the group. Similarly, they take care not to use their success to threaten group solidarity. Salim again:

> Chris is like that, he is very careful not to show other people up. If he got a better score than you on an exam, and you ask him what he got, he would try and avoid telling you. Chris would just use the phrase, 'I can't even remember, I think I'm losing my mind now'.

In keeping with the value attached to hard work in school, the boys generally value clean living and modest presentation of self; Jamie said, 'the group we're in is a bunch of good boys'. They reinforce valued behaviours through negative sanctions (joking, ridicule, ostracization) as well as persuasion (Salim: 'we'd definitely try to talk him out of it'). Some deviant behaviours are tolerated with the rationalization that they predated the formation of the group.

As Salim says:

> (. . .) none of us really use drugs and we don't agree with people who do. [A former group member] used to be a friend of ours, but he got into drugs and we didn't hang around with him too much after that (. . .) I don't drink, Bill doesn't drink, Chris will

drink a couple of beers, Jamie sometimes gets pretty drunk. Chris
and Jamie's drinking pretty much started before our group was
formed (. . .) If you swear too much, f'n this and f'n that, not
many people [in our group] will laugh, the way it's put across to
people if you swear too much. Malcolm [an occasional member
of the group] likes to swear a lot, but that, he learned that from
his old school, and he already swore when he joined the group.

Similarly, appearance is designed to take the middle road. Salim:

Anything loose, nothing with a classy brand name, no Armani,
sport brands or teams are okay (. . .) Gap is too JAP [Jewish
American Princess] (. . .) no Cross Colours because a lot of
Blacks in our school have taken some serious attitude (. . .) like
one [pant] leg up, and all bad. If you dress like that and it's not
your attitude, it looks stupid. We don't like that, it's pretty
hard core.

In their music preferences, the phat boys recognize that they
orient towards music that is stereotypically considered 'black', but
insist that they also listen to other kinds of music (jazz, 'slow',
'mood music', classical). Jamie says: 'I don't necessarily hate all
rock, I actually like some heavy metal songs.' Chris says: 'I can
listen to it (rock) if it's on, but it's not like I'm going to go to the
store and buy an AC/DC CD.' Here again, they chart out a middle
position, with clear hip-hop values that allow them to state their
preferences but be open to all other things.

In sports, they share the Somali and Haitian love of basketball.
It provides them with something in common, although for the
moment at least that is not enough to overcome the linguistic and
cultural barriers they feel are present. Above, Jamie talked about
the limits to social interaction even within the school basketball
team. In addition, the boys are sensitive to the racial categorization
of sports that operates to categorize groups in the school. Just as
hip-hop is seen to be black music, and rock white music, basketball is seen to be a black sport, and volleyball and hockey are seen
as white sports. Farah, for example, reported one day that she had
seen her brother, Salim, who was on his way to an English class.
Groups had been asked to prepare an example of an advertising
slogan. Salim's group's was: 'Basketball is not just a black thing.'

Perhaps most importantly, the boys share linguistic practices,
which, to them, not only reflect their solidarity as a group, but

also their shared outlook on life. In many of the above examples, the solidarity among the boys is reflected in their ability to finish off each other's sentences, to speak simultaneously in harmony with each other, and to support each other's statements with new information that attaches right onto a friend's affirmation. Salim:

> The way we think is generally the same, it is actually (related) a bit to our language, the way we talk and everything, and maybe a bit to our environment too (. . .) we all speak the same dialect (. . .) we all speak rather the same, along the same lines. We all speak what's on our minds (. . .) the way we speak is, well, we generally have the same taste, so we can speak on the same level.

They develop code words ('FIA means "foot in the ass", like if one of those guys are really acting like a chimp, one of us would just say "FIA", and we all know what that means' – Salim), and engage in word play derived from African-American street language.

This word play is an important part of the phat boys' image and ethic. While in many ways they are, in Jamie's words, 'good boys', they equally nurture an image of themselves as hip, plugged into popular culture, and even involved in creating that culture. This stance, which may well derive in part from their marginal status in school life, is important, because it provided grounds for the development of a consciousness of the margins, and a basis for an alliance with the hip-hop and reggae culture of the students of African and Caribbean origin.

Because most of official school life occurs in French, the only classroom space where this knowledge and these practices can emerge is in the English class. Indeed, in that class, the teacher, Derek (known to the students as Mr Baxter), used as a pedagogical practice the method of translating literature (especially notoriously inaccessible literature such as Shakespeare) into the everyday language of the students. In this regard, Derek often looked to the phat boys as a source of translation:

Example 6.4   11th and 12th grades (combined) advanced level English, 1994

Derek:	'You have me, have you not, my lord?' Well, what does that mean in the regular language of today?
Jamie:	You have me, dig it, Jack!
Class:	(Laughter)

Example 6.5 11th and 12th grades (combined) advanced level English, 1994. Derek is handing back corrected writing assignments. Chris had written: 'I'm not dropping phat lyrics.' Derek had commented: 'It does run on in a certain fashion, as you say, but nonetheless, you put down some phat words here.' After reading Derek's comment, Chris says:

Chris: Mr Baxter, what do you mean by 'phat' here?
Derek: I'm writing, I mean I'm speaking the same language you're speaking.
Salim: (laughs) He's speaking blackenese.
Jamie: (laughs and claps)
Derek: I don't want to be accused of not being able to speak the same way you can.
Chris: all right!
        (A few minutes later)
Derek: Oh man, this was a lot of writing.
Chris: It's phat though.
Salim: Phat, it's phat.

Example 6.6 11th and 12th grades (combined) advanced level English, 1994

Derek: Polonius is saying to his daughter, 'I thought he was after your body for a little bit of time'.
Chris: That's phat.
Jamie and Salim: (laugh)

Similarly, the boys formed part of a group which self-consciously engaged in the African-American verbal duelling ritual of *dissing*. While these nice boys don't swear, they do engage, as we have seen, in ritual behaviour which allows them to do things that would otherwise be too threatening either to their ethic or to the solidarity of their group. Dissing is useful for them, since, at the same time, it allows them to establish their bona fides as members of the hip street culture, and also provides a ritual means of defusing dangerous conflict.

In one such incident, tension mounted between Salim and Sam, a Jewish boy of Israeli origin (but who came to Champlain from Montreal), and a friend of Salim's older sister, Farah. Since Salim observed Muslim dietary regulations, he did not eat in the cafeteria, but instead kept food, including candy, in his locker, and occasionally shared it with others. One day, in drama class, he passed out some liquorice. Sam asked for some too, but Salim said, jokingly, 'Not for you, you're a Jew'. Rafi responded by calling Salim a Muslim terrorist. Salim continued to offer liquorice to others, but not to Sam. Sam said, 'Come on, please man, please give me a piece, give me a piece'. Salim replied again, 'No way, no way, not for you, you Jew'. At this point Jamie made a comment about Sam's girlfriend, to which Sam replied in kind. The discussion between Salim and Sam about religion and candy, then broadened out to include ritual insults about girlfriends. At one point some-one said, 'Don't diss me, man!', at which point four boys decided to engage in a formal diss. Sam and Chris formed one team, and sat facing their opponents, Jamie and Salim. Mark (with his tape-recorder) and Bill were also present, as were two Somali students, Hassan and Abdi.

Example 6.7   11th grade, Art dramatique, *1994*

Jamie:	I get, you gotta pick you gotta pick your team-mates, pick a team-mate, I pick Sal
Sam:	no not him
Mark:	judges here, partial audience, partial judges
Jamie:	I pick a team-mate, Sal's my team-mate
Sam:	okay, Chris, does he know how to
Salim:	hell yeah he knows
?:	he's black, you think he don't know how to diss
Chris:	African-American chicken, Kentucky Fried Chicken (*name of a fast-food chain selling fried chicken, a stereotypically African-American food*)
?:	your mother is so big and fat
All:	(laughter)
Sam:	you guys, shut up, shh, go
Salim:	not my mothers, number one
?:	wait, let me take my drink out
Sam:	you know mother jokes too
Chris:	this session part one
Sam:	allright, your girlfriend's armpits are so hairy, it seems like she has Snoop Doggy Dog with an Afro in a headlock
All:	(cheers, laughter)
Jamie:	okay, okay
Sam:	yesterday night
Jamie:	no, you only get one, you only get one
All:	you get one, you get one
Jamie:	okay, okay

Salim:	you go, you go
Sam:	no, you have to say, you can help him out
Jamie:	I was gonna like, your girlfriend's armpits are so long and nasty she has dread
Sam:	all right, go
Jamie:	okay, okay, your girlfriend's armpit hair is so long and nasty that she could tie dread and swing from it
Sam:	what, okay, I got one, your girlfriend's legs are so hairy that if you give her a fur coat and a banana they'd mistake her for a monkey and put her back in the zoo
All:	(laughter)
Jamie:	ha, ha, oh my God, ha, ha
Sam:	I did it, take it back, okay I got one, okay, can I go now?
Jamie:	no, your mama's so fat
Sam:	my girlfriend, my girlfriend
Chris:	no, your mama, your mama
Salim:	same person, what's the difference
All:	(laughter)
Chris:	who cares
Jamie:	you're both related to them anyways. Okay, your mother is so fat I roll over her twice and I'm still on top of her
All:	(laughter)
Sam:	okay, okay, I'm gonna go, your mother's so hairy, that when you see her ass on the street, your daddy goes 'Lassie, Lassie come back home' (*Lassie is the name of a collie dog star of American 1960s movies and television*)
All:	(laughter)
Jamie:	okay, we're getting into hairy ones, right, your sister, no, you don't have a sister, right
Sam:	no
Jamie:	your grandma, no, your girlfriend's better, let's see, lesbians and, no, I got to think of a good one, I've got to think of a good one, that was good, you got me
Sam:	okay, had enough
Jamie:	pass
Salim:	pass, say something Chris
Chris:	aahhh
Sam:	yeah, yeah, yeah, your mother is so stupid that she failed a blood test
All:	(laughter)

Salim:	okay, well then, you may be handsome and smart and all that, but you're not a very nice person
Chris:	not a nice person
Jamie:	not a nice person (squeals) these guys are like, hey, I want to trade partners, I want Chris on my team
?:	you guys are terminating them
Sam:	yeah, no, I know (pause) all right, all right
Jamie:	okay, okay, go
Sam:	your mom's so fat that on her driver's license it says 'Picture continues on next side'
All:	(laughter)
Chris:	that's old
Salim:	that's old
Jamie:	your mom, speaking of driver's license, your mother is so fat that she couldn't just stop with a G, with a G license, because she couldn't fit in any of those cars (*in Ontario, a G license is for driving the largest, heaviest vehicles*)
Hassan:	(laughs: the others look at him)
All:	(laugh at Hassan for having laughed)
Jamie:	thanks, Hassan, my man
?:	(xx)
?:	(xx)
Sam:	yeah, we won, man (xx) keep your word
Salim:	here you go
Jamie:	they won, they kicked our ass
Salim:	who won, who won, who won
Jamie:	they won, they kicked our ass, that wasn't fun
Salim:	I want to go with Sam for a little while

At this point, Sam reiterates his request that Salim give him some liquorice. After making Sam say 'please' and kiss his hand, Salim finally relents. The teams reform (Salim and Chris against Sam and Jamie). They attempt further rounds, but have even more difficulty keeping the momentum up (at one point, Chris says, 'Nobody has any new ones here, I'm afraid there aren't enough black people to go around'). Eventually, the occasion deteriorates into making fun of Salim, and then the group disperses, the focus not interesting enough to hold their attention.

At one level, the diss provides a means for the phat boys to defuse the danger of the dispute between Salim and Sam. It ritualizes it and refocuses attention away from explosive religious differences, and onto the safe grounds of sexist male display that all the

boys can relate to, as males (as Jamie says, let's see, should it be about mothers, sisters, girlfriends, lesbians . . . ?). It allows both Sam and Salim to save face; Sam won his liquorice by demonstrating his prowess, but Salim still made him beg. At another level, the diss is another way in which the phat boys demonstrate their affinity with black American culture, something which they also have in common with the Somalis. Now, they are not very good at dissing. They hesitate, they have to think, their turn-taking sequences are anything but smooth. Almost all their disses are routinized, and already well known in their circles. Jamie makes one attempt at constructing an original, innovative diss, based on knowledge of Ontario driver's licence categories, but this falls

completely flat. While Hassan laughs, the others seem to feel that his laughter betrays total ignorance of the content of Jamie's diss, and they mock him for having laughed.

So, in 1994, what we have is a set of small groups, like the phat boys, or Sam's group, or, occasionally, loners who try to make connections in one direction or another. The phat boys situate themselves in the intersection between the dominant culture of the school and that of the Somalis; as we shall see below (section 4), Sam's group (consisting of Sam, Frantz, a Haitian boy, and Juan, a

boy of Colombian origin, both of whom also came to Champlain from Montreal) makes the same bridge through hip-hop. Sam is friends with Farah, who hangs out alternately with members of the dominant group, or with other marginals. Others try harder to penetrate the Somali group, especially girls who would like to, and sometimes succeed in, dating Somali boys. What began to emerge at that time was a culture of the margins, but a culture focused on making the bridge between school success and institutional legitimacy, and the popular culture of resistance. Practised initially in the small spaces groups like the phat boys could carve out for themselves, this culture began to take a greater and greater place in the life of the school.

3   A view from Africa

One spring day in 1993, Mark came to Champlain only to find a
large group of students, almost all of them Somalis, outside the
school, despite the fact that, according to the clock, they should
have been in class. Some of the students explained to Mark that
they were on strike ('*on fait la grève*'). The event that triggered
the strike, they said, was something that had happened in a game
played by the boys' soccer team. According to several accounts
(none of them eye-witness), the coach had kept one particular
player, a boy of African origin, on the bench, despite requests on
the part of some other players of African origin (or perhaps from
that player himself) to allow him to go on the field. The boys felt
that there was no clear reason for the coach to make that decision,
and that therefore the coach's gesture was a racist act. They called
for the coach's dismissal from the teaching staff, and mobilized
other students of African origin to join them in a strike. Hodan, a
Somali girl, said in an interview that all she knew was that she
was in class when some female students came in to say that the
Somali students were going on strike, and that the Somalis in the
class should join them. Hodan asked her teacher for permission to
leave class, and went to join the others, who told her what was
happening. Eventually, the principal came out to talk to the students, and they went back to class. The teacher was transferred to
another school, and a short while later the principal organized a
day-long workshop on anti-racist education.

Interestingly, many of the white students had no idea of what was
happening while their schoolmates were on strike. The mobilizing
agents targeted classes that contained large numbers of Somalis,
and left the others alone. The fact that this was even possible is
revealing of the social distance between the Somalis (and other
students of African origin) and the other students at Champlain.
We have already seen (Chapter 2) how the Somalis felt excluded
by the bilingual practices of the majority of Champlain students,
and by the monolingualizing, French-Canadian world view of the
school authorities. This feeling of exclusion quickly provided grounds
for conflict and tension, and was understood by the students of
African origin as a clear manifestation of racism. The soccer incident may simply have been the proverbial last straw, or it may
have served as a trigger for mobilization because it involved both

a confrontation with school authority and a significant number of students (unlike playground confrontations among students, or incidents involving one or two students and their teacher). In addition, it was in the context of a soccer game, which is a form of public display (unlike, say, a classroom or the corridors). In any case, it provoked the Somali students into their own public display of anger at their marginalization from school life.

Somewhat like the phat boys, although obviously on a much larger scale, the Somalis were unable to penetrate the closed social networks of Champlain. For them, of course, the problem was also aggravated by the much greater differences in language, culture and race. At the same time, these students were determined to make their way in the Canadian school system, since most of them had come to Canada in order to pursue their education. As Amran said:

(. . .) c'était comme euh on avait pas d'autres possibilités euh d'aller, parce que tu sais que dans notre pays il y a la guerre, qu'il y a, il fallait qu'on (prend?) quelque part pour nos études, parce que on était euh tout ce qui compte pour nous c'est les études, pis fallait vraiment qu'on continue nos études. Puis donc euh on est venu au Canada parce que c'est la seule chance qu'on avait.

(. . .) *it was like uh we had no other possibilities uh to go, because you know there is a war in our country, there is, we had to (take?) somewhere for our studies, because we were uh all that counts for us is studying, and we really had to continue our studies. And so uh we came to Canada, because it was the only chance we had.*

And Amran was far from the only one to point out to us that the main reason they were at Champlain, indeed in Canada at all, was that they had to have access to a good educational system, one that would allow them to prepare for post-secondary education and professional careers in areas like law, medicine and accounting. If they could have done this at home, or in Europe, or in the United States, they would have done so.

Also, as we saw in Chapter 4, despite the ambiguity of their feelings towards that language, these students also shared with the bilinguals and the phat boys an interest in acquiring French through schooling. However, unlike those groups, they had no reason to play along with the school's idea that French should be a first language for its students. For them, the job of the school was unequivocally to provide them with access to a language they would otherwise not master, and to do so in a way which would take into account, in a straightforward manner, the nature of their linguistic repertoire.

They therefore reacted negatively to what they felt was a narrow French-Canadian focus on the part of the school, and a narrow local bilingualism on the part of the students. The kind of school they had in mind would be more open to the world, less socially fragmented, and more focused on the kind of French they felt would be prestigious anywhere in the world. Here are some formulations of these concerns, from interviews with Monica, Laurette and Awad:

Example 6.8   Interviews with Somali students, 1992 and 1994

Monica:	au niveau des matières, est-ce que c'est à peu près les mêmes matières, le même contenu (que chez vous)?	*as far as the subjects go, are they about the same subjects, the same content (as at home?)*
Aïcha:	je crois pas, parce que nous on était le même comme la France, donc les mêmes études comme la France	*I don't think so, because we had the same as in France, so the same studies as France*
Monica:	c'est exactement le même programme?	*it's exactly the same programme?*
Aïcha:	que la France. Mais ici c'est un peu plus, c'est pas la même. Je veux dire que (xx) les cours français sont plus améliorés que les cours canadiens, ici c'est un peu faible, comme je le vois, de mon point de vue c'est un peu faible.	*as France. But here it is a little more, it isn't the same. I mean that (xx) the French courses are more improved than the Canadian courses, here it's a bit weak, the way I see it, in my opinion it's a bit weak*
Monica:	parce qu'il y a pas assez de contenu, parce qu'il y a pas assez d'examens?	*because there's not enough content, because there aren't enough exams?*
Aïcha:	il y a pas assez d'examens, oui. Nous on doit passer des examens quand on, et puis le travail on faisait des dictées, ici j'ai rien vu, il y a pas de dictées, il y a pas,	*there aren't enough exams, yes. We have to take exams when we, and then the work, we did* dictées, *here I've seen nothing, there are no*

il y avait des exposés écrits, oraux, on faisait tout ça, des lectures, ici on fait rien. (...) même en histoire, géo, tu vois, on faisait sur, dans tous les pays, comme la France, l'agriculture française, ici ils parlent que du Canada! Tu vois, si on n'est pas habitué, c'est pour ça que je vais échouer mon cours d'histoire, l'histoire du Canada, parce que je savais rien du Canada. Si ils me parlaient de la France, comme l'agriculture française, ou bien l'industrie, tout ça

dictées, there are no, we had written essays, oral ones, we did all that, readings, here we do nothing (...) even in History, Geography, you see, we did, on all countries, like France, French agriculture, here they only talk about Canada! You see, we aren't used to it that's why I'm going to fail my History class, History of Canada, because I knew nothing about Canada. If they talked to me about France, like French agriculture, or industry, all that

Monica:	ou bien de l'Afrique
Aïcha:	ou bien de l'Afrique, comme ça, oui, mais ils parlent que du Canada. Je ne comprenais rien.

or else about Africa
or else about Africa, like that, yes, but they only talk about Canada. I understood nothing.

–

–

Laurette:	okay, si euh vous aviez des choses que vous pouviez changer dans l'école, imagine un rêve (rires) qu'est-ce que tu changerais dans l'école?
Amran:	ah surtout les activités (...) comme une africaine qui vient d'un autre pays puis je trouve que lorsqu'ils font des activités dans cette école on dirait qu'ils font juste à leur goût, parce qu'eux ils ont le même goût, ils ont tu vois pas la vraie culture, mais ils ont comme le tu vois les mêmes

okay, if uh you had things you could change in the school, imagine a dream (laughter) what would you change in the school?
ah, mainly the activities (...) as an African who comes from another country, and I find that when they do activities in this school you'd say they just do what they enjoy, because they have the same taste, they don't you see have real culture, but they have like you see

idées, parce qu'ils sont, ils viennent tous du Canada, puis tu vois, j'aimerais bien que des fois ils demandent aussi à d'autres personnes qui viennent d'autres pays, qu'est-ce que vous aimez (...)

the same ideas, because they are, they all come from Canada and you see, I'd really like it if sometimes they also asked other people who come from other countries, what do you like? (...)

Laurette: est-ce que tu pourrais participer au conseil étudiant, non?

could you participate in the student council, no?

Amran: hum, oui, mais

um, yes, but

Nouria: ils vont pas te choisir

they won't choose you

—

—

Rahman: (...) et t'sais il y a une chose qui est p qui est pas bien, dans le système canadien par exemple

(...) and you know there is something which isn which isn't good in the Canadian system for example

Awad: lequel?

which?

Rahman: ce qui leur pose être ah amener la discrimination raciale, tu sais pourquoi?

which brings them to be uh racial discrimination, you know why?

Awad: pourquoi?

why?

Rahman: par exemple, nous en Afrique, ah c'est un exemple que en Afrique quand on étudie l'histoire, (ou?) la géographie internationale, on commence depuis l'âge de cinq ans, tu vois? et c'est déjà bien quand tu es déjà petit et que tu apprends des choses, ça te permet d'avoir l'esprit plus large, tu vois? et plus que tu continues. Pourtant le système canadien, c'est pas ça. C'est normal qu'ils discriminent, parce qu'ils ne connaissent rien de nous (...)

for example, we in Africa, ah it's an example that in Africa when we study history, (or?) international geography, we start from the age of five, you see? and it's already good when you are already small and you learn things, it allows you to broaden your mind, you see? and the more you continue. However, the Canadian system is not like that. It's normal that they should discriminate, because they know nothing about us (...)

These students talk about feeling excluded not only by English, but by the narrow Canadian focus of the curriculum, which they feel contributes to an atmosphere of general lack of understanding of (or interest in) anyone who is different. They are demotivated by this devaluing of their knowledge, a devaluing also manifested in their course placement. While they understand the problems posed by the fact that they arrived without school documents, they do not accord much legitimacy to the placement tests or other means of classification which, as far as they are concerned, do not test what they know. They are discouraged by lack of institutional support for the activities that interest them, such as basketball (several students mentioned that they were often evicted from the basketball court by school teams, and that their attempts to gain official support were thwarted by lack of a staff member willing to supervise them). They are convinced that they stand little chance of entering school power structures, and hence bringing about change that way. So they ended up feeling that the knowledge they brought to the school was knowledge the school should have valued and didn't; that the sad segregation of blacks and whites was a product of Canadian ignorance and narrow-mindedness; and that the result was predictable discouragement on the part of the African students. The problem was where to put these feelings.

The strike was probably the most dramatic attempt on the part of these students to protest their exclusion from school life. However, in many other ways the Somali students attempted to formulate their alternative vision of Champlain, and to express this vision on the public floor of the school. Their initial attempts focussed on using discursive spaces made available by the school, indeed by the Ontario school system, expressly for marginalized groups of black students or in the context of anti-racist and multicultural education policies. These attempts served to create a certain solidarity among at least some Somali students, and between Somalis and other black students (most of them of Haitian origin). They also served to bring the African perspective onto the public floor. Finally, it is likely that they paved the way for an integration of this perspective into the mainstream power structures of student life, as the Somalis and the 'multiculturals' joined forces to win the 1994 student council elections (see section 5, below).

There were three kinds of institutional spaces made available to these students. The first was the annual multicultural lunch, instituted at the beginning of the 1990s. The multicultural lunch was a type of event which had been gaining in popularity in Toronto's English-language schools throughout the 1980s, and can be traced fairly directly to local manifestations of Canadian federal initiatives to promote the notion of Canada as a bilingual, multicultural country. They became especially popular in Toronto because of the diversity of the student population in so many of its schools (although similar diversity in Montreal did not lead to the same practices, because of the vastly different ideology of integration into the francophone community prevalent in Quebec). Despite being in an autonomous French-language board, Champlain was never immune from influences from sister anglophone schools, in part because Ministry of Education policy rarely was made separately for French- and English-language schools, in part because those schools constituted direct rivals for student enrolment, and in part because there was one sitting not a hundred paces from Champlain's back door. The multicultural lunch proved to be immensely popular. It also became the special domain of a group of Somali girls, who worked hard with the supervising teacher to organize it, who attended in Somali dresses, who acted as servers at the buffet tables, and who provided vast quantities of Somali food, covering almost one-third of the available table space.

The second was an organization for students of African descent, created under the auspices of a youth worker, employed by the school board with funding from a province-wide programme aimed at helping school boards help black students stay in school. In the English-language school system, black students, most of them of Caribbean background (and perhaps first- or second-generation immigrants), were statistically highly over-represented in the lowest high school streams and among the ranks of drop-outs. The programme was developed primarily for this population, but was made available also to French-language schools, whose student population was beginning to include increasing numbers of black students, albeit from a different background and set of circumstances. The youth worker, among many other contributions, encouraged the students to form a group where they would be able to discuss matters of concern to them, and take action on them. One of the major concerns to emerge from this group was the importance of being able to express their point of view, their experiences, and their interests on the public stage. They wanted to be a part of school life.

What this group did was to take advantage of further existing dimensions of institutionalized opportunities. First, they exploited the occasion of Black History Month, an import to the Ontario school system from the United States, where it was initially developed to facilitate and highlight the integration into the History curriculum of the forgotten and ignored contributions of blacks to American society, as well as the history of the black community in its own right. In Ontario, as in the United States, February became the moment designated for the creation and execution of projects specifically designed to foreground black history, both global and local. In the autumn of 1992, the group of Champlain students of African descent (most of them Somalis, but also some of other origins) decided to aim at February 1993 as a moment for making a statement to the broader Champlain community.

The kind of statement they decided to make was modelled on existing formats of public discourse. As we have seen, the major form of public display at Champlain involved the use of the main stage for presentations to the assembled student body and staff, whether this was for student-council-led *réunions générales*, for invited artists, for the *Soirée cabaret*, or for the fashion show. The presentation of February 1993 in the end involved elements of most of these: a show of African traditional dress, presented in the same format as the fashion show; displays of African dance; readings of student poetry; and, most importantly, a skit. Later, several students involved in the development and presentation of the skit told Awad that they had a specific goal in mind, namely, to show the history of Africa, from the times before the European colonizers came until the present day. Moreover, they wanted especially to point out the destructive effects of colonization on African society.

They did this by showing a series of four brief skits. As Abdi put it: '*parce que les élèves ils ne savent rien du tout de l'Afrique, vous voyez, là il fallait les montrer*' (because the students know nothing about Africa, you see, so we had to show them). The first showed an African village council, and its deliberations concerning the rumoured arrival of whites in the area. The second showed the Europeanization of Africans through participation in the military. The third showed today's Africa, with its tensions between pre-colonial and European ways of doing things. The fourth showed an African family in the diaspora, equally wrenched between attachment to traditional values and those of the societies in which they now live. The central problems presented had to do with the nature and locus of authority and decision-making, both within a community and within a family. For example, in the last skit, a father attempts to control his children, who are learning in their new home to act too independently. He then tells his wife to bring him coffee. She throws down her broom and stalks out, saying that he can't order her around like that any more. She then returns, and cries, holding her head, '*Qu'est-ce qui se passe? Je suis en train de perdre mes valeurs!*' (What is happening? I'm losing my values!). There is no resolution offered, simply the expression of the profound tensions and ambiguities of African identity.

The skit prepared for 1994 returned to the theme of the diaspora, this time focusing on the problems of intercultural communication. Entitled *Diallo le Torontois*, the skit tells the story of a young man who dreams of going to Canada to study medicine. While he awaits news of his scholarship and visa applications, his father, whose wealth and interests are concentrated on his herds ('*Une bonne nouvelle? Tes chameaux ont eu des petits?*' – Good news? Your camels had foals?), arranges for him to marry his cousin, Leila. Diallo likes Leila well enough, but does not love her, although he knows that his best friend, Hussein, does. Without daring to challenge the authority of his father, Diallo goes off to study medicine in Toronto, with the understanding that he will marry Leila on his return.

Upon arrival in the midst of a Canadian winter, Diallo goes to the apartment of his cousin Osman, who has been in Canada for some time already, and has learned the peculiar variety of French spoken there. Here, he has his first intercultural encounter.

Example 6.9   Extract from the script of Diallo le Torontois, *1994*

1	*Osman:*	(en voyant Diallo)	*(sees Diallo) Diallo,*
2		Diallo, cousin, (les	*cousin (they exchange*
3		deux s'échangent les	*the customary*
4		salutations d'usage)	*greetings) But come in*
5		Mais entre voyons	
6		(Diallo entre)	*(Diallo enters)*

7	*Diallo:*	(grelotte de froid et	*(trembling with cold*
8		claque des dents) J'ai	*and with chattering*
9		pris un taxi, je suis	*teeth) I took a taxi, I*
10		arrivé plus tôt que	*got here a bit earlier*
11		prévu.	*than expected*
12	*Osman:*	Enlève ton coupe-vent.	*Take off your*
13			*windbreaker*
14	*Diallo:*	(en claquant des dents)	*(teeth chattering) I'd*
15		Je préfère le garder	*prefer to keep it on for*
16		encore un peu, merci,	*a bit, thanks, it's so cold*
17		ce qu'il fait froid ici!	*here! It's hell at the*
18		C'est l'enfer au pôle	*North Pole!*
19		nord!	
20	*Osman:*	T'en fais pas, tu t'y	*Don't worry, you'll get*
21		feras. Demain nous	*used to it. Tomorrow*
22		prendrons le choar et	*we'll take the* 'char' (car)
23		nous irons t'acheter une	*and we'll go buy you a*
24		canadienne, des mouffes	'canadienne' *(a heavy*
25		et des bottes.	*coat), mitts and boots*
26	*Diallo:*	(qui reprend du mieux)	*(pulling himself*
27		Un char? Une	*together) A* 'char'
28		canadienne? Te voilà	(tank)? *A* 'canadienne'
29		qui fais le commerce des	(Canadian woman)?
30		femmes pour l'armée	*You're trading women*
31		maintenant?	*for the army now?*
32	*Osman:*	Bien non, ici, l'auto	*No no, here, a car*
33		c'est un choar et une	*is a* 'choar' *and a*
34		canadienne c'est un	'canadienne' *is a coat.*
35		manteau.	
36	*Diallo:*	Si les canadiennes sont	*If* 'canadiennes' *are*
37		des manteaux, elles	*coats, they must be*
38		doivent être chaudes.	*warm*
39	*Osman:*	Bien non, pourtant ça	*No no, just the same it*
40		ne prend pas la tête à	*doesn't 'take a Papineau-*
41		Papineau . . .	*head' (a genius)*
42	*Diallo:*	Et de quoi a l'air une	*And what does a*
43		tête de Papineau?	*Papineau-head look like?*
44	*Osman:*	Laisse tomber, quand	*Never mind, when*
45		tu seras revenu de ton	*you've gotten over your*
46		choc culturel, tu	*culture shock, you'll*
47		comprendras.	*understand*

Two aspects of culture shock are highlighted here: the cold of
Canadian winters, and the strange French spoken in these lands.

The humour comes from the misunderstanding over the meaning of *char* (spelled *choar* in lines 14 and 21, in what appears to be an attempt to render the diphthongized vowel /aw/ typical of Canadian French and picked up on by the Canadianized Osman), Canadian French for 'car', European French for 'military tank', and of *canadienne* ('coat' versus 'Canadian woman'), as well as the opacity of the expression '*tête à Papineau*' (genius). But this culture shock is nothing compared to what is coming.

In the next scene, Diallo is sitting alone at a table in the university cafeteria. A girl sits down next to him, and strikes up a conversation.

Example 6.10   Extract from the script of Diallo le Torontois, *1994*

Isabelle:	Il y a quelqu'un ici?	*Is someone sitting here?*
Diallo:	Non, allez-y, asseyez-vous.	*No, go ahead, sit down.*
Isabelle:	T'es nouveau, je t'ai remarqué qui grelottait l'autre jour dans la bibliothèque.	*You're new, I saw you the other day shivering in the library.*
Diallo:	Oui, je viens d'arriver d'Afrique, d'Éthiopie.	*Yes, I just arrived from Africa, from Ethiopia.*
Isabelle:	Ah oui, je connais. C'est là où il y a la famine. Je l'ai vu à la télé. Mais tu me sembles en état de marche.	*Oh yes, I know about (Ethiopia). That's where there's a famine. I saw it on TV. But you seem in working order.*
Diallo:	Oui, je me porte bien. Mais en Éthiopie ce sont seulement ceux qui n'ont rien à manger qui meurent de faim. La famine sévit seulement au nord, à cause de la guerre civile. Mais nous sommes un peuple très fier. Je crois que c'est l'image que les médias nous donnent, comme celles que j'ai eu au sujet du Canada.	*Yes, I'm fine. But in Ethiopia only those who have nothing to eat die of hunger. The famine is only in the north, because of the civil war. But we are a very proud people. I think it's the image the media give us, like the ones I got about Canada.*
Isabelle:	Que veux-tu dire?	*What do you mean?*
Diallo:	Lorsque j'étais petit, je croyais que tous les Canadiens vivaient dans des igloos et qu'ils mangeaient du phoque et du poisson séché.	*When I was little, I thought that all Canadians lived in igloos and ate seal and dried fish.*

The point the students are trying to make is clearly aimed at their non-African fellow students (or why else would they ask the audience to suspend its knowledge of real-world Toronto in order to believe that the normal language of communication in public there is French?). They are trying to show how misunderstandings arise because of the stereotypes people have about each other, stereotypes fed by the media, and compounded by cultural and linguistic differences. They are also demonstrating that it is not only white Canadians who are allowed to judge Africans; Africans are on an equal footing, and can judge white Canadians. They can judge their odd French, their unfortunate propensity to believe everything they see on television (like little children), their readiness to jump to mistaken conclusions, and their lack of knowledge of the world.

The subsequent scenes provide a message of hope for cross-cultural understanding: Isabelle and Diallo (who has learned in the meantime to call a car a '*choar*') fall in love, and decide to marry, despite Diallo's promise to his father to marry his cousin Leïla. Diallo brings Isabelle back home, thus nicely reversing the power relations obtaining between African and Canadian, immigrant and host. The proposed ending (the script was never completed) provides an interesting resolution: The fathers of Diallo and Leïla accept the power of love, allowing Diallo to marry Isabelle, and Leïla to marry Hussein.

In the spaces provided by Black History Month and their youth group, the students formulated a response to their experience of exclusion at Champlain. The message they sent to the school was that the other students were wrong to exclude them and the school was wrong to undervalue them: wrong because their exclusionary and devaluing practices led to discouragement and anger among the students, putting their future in danger; wrong because those practices were based on a lack of understanding, or a misunderstanding of the African students; wrong because the knowledge the school and its population possessed was only different, not better, and maybe even less valuable, than that possessed by the African students; wrong because learning to understand the African students would allow Champlain to broaden its narrow horizons in ways that could only be beneficial to it.

At the same time, a few students began to make attempts to penetrate the official power structures, in order to have a more direct influence over the school, and despite the conviction of many that trying to do so would be a thankless and vain task. A few girls penetrated the structure of the fashion show and the *Soirée cabaret*, using beauty and talents for dance and song that could be universally appreciated. Their performances were built around musical forms from French mainstream pop culture which even the school authorities could approve of, or house music which could provide a common meeting ground in dance for students of all origins. They remained at the margins of these activities, but pointed out that afterwards other students did notice them, and talk to them, something that had not happened before. Two boys managed to win positions on the student council, one as councillor responsible for culture (a position which typically would go to a minority group member, since the portfolio was thought of as principally being about multiculturalism), and the other as councillor responsible for the environment (a mainstream, but marginal, position). While the first did not last long, the second, Saïd, had his sights set on acquiring experience which would be useful for the career in political science which he had in mind for himself. It would be Saïd, in the end, who would act as the catalysing link in bringing the interests of marginalized groups into the mainstream, where they had always wanted to be.

4 Music and consciousness

Music was a central terrain for the development of cultural identities at Champlain. We have already noted some of the ways in which affinities for music styles, in particular, hip-hop/rap, reggae, soul and rock, served as boundary markers for social networks, and some of the ways in which these affinities connected to, and indeed became symbols for, class or race distinctions. Notably, students in the bilingual mainstream could frequently classify their music tastes as 'normal', or 'just everything', so central were they to the definition of taste in the school. Other students more clearly identify with musical styles as a form of oppositional practice, and indeed, the very content of the music styles preferred lends itself to the expression of this stance.

When we first met them, Sam and Juan were hanging out together, sharing an interest in what was then marginal music. In the autumn of 1991, Frantz appeared on the scene, just arrived from

Montreal. In short order, he had joined up with Sam and Juan in a DJ/MJ operation, looking for gigs. Frantz had already learned how to rap, Sam knew how to DJ, and together they found a way to make a name for themselves: multicultural French rap. Here is (one version of) the rap that put them on the map:

Example 6.11   Frantz, with Juan and Hussein, performs for Awad Ibrahim, a member of the research team, in front of the school. Frantz establishes the rhythm, which Hussein and Juan attempt to keep by stomping or finger-snapping. Frantz raps. June 1994

on parle d'aujourd'hui, on parle de demain	*we talk about today, we talk about tomorrow*
c'est pour ça qu'on dit qu'il faut se donner les mains	*that's why we say we have to give each other our hands*
quand je parle comme ça c'est pour nous qu'il faut nous parler	*when I talk like that it's for us we need to talk to each other*
c'est pour ça que je suis en train de chanter	*that's why I'm singing*
je chante en partant en pensant de toi de toi à moi	*I sing from the beginning, thinking of you of you of me (for me)*
et tout est fait en chocolat	*and everything is made of chocolate*
je suis comme moi et tu es comme ça	*I am like me and you are like that*
et c'est pour ça qu'il faut pas être séparé	*and that's why we should not be separated*
toujours être ensemble	*always be together*

This rap, with its lyrics expressing precisely what school and community authorities were trying to project as a new public image, got them invited to a number of francophone community events. For example, they were invited to perform at the annual St-Jean-Baptiste Day celebrations in Toronto, at a community event on the day which began as the feast day of the patron saint of francophone Canada, and which has recently become a francophone 'national' holiday. In addition, through a member of our research team, they were given a French-language slot on a community radio station. Once a month, starting in 1993, they ran *Back to the Old School*, a programme in which most of the chat was in French, but most of the music English hip-hop/rap. They continued to develop their own original repertoire, in English (which Frantz says is best for hip-hop), but also continued to project their original image, using the fact of their different origins and collective wide linguistic repertoire. The collaboration was thus built on the common ground of English-medium hip-hop, projected through the multicultural French filter of their public image.

In addition to their outside gigs and radio show, Sam and Frantz (with Juan alongside) began to establish a higher profile inside the school as well. They advertised their show, and made efforts to bring their music into the school. Eventually, the school hired them on several occasions to DJ music for school dances, first for the younger students, and later for the older ones. Through this work, Sam and Frantz were in a significant position to influence taste.

But for Sam and Frantz, their music was not just about music. Frantz says:

> Maybe, just like I said, there's a lot of like people from this school, they don't really listen, they don't really listen to music from their countries, they like listen to popular music, like American music, you know, the most pop popular music, the popular music which I know which is make a lot of, a lot of people appreciate it, is uh like R&B and hip-hop, and that's what I think is the most popular now, in in um in our school, 'cause like a lot of people in our school like Boyz to Men, and this is the type kind of R&B, so and uh hip-hop mostly, like just hip-hop, like hip-hop can just, hip-hop you know 'cause like rap it's something you do, and hip-hop is something you live (. . .) hip-hop, hip-hop, exactly, hip-hop, knowledge, power, communication, understanding, that's, that's hip-hop.

And:

Example 6.12   Interview, Mark and Frantz, school library, January 1995

> *Frantz:*   Yeah, like also I have uh I have a couple of songs by myself, like like (begins to use rap rhythm) I walk around with a bigger one it's like let's say my my my let's say it's like I walk around with a bigger one, which which is knowledge
>
> *Mark:*   with a what?
>
> *Frantz:*   I walk around with a with a bigger one, a bigger one, let's say you're walking around with a Mac Ten, a gun, a knife, or whatever, I'm walking with a bigger one 'cause I have knowledge

Mark: so you're using then knowledge as a metaphor for
         power?
Frantz: yeah, that's, that's what I'm um, that's that's the kind of
         thing that you can use to make people appreciate you,
         people who know hip-hop

Frantz certainly saw it as socially and politically important to establish hip-hop in the school:

Example 6.13   Interview, Mark and Frantz, school library, January 1995

Mark: oh, I know, the other thing, the association between the
         school as hip-hop now, but the school before as rock
Frantz: the this school was more rock, the hip-hop was more,
         kind of like well uhhh you know, 'cause people didn't
         know about hip-hop, you know what I'm saying, it's
         like me and Sam, me and Sam brought it in the school
         and around the school, you know, because people would
         hear, hearing about hip-hop, hear about you know, and
         we try and make them know about it, hip-hop, that's
         why you know we did our thing outside, and Sam and
         and S Sam Sam's doing uh uhn the grade seven and
         eight DJ, dance I mean, you know that you know and
         it's mostly hip-hop
Mark: um, before the school was mostly rock, is rock
         associated with the White kids?
Frantz: of course, I don't see no Black people jumping for rock,
         I don't see no Black people jumping for rock, annn
         Metallica, maybe outside some somewhere else, but not
         in this school, in this school it's mostly uh it's mostly uh
         reggae or hip-hop
Mark: okay, where's the rock now in the school, is there rock
         in the school still?
Frantz: that's it   rock   yeah
         it's still in the school, of course, of course it's in the
         school, but now you have d d d you have more hip-hop
         for the last year   you know more people will
Mark: okay
Frantz: appreciate hip-hop and like hip-hop than last year, you
         know what I'm saying, like things changed   things
Mark: okay
Frantz: changed, you know, the school, the school, the school's
         getting higher and higher, and it's going to be a level
         which is the level that I want

Mark: which is what?
Frantz: hip-hop
Mark: okay, and what is, what do you mean by that?
Frantz: I mean the level that I want the school to have is is the level that the school never used to have, you know, hip-hop, that's it
Mark: okay, sooo, the black kids, the brown kids, the yellow kids, the white kids can
Frantz: whatever
Mark: they do freely
Frantz: hip-hop, I I I want them to appreciate hip-hop, about hip-hop, 'cause they can't understand hip-hop, you know they don't try to understand the words like that, blu blu blu, you know they making fun of it, yeah you know, it's like me making fun of Metallica, you know, whe whe when I did did Metallica in front of you, I don't go like blu blu blu ahhh, you know. Of course it's it gets noisy, of course it gets, and noise for me, you know, don't criticize my style, 'cause if you criticize my style, I'll criticize yours, an an and that can turn to a war, you know what I'm saying?
Mark: so there still is a division, there still is a division between the rockers and the hip-hoppers in the school?
Frantz: yeah

For the marginalized 'multiculturals' then, hip-hop was about challenging the hegemony of rock, and about bringing an ethos of inclusiveness into the school: 'knowledge, power, communication, understanding'. While Frantz seems unprepared to say anything definitive about the relationship between race and music tastes, he does go so far as to say that he doesn't see any 'Black people jumping for rock'. But perhaps more importantly, his hip-hop challenge is not about replacing a white hegemony with a black one (in any case, as Frantz well knows, it would be simplistic to make that equation), but rather about replacing a system which hegemonizes and marginalizes with one that is inclusive. This emerges more clearly in the following example. Sam and Farah are discussing a school dance with Mark; Farah (by now vice-president of the student council) is making the point that it is difficult to find common ground, since students will only participate when 'their' music is playing:

Example 6.14   Discussion, Mark, Farah and Sam, 1995

Farah: (. . .) but like when they were playing the hip-hop music and the some of the reggae, stuff like that, while that was going on, the people who like a lot of heavy metal were very discouraged too. Two little girls were sitting outside in the foyer, and they were saying to me, 'Farah, when are they gonna get this stuff off, it's scaring me, I want more Metallica', and they were saying 'ah, I haven't heard any Metallica for the whole dance'

Sam: that's the key to racism, is fear

Mark: okay

Sam: that's what I think, 'cause most people today, they would say they hate rap because it generally represents a black ah a black crowd which is violent, which is like so untrue, because not because of how much hip-hop I've heard, or like how I dress here, like 'cause the way I dress I don't represent nobody but myself. No, I don't tend to put hip-hop clothes, and I'm a hip-hop fanatic, like like I practically know everything about hip-hop. And people tend to generalize, like white trash, black music, bla bla bla. Well, like, you know me, if I enjoy some music, you know, I like it, that's why like people say 'rap is for black people', I totally disagree, because like I'm the type of guy, I have like so many, you see me go, I can talk to any single crowd here, because I show them respect in their music, and I tell them all, like I can talk to like a lot of heavy metallists, and I say 'ah, that's cool', like you know, but I don't like heavy metal, I wouldn't listen to it, but I don't disrespect it, that's the way it comes if you you disrespect somebody you will have a problem racially

For Sam, then, music is associated with race; it can be used destructively to highlight racial divisions and to create tension, or it can be used to cross boundaries, to increase understanding. Sam's take is different from Frantz' in that he does not invest himself in the notion of hip-hop as inherently inclusive, but he does consciously engage in practices which are designed to help him to cross boundaries and to ease interaction across them. Being a DJ is more than simply playing music for a dance; for Sam it is an exercise in social engineering.

Over the years, from 1991 to 1994, the hip-hop movement slowly built steam. By 1995, Jamie, the marginalized multicultural hip-hop and R&B enthusiast, had won a position on the student council as co-ordinator of school social activities. In an interview with a local television station, he was able to say: 'This is a hip-hop/rap school, but we like a mix of pretty much everything.' The vision of inclusiveness had come to dominate the public discourse of the school. In the next section we shall take a closer look at the political process which brought Jamie, Farah and other formerly marginalized 'multiculturals' to centre stage in the student council.

5   The Angels

In the spring of 1994, two students, Mireille and Kate, volunteered to organize the events celebrating the twenty-fifth anniversary of Champlain. They had no position on the student council, or any other official capacity, just the time and interest. The girls were close friends; Mireille was from a family originally from Quebec, Kate from an anglophone background. They belonged to the bilingual practices network, were relatively academically successful, and generally socially active. They successfully organized a *Soirée cabaret*, showcasing school talent, a garage sale, and other events. Their work was supported by the principal, who gave one of them the honour of unveiling the statue of Champlain at the crowning ceremonies of the anniversary celebrations.

A month later, elections were held for the following year's student council. The girls decided to buck convention, and rather than run individually they formed a list. This list consisted of Mireille and Kate as candidates for a co-presidency, and other 'bilinguals' in the other positions, except for the position of multiculturalism councillor, for which they recruited a girl of Indian origin who had long been friendly with many of the bilinguals. They gave themselves a name, TACK, which stood for *Tripper avec un conseil kapotant* (more or less, Have a blast with a krazy council) or, later, *Triompher avec un conseil kapotant* (Triumph with a krazy council). They organized a slick, almost professional campaign.

Other students had also decided to run for council, but as individuals. Among them were Farah, who said she realized it would have to be this year or never, and who was motivated by a combination of an excess of ideas for how to make the school a better place, and the thought that a student council position would probably look good on a university entrance application. Another candidate was Saïd, a Somali boy who had already served one year on the student council, as councillor for environmental issues. Once Saïd realized that Mireille and Kate were organizing a slate, he decided that it would be politically astute to do the same.

Saïd therefore approached Farah, who agreed to work with him. Together they put together a list of candidates which consisted exclusively of students who had been heretofore marginalized from the mainstream power structures. In addition to Saïd as candidate for president and Farah as candidate for vice-president, the slate included Jamie as candidate for social director (heavily supported by Sam and Frantz, who figured that Jamie would be in a position to throw a number of gigs their way if he were elected), a boy from Quebec whose mother was French and whose father was Indian, a francophone Québécois, and a boy from Belgium whose father was Belgian and whose mother was Thai. (Probably not coincidentally, Sam and Frantz devoted an evening of their *Back to the Old School* show to the election campaign, inviting students to call in; most of the calls were from supporters of Saïd's and Farah's list.)

This list also gave themselves a name, the *Anges* (Angels), which was meant to stand for *Animation par un nouveau groupe extraordinaire* (Organization/development by a new extraordinary group). The name positions the group as outsiders, and presents it as offering something new because the members themselves are new to the power structure.

Saïd also made an explicit attempt to position the slate as multicultural, and to enlist a broad base of support. Here is his account of how he prepared for the elections, given in an interview with Awad, a member of the research team, shortly after the elections (but before the results were announced).

Example 6.15   Interview, Saïd and Awad, June 1994

Awad:	ahm, cette année je pen j'ai remarqué que les élèves de race noire en particulier étaient étaient comme i étaient pas tellement organisés comme l'année	*um, this year I th I noticed that the black students in particular were were like they were not as organized as last year, the year before, that*

dernière, l'année d'avant, c'est-à-dire dans un sens ahm, est-ce qu'ils étaient vraiment organisés? *is in a way um, were they really organized?*

Saïd: organisés pour faire des activités? *organized for doing activities?*

Awad: organisés pour ah, c'est pour les élections c'est-à-dire est-ce qu'ils ont travaillé avec toi? *organized for ah, it's for the elections, that is did they work with you?*

Saïd: pour m'aider? *to help me?*

Awad: oui *yes*

Saïd: tout le monde m'ont aidé, tous les tous les groupes ethniques qui sont là m'ont aidé, il y a des Somaliens qui m'ont aidé, je suis allé, j'ai parlé avec chaque groupe ethnique *everyone helped me, all the all the ethnic groups that are there helped me, there are Somalis who helped me, I went, I spoke with each ethnic group*

Awad: ah okay *ah okay*

Saïd: j'ai pris une feuille, j'ai écrit tous ses besoins, et je l'ai j'ai ça, j'ai [cette feuille-là?] dans mon cahier, dans mon cahier que j'ai [pris?]   et c'est *I took a sheet (of paper), I wrote all its needs, and I have it, I have it, I have [that sheet?] in my notebook, in my notebook that I [took?]   and*

Awad: okay *okay*

Saïd: que je vais faire. J'ai tout le presque tous les groupes ethniques, je les ai parlé, et c'est ça que je vais faire, des activités pour tout *that's what I'll do. I have all the almost all the ethnic groups, I spoke them (sic), and that is what I'll do, activities for all*

Awad: euhm, euhm, oui, ça c'est très intéressant parce que dans un sens euhm *um, um, yes, that's very interesting because in a way um*

Saïd: il faut il faut pas dire seulement, que j'ai travaillé seulement avec les Somaliens, parce que ça c'est pas juste. Si je vais dans un truc multiculturel, je dois m'entretenir avec tous les élèves de cultures différentes *you can't you can't say only, that I only worked with the Somalis, because that's not exact. If I get involved in a multicultural thing, I have to deal with all the students of different cultures*

Awad:	ah okay	*ah okay*
	oui, mais est- ce que là,	*yes, but there, are you*
	est-ce que tu tu penses à	*you thinking of also*
	travailler avec les élèves de	*working with the white*
	race blanche aussi?	*students?*
Saïd:	pourquoi pas? Dans mon	*why not? In my in my*
	dans mon conseil il y a trois	*council there are three*
	blancs (il rit) et je trouve	*whites (he laughs) and I*
	pas, je ne sais pas pourquoi	*don't find, I don't know*
	pas je vais pas travailler ave,	*why I won't work wi,*
	pourquoi je je peux pas	*why I I can't work I will*
	travailler je vais travailler	*work*
Awad:	travailler aussi pour les	*also work for the white*
	élèves de race blanche aussi	*students also*
Saïd:	pour les élèves avec qui moi	*for the students with*
	(bruit)	*whom I (noise)*
Awad:	vas-y	*go ahead*
Saïd:	(bruit) mais moi (bruit) moi	*(noise) but I (noise) but I*
	c'est c'est je regarde pas	*it's it's I don't look*
	outside, je regarde	*outside, I look inside*
	inside (bruit)	*(noise)*
Awad:	vas-y	*go ahead*
Saïd:	encore comme je sais, moi je	*again like I know, me I*
	travaille avec tout le monde,	*work with everyone, and*
	et j'aimerais travailler avec	*I would like to work with*
	tout le monde si tout le	*everyone if everyone, that's*
	monde, c'est ça ce que je	*what I will, and what I'll*
	vais, et ce que je vais	*change is the separation*
	changer c'est la séparation	*of the white students and*
	des élèves blancs et noirs, je	*the black students, I'll*
	vais les recouper, je vais faire	*mix them, I'll do*
	tout, je vais faire des	*everything, I will create*
	activités qui regroupent les	*activities which bring the*
	deux groupes	*two groups together*
Awad:	ah oui, est-ce que t'as t'as	*oh yes, do you have you*
	des idées (xx)	*have ideas (xx)*
Saïd:	oui j'ai des élèves blancs	*yes, I have white students*
	qui veut qui	*who*
Awad:	aha	*aha*
Saïd:	me supportent pour cette	*want to who support me*
	idée-là, et veulent faire une	*for that idea, and who*
	différence dans notre école	*want to make a difference*
		in our school

Awad: ah oui?   *oh yes?*

Saïd: oui, et c'est ça que je vais commencer avec nos élèves
  yes, and that's what I will start with our students

Awad: euhm, qu'est-ce qu'il   *um, what do*

Saïd: c'est ça un de mes premiers   *that's one of my first*

Awad: qu'est-ce qu'ils ont comme   *what do they have like*

Saïd: comme dans les classes lorsqu'on rentre on (voit?) partie somalienne ici, partie blanche ici   je vais
  like in the classrooms when you enter you (see?) Somali part here, white part here   I will arrange I will

Awad: oui   *yes*

Saïd: arranger je vais commencer, même aujourd'hui, même si je suis pas le (président?), même si je ne suis pas, je vais former un groupe un conseil qui va faire ça, un conseil anti-racial
(...)
  start even today, even if I am not the (president?), even if I am not, I will form a group, a council who will do that, an anti-racial council
(...)

Awad: (...) les élèves de race blanche étaient avaient avaient déjà le c'est la dominance de l'école
  (...) the white students were had had already the it's the dominance of the school

Saïd: dans le conseil?   *in the council?*

Awad: par exemple   *for example*

Saïd: c'est ça que je vais changer, c'est pourquoi je suis rentré dans le conseil un des premiers, je veux que tout le monde participe, je veux que tout le monde soit dans le conseil, je veux que tout le monde soit égaux
(...)
  that's what I will change, that's why I joined the council, one of the first, I want everyone to participate, I want everyone to be on the council, I want everyone to be equals
(...)

Awad: est-ce que t'as t'as des raisons pourquoi par exemple euhm les groupes ethniques euhm travaillent avec toi ou vont voter pour toi?
  do you do you have reasons why for example um the ethnic groups um work for you or will vote for you?

Saïd: parce que mon conseil est multiculturel
  because my council is multicultural

Saïd's political vision is thus staunchly inclusive. He refuses to fall into the black–white polarization offered by Awad, and which he recognizes as operating in the school (he refers, for example, to the way the groups occupy different physical and social spaces in the school). Rather than attacking 'white domination' of the council by replacing whites with blacks (or in any case, non-whites), Saïd prefers to substitute a racialized vision of the school with an inclusive, non-racial one. He himself continues to use the discourse of difference (he talks about consulting each ethnic group, for example, and sees the members of his slate as representing different groups), but means this to be the beginning of a dialogue among groups, and the creation of a colour- and culture-blind form of social organization of school life.

The student council constitution called for each candidate to make a speech presenting himself or herself in front of the assembled student body just before the elections. Shortly before the day appointed for the speeches, Saïd discovered that TACK had decided to present a skit as well as their individual speeches, and decided that the *Anges* had better do the same. There was some dispute about this within the group, with some members arguing that TACK's collective strategy (including its proposed co-presidency) was unconstitutional. These objections were over-ruled by the presiding officer (a fellow student, working with a teacher), and the *Anges* decided to go ahead with a parallel strategy (if you can't beat 'em . . .).

The day of the elections assembly the students flooded into the auditorium. As usual, they sat in relatively segregated groups. TACK began with a lively skit: the members of the group entered the stage to rock music, hidden behind four large white panels they were carrying. They then came out and, moving to the rhythm of the music, spray-painted T-A-C-K on the panels (unfortunately, one of the aerosol cans didn't work, but the pair saddled with this problem carried on professionally as though they were able to paint). They flipped the panels around, revealing the group slogan: *94–95 Triompher avec un conseil kapotant! TACK.* Finally, the music stopped, they let the panels fall, and they shouted: '*Triompher avec un conseil kapotant!*' The effect, at least as far as we were concerned, was of a well-organized, professional team, who knew how to work together and how to produce something catchy and innovative.

The Angels' skit began with the group dressed in white, entering from the back of the auditorium, each carrying a candle or a lighter. They moved up to the stage, which was decorated with an angel made of styrofoam and other materials, and knelt down. A voice off-stage (Sam's) boomed: '*Que voulez-vous?*' (What do you want?). The Angels replied in chorus that they wanted to be elevated to the council. In that case, replied the voice, they would have to prove themselves. The Angels responded, '*Amen*', and left the stage.

Each candidate in turn then presented a speech, with Mireille and Kate, on the one hand, and Saïd and Farah, on the other, presenting theirs together. Most of the speeches concentrated on the qualifications of the individual (or, in the case of Mireille and Kate, of the pair) for the position in question. However, the Angels' candidate for sports director included a question of inclusiveness, arguing that one of his priorities would be the extension of sports activities for girls: '*Il doit y avoir plus de participants et surtout de participantes, oui, parce qu'il n'y a pas assez de filles!*' (There should be more participants and especially more female participants, yes, because there aren't enough girls!). More importantly, Saïd and Farah characterized their slate of candidates explicitly as multicultural, and proposed integrating multicultural activities more broadly into school life, going beyond the annual multicultural lunch to establish a national theme for each month, or an international day each month.

In contrast, multiculturalism was confined in the TACK slate to the speech of the candidate for multicultural affairs, who, significantly, ran unopposed by the Angels, who had integrated multiculturalism into the heart of their platform (and who may have been concerned that it would have been unseemly to seek conflict over this issue in such a direct way as running a candidate against that of TACK). The TACK candidate's speech was not unlike Saïd's and Farah's, insofar as she focused on the need for more multicultural activities. In addition, while she could not appeal to her own list diversity, she did make reference to the school's motto, *L'Unité dans la diversité*.

There was a great deal of audience reaction to the speeches. Supporters of each group cheered their candidates, and it was clear that the room was divided into camps which were at least in part defined by race. Supporters of the *Anges* also booed some

TACK candidates, and some mentions of the incumbent council, despite efforts on the part of the presiding officer to quell them.

After the students had voted, they were to meet in their classrooms. Sidiqa, a young Somali girl, came running into her classroom shouting 'Help me! Help me!'. She said she was being pursued by older Somali boys who were angry with her because she hadn't voted for the *Anges*. An Ethiopian classmate commented that some people thought Sidiqa should have voted for the *Anges* 'because they're black, and she's black, but that's racism!'. Later, Sidiqa and other members of her group, all Somali girls, had lunch in the cafeteria, where several people came by to ask who had voted for whom. One of Sidiqa's friends said that she told people what they wanted to hear, since passions were running so high over this election. Most of the group said that they had in fact not voted by list, and resented the pressure to do so placed on them by other students. They particularly were appalled by the booing of Mireille and Kate, which came from the same people who were pressuring them to vote for the *Anges*. Nonetheless, a number of minority students expressed the view that they felt that the *Anges* represented them, and that, for the first time, there would be someone on the student council to whom they could talk. For example, Abdi, a Somali student, said this after the results were announced:

moi d'abord j'étais pour les Anges parce que c'est un groupe multiculturel, qui représente presque toute l'Europe, qu'est-ce qu'on dit Somaliens, Chinois, je ne sais pas Bangladesh ou Arabes, ils étaient tous là, c'est un groupe très très hétérogène. En plus, il y avait des élèves de différents niveaux, de 10e, de 11e, de 12e, et jusqu'à CPO, donc ils représentaient très bien notre école, et particulièrement notre groupe, les Somaliens, donc j'étais très content que qu'ils gagnent, parce que j'ai eu quelqu'un enfin quelqu'un à qui m'adresser. Moi, les anciens, conseil des élèves je ne	*me, first, I was for the Anges because it's a multicultural group, which represents almost all Europe, what do we say, Somalis, I don't know, Bangladesh or Arabs, they were all there, it's a very very heterogeneous group. In addition, there were students from different levels, 10th grade, and 11th, and 12th, up to OAC, so they represented our school very well, and in particular our group, the Somalis, so I was very happy that they won, because I finally got someone finally someone I could speak to. Me, the former students, student council, I*

les connaissais pas, maintenant   *didn't know them, now happily*
heureusement je connais   *I know someone I can speak to*
quelqu'un à qui m'adresser et   *and tell my problems to*
dire mes problèmes

(Nonetheless, when Awad reported this to Saïd, Saïd's reaction was to say that this was good, but of course, Saïd felt himself to be approachable by members of any of the school's ethnic groups, 'qui sont minoritaires, qui sont majoritaires' (*who are minorities, who are majorities*).)

And so the *Anges* won, quite handily, with the exception of course of TACK's unopposed multiculturalism councillor candidate, who, apparently without any problems on either side, joined the new *Anges*-dominated student council (which as a result counted, in the end, four members of at least partial Indian origin, thereby vastly over-representing their group's share of Champlain's population). In addition, a few weeks after the election, Mireille was outside helping the new student council distribute hot dogs at its first school-wide social event, so someone had done some important work on healing the breaches.

Nonetheless, there remained widespread concern that the election had been hijacked on either side by specific political interests, and that it had had the effect of polarizing the student body. Despite recognition of the value of the *Anges*' platform of inclusiveness, and of that of the experience and commitment of TACK, some felt that marginalized students had reacted too strongly against TACK, or that TACK paid a price for having been too closely involved with the school administration. Clearly, the elections had brought to the fore some central questions about the school: Whom is the school for? Who gets to make decisions about the school, about its image, and about who belongs?

6 A hip-hop school

By the summer of 1994, the ethic of bilingualism had been replaced by the ethic of inclusiveness in the public space of Champlain. There are a number of reasons, beyond the vagaries of personality conflicts and local political concerns, that might help explain how this came to pass.

First, we must account for the frustration of students who had long been marginalized, but who felt strongly that they had something to contribute to the school, and the right to a place there. The discourse of anti-racist education, and the politics of inclusiveness, provided students with a vocabulary for expressing their frustrations and their hopes, and a means to finding their place in the school. Their success seems to us to be due in part to the fact that they were able to avoid reproducing the structures of exclusion against which they fought; they did not argue that they should replace the incumbent power brokers, but rather that power should be more equitably shared.

Second, it is important to understand the cultural basis of inclusiveness. In a school where music provides the major trope of identification, hip-hop provided ideological meeting grounds. Its own ethic, at least as practiced by Champlain students, precludes conflicts. The idea is precisely to find through music a way of living that tolerates difference, your own and others'. Sometimes this means listening to music you can't stand, but for most of these students that is a small price to pay.

At the same time, the fundamental differences acknowledged in the ethic of inclusiveness, gives way to the commonality of shared musical tastes, and a shared appreciation of the value of multilingualism, and especially of a command of French and English. Here, those who subscribed to the formerly dominant bilingual ethic can also find themselves. In addition, their interest in finding a path to the global village is clearly compatible with the *Anges'* vision of inclusiveness. How better to learn how to live globally than in one's own school? At the same time, the Phat Boys themselves are conscious of the ways in which their explicit assault on exclusiveness could have dangerously backfired. In the following retrospective account, Jamie points out that a challenge made in the name of inclusiveness runs the risk of paradoxically contributing to polarization.

Example 6.16   Discussion in a restaurant, Mark, Bill, Chris and Jamie, January 1995

> *Mark:* okay, when you guys ran for election, one of the things on your platform was, you spent a great deal of time talking about multiculturalism and   presenting
> *Jamie:*   yeah
> *Mark:* yourself as the only truly multicultural

Jamie: I don't think we
should have done that
Mark: party, please, your comments
Jamie: ah, well, I didn't like the way, ah, I thought the last
election last year, see a lot of people were saying, well,
it's the best elections we've had in years and years, right,
because like they actually went up there and they really
tried, they wanted to be on it, but I think it created a lot
of hostility between the two groups, and it brought up a
little bit of like racial ugliness that shouldn't have been
brought up, I think
Mark: between what two groups?
Jamie: I think between uh white groups that felt that ah felt
threatened, and coloured groups that were pretty much
ignorant if you ask me, like for instance, we had
Mark: okay
Jamie: this girl call up at Sam's, we did a show one time, and
(she) said, oh, well, you know, like my group is Angels,
they're the only group with any coloured people on it,
right, and Sam said, 'What the hell are you talking
about? Who even cares what colour you are?', you know,
it's true, it doesn't, like it doesn't, it shouldn't matter at
all what colour you are, as long as you represent, it's a
stu, first of all, you're a student body, I don't think our
student body should be divided already into racial, like
you know, racial divisions for, what the hell am I talking
about? (laughs)
Mark: please go on
Jamie: but it really shouldn't be, um, like divided already, and
the thing is, I think some people don't think about things
properly, like that stupid girl that called up, like that
was, that was, it's dumb to make divisions like that
already

At the same time, Saïd had this to say as a retrospective account:

Example 6.17   Interview, Saïd and Awad, June 1994

(. . .) il y a un grand écart là par rapport à 90 parce que les profs se sont améliorés, les élèves sont plus sociables, les blancs et les noirs les Indiens et tout ça, parce que c'est une	*(. . .) there is a big difference with respect to 90 because the teachers have improved, the students are more sociable, the whites the blacks the Indians and all that, because it is a*

diversité culturelle c'est c'est	*cultural diversity it's it's like a*
comme une sorte de mosaïque	*kind of mosaic that exists at*
là qui existe à l'école, et je	*the school, and I think now*
pense que maintenant il y a une	*there is a big change for the*
grande amélioration à l'école	*better at the school*

Obviously, it would be easy to make too much of the *Anges'* victory, and we must be careful about making claims about their impact on the ideology of *francitude* at Champlain. Nonetheless, by 1995, many of the Somali students talked about the days of the major problems of segregation and racist discrimination at the school as a thing of the past, saying yes, things had been difficult, and they still weren't perfect, but they were much, much better now. Members of the bilingual group started to open up their friendship networks, and the occasional mixed-race couple could be seen holding hands in the corridor (well, maybe not just holding hands . . .), although the general tendency towards segregation remained, and the progress made was fragile.

Perhaps what this story reveals best are the fundamental ideological fault lines within the school's ideology, and some of the processes whereby the school might avoid a major earthquake. In the next, and last, chapter, we shall consider in greater detail what some of these processes and their consequences might be, not just for Champlain, but for the Franco-Ontarian community, and indeed for linguistic minorities elsewhere in the global city.

PART III

7 The distribution of linguistic capital

1 L'École Champlain and the politics of identity

In an opinion piece published in *La Presse* (a major Montreal French-language daily newspaper), Gérard Bouchard, a professor at the Université du Québec à Chicoutimi, reflected on the nature and consequences of the transformation of the idea of the nation in French Canada over the last several decades:

> *Depuis un demi-siècle environ, la francophonie québécoise a effectué un gros travail de transformation sur elle-même en redéfinissant substantiellement ses références principales. Par exemple, la nation, jusque-là exclusive, s'est délestée de plusieurs attributs particularistes, comme la religion, la référence ancestrale, les traditions coutumières. On dit couramment qu'elle est passée d'un modèle ethnique à un modèle civique. (. . .) cette nation civique (. . .) devrait être considérée comme un point de départ. En effet, la situation civique qu'elle crée (au Québec comme ailleurs) soulève plusieurs questions de fond (. . .) et comporte quelques urgences.*
>
> (*La Presse*, 25 November 1997, p. B3)

(For about the last half-century, the francophone community of Quebec has engaged in a major transformation of itself through a fundamental redefinition of its main points of reference. For example, the nation, up until that time exclusionary, left behind its particularistic attributes, like religion, the reference to ancestry, customary traditions. It is frequently said that it has passed from an ethnic to a civic model. (. . .) this civic nation (. . .) should be considered a point of departure. In effect, the civic situation it creates (in Quebec as elsewhere) raises many basic questions (. . .) and some pressing ones.)

While Bouchard is concerned with Quebec and its counterpart proto-nation-states, we have seen here that the same processes and logic apply to linguistic minorities without aspirations to traditional statehood. In his text, having established the importance of the civic model (that is, one based on citizenship rather than on blood), Bouchard goes on to discuss the urgency of reinventing the nation, and the necessity of finding a way for French to prevail over English as the common language of all civic constituents. Without necessarily intending to, he points out the fundamental problem of inventing a civic nation; while he argues that it is possible, even essential, to invent a nation 'without the fiction', the very process of inventing a nation is centrally a process of creating fictions, insofar as any national ideology is socially constructed. This is not to say that fictions are not real; clearly, they are, in that the stories we tell ourselves serve as our ways of understanding our world, and orient our actions. What is at issue, then, is not whether the nation is fictive or real, but whether the nation we invent is credible and legitimate in the eyes of those affected by it. In the particular case which concerns us, if we are to accept that the heretofore minority language (we happen to be talking about French in Canada, but the same could be applied to Catalan, or Welsh, say) should act as a common language of civic participation, and no longer as an ethnic emblem, then there has to be some compelling reason to do so. For a nation founded on shared language, this reason, as Bouchard points out, has to be more than pragmatic, it has to be linked in some way to a legitimate political ideology. But so far, the only legitimizing political ideology we have encountered is precisely the old ethnic nationalism which the emerging nation wishes to disavow. At best, we have the glimmerings of some new pluralistic pragmatism.

How did we come to this? The fading power of the nation seems to have opened, after the Second World War, a gap permitting the development of resistance to the domination of the majority. But the same conditions which allowed for linguistic minorities to mobilize to attain the right to self-determination, that is, to set up their own nation-states, undermine the very logic of ethnic state nationalism. In the meantime, there have nonetheless been some very real gains. People who formerly were marginalized now wield power in regionalized domains of political and economic activity, and position themselves to take advantage of the need for multilinguals in the global economy. The problem, then, is to how to preserve these gains while accomplishing a shift to a new basis of legitimacy of that position of power.

As is the case for all linguistic minority institutions of its era, l'École Champlain is a creature of the politics of identity as they developed in the 1960s. Its existence is a testimony to the power of the argument that French Canadians have some right to self-determination (although the extent of that right is still the subject of heated debate). But its existence is also a testimony to the concern of the Canadian federal government to establish itself as the legitimate representative of all Canadians; failure to do so would mean the collapse of the federal structure itself. Significantly, the federal government chose to rise to Quebec's ethnic nationalist challenge not by attempting to redefine the nature of nationalism, but by accepting the terms of the argument as set by Quebec. Canada was forced to reinvent itself as a nation (with a culture, if not one single language), and ever since we have been treated to a search for national identity. In the meantime, as Bouchard points out, Quebec (and the rest of French Canada) has come up against the contradictions of an ethnic polity which is also committed to democracy and equity, augmented by the very real problems of reproduction faced by a group whose birth rate is below the minimum needed to maintain its numbers. The mobilization of linguistic minorities was made possible by a weakening of nation-state hegemony in the face of economic transformations; the success of linguistic minorities has also contributed to changing the conditions of their existence, namely, to rendering pluralism respectable, and to strengthening forms of social organization which by-pass the state. But their success entails an investment in the politics of identity.

Schools like Champlain are meant therefore to contribute both to emancipation and to social and cultural reproduction, even though the conditions of their existence make this mission more than problematic. The ways in which Champlain has confronted the problems inherent in its framework shed some light on the problems faced by linguistic minorities, linguistic minority education and pluralist polities in the hyper-modern world in general. What Champlain shows us is a vision of pluralist pragmatism, in which language becomes capital and not emblem, and in which the school, as a social institution, plays a key role in producing and distributing that newly valued capital. The old politics of identity at the root of Champlain fade away; what emerges instead is an economics of language, which can be used pragmatically by individuals to position themselves advantageously in an international world. This is not a new political ideology, but it shows us the direction in which things may be moving.

The school itself is clearly situated in the transition from the politics of identity to an economics of language. Its own legitimacy is based on contradictory things: it needs to be authentically French (which implies some processes of inclusion and exclusion) and both democratic and meritocratic. These contradictions, which flow from the historical conditions of the politics of identity out of which Champlain emerged and from the ways in which that politics both changed the world and has been shaped by a changing world, are played out on the terrain of language, in the form of contradictions between monolingualism and bilingualism and between the economic value of the standard as opposed to the authenticating value of the vernacular.

They are felt in a particularly acute way in schools because of shifts in the ways in which linguistic resources are produced and distributed in Canada. In the past, French was produced and reproduced in relatively homogeneous, monolingual communities; while schools were important, so were home and Church. Those community-based processes have crumbled, as part of the very process which has led to the rise in the value attributed to (at least one form) of the linguistic resources produced there. In community after community in Ontario, the numbers of people speaking French at home drop (as measured by the census), while the numbers enrolled in French-language minority schools rise. The school is replacing the home and the community as the privileged site for the production and distribution of the linguistic resource that is French. As a result, the criteria of, and means for getting access to, French have changed; it is no longer necessary to be born into a French-speaking family, or to live in a French-speaking neighbourhood. It is only necessary for you or one of your parents to possess the right kind of linguistic capital, however that might be acquired; and even that criterion is not always rigidly adhered to.

In the centre of all these contradictions, the school has to function. The school's strategies for dealing with what might otherwise be crippling contradictions entail actively working to incorporate a civic, pluralist vision of the French-Canadian nation, while maintaining an investment in the politics of identity which legitimizes its existence. By juxtaposition they construct a public face, a front stage, which is both authentically French Canadian and pluralist: it is Champlain surrounded by the banners of different places of origin around the world; it is the maple leaf mosaic with the flag of French Ontario in its centre, surrounded by the flags of eight different countries; it is the multicultural lunch with *tourtière* and couscous. On this stage, one part of Bouchard's vision is realized: French is the common language of a variety of groups, who come together with the common cause of getting ahead by acquiring what the school uniquely offers: an education in French. The contradiction between ethnic authenticity and pluralism is resolved only through juxtaposition; the substantive nature of the consequences of pluralism for authenticity, or of authenticity for pluralism, are not confronted. Nonetheless, it is clear why pluralism is necessary to the school's image: it is consistent with the aims of mobilization, namely, the construction of access for francophones to the wider world and its resources; it is consistent with the democratic and meritocratic ideology of the school; and it is proof in itself of the power of attraction of the francophone community, and hence of its ability to reproduce itself, albeit in some kind of new guise.

More difficult contradictions are dealt with by discursively placing them off-stage. The discursive options open to school staff are mainly available through the discursive organization of social relations in schools; the social organization of school communication has its origins in ideologies of learning and schooling, but becomes available as a way to manage the particular sociolinguistic concerns of minority education. In this case, the concerns have to do with the problems of creating a monolingual space in a bilingual world, and with valuing 'standard' French without losing the authenticating value of the vernacular.

If French is attractive to people, it is as part of a bilingual repertoire which includes English; yet, the logic of the politics of identity excludes English from the discursive space of the school. The real presence of English must therefore be managed. The management is double: on the one hand, the presence of English is acknowledged but constructed as a threat, and as proof of the necessity of being vigilant about protecting the monolingual space of the school; on the other hand, English is relegated to off-stage zones, in student-controlled spaces and in whispered asides, or in codeswitches which set off English from French through discursive devices which relieve the speaker from responsibility for having spoken English. Similarly, the school needs to recognize the authenticating value of Canadian French, but must cope with the fact that this linguistic variety is not valuable in the international market to which the school's clientele wants access. The school's strategy here is to adopt a universalizing discourse focused on language quality, which mystifies the class origins of the variety the school prefers by labelling it 'better French'; that is, the preferred variety is held up as preferable by virtue of its quality, and should therefore serve as a model for everyone. The fact that it is the élite who define what counts as 'quality' is hidden. The second dimension of the school's strategy is to neutralize the tension between the prestige of the standard and the authenticating value of the vernacular by accepting into the standard a few unthreatening characteristics of the local vernacular, thereby symbolically appropriating its authenticity.

The result of these strategies is to protect the market in which school staff have invested; if the school cannot cope with the contradictions it faces, the people who work there lose the meaning they attach to their jobs, and perhaps even the jobs themselves. As Bourdieu (1977: 651–2) argues:

> Those who seek to defend a threatened capital, be it Latin or any other component of traditional humanistic culture, are forced to conduct a total struggle (like religious traditionalists, in another field) because they cannot save the competence without saving the market, i.e. all the social conditions of the production and reproduction of producers and consumers. The conservatives carry on as if the language were worth something independently of its market, as if it possessed intrinsic virtues (mental gymnastics, logical training, etc.); but, in practice, they defend the market, i.e. control over the instruments of reproduction and competence, over the market. (. . .) The educational system is a crucial object of struggle because it has a monopoly over the production of the mass of producers and consumers, and hence over the reproduction of the market on which the value of linguistic competence depends, in other words its capacity to function as linguistic capital.

Neutralizing contradictions, therefore, also allows the school to produce and distribute the linguistic capital which has become valuable to certain kinds of people, people who are poised to take advantage of what the politics of identity has achieved, although not all have reason to engage in such a politics themselves. Inadvertently, the school acts to serve the interests of those who come by French the new way, through institutions like schools, as opposed to those who come by French the old way, through participation in an ethnically defined social group. It actively embraces the new, pluralist and globalizing image of the francophone world, emphasizing the value of French in international business and trade, and its value of distinction in the increasingly bitter competition for access to higher education. But it is not quite sure what to do with the problem of identity; to abandon it is to risk losing both legitimacy and a privileged position, to adhere to it too strongly is to return to what increasingly appears to be a discriminatory and narrow outlook.

2   Bilingualism, language norms and social selection

Recently, I was sitting in a kitchen in Berlin, listening to a radio station in Potsdam give us its take on the morning world. I was struck by a song which vaunted (albeit sarcastically) the advantages of being young, free and bilingual in the new Europe. The song turned out to be *Single*, by a British group called The Pet Shop Boys (Cage Music Ltd, 1996).

> They call this a community
> I like to think of it as home
> Arriving at the airport I am going it alone
> Ordering a boarding pass
> Travelling in business class
> This is the name of the game
> I'm single bilingual
> Single bilingual
> I come to the community from U.K. p.l.c.
> Arriving at my hotel there are faxes greeting me
> Staying in a junior suite so there's room to meet and greet and
>   after work explain how I feel
> 'Perdoneme me llamo Neil' (sic)
> I'm single bilingual
> Single bilingual

In Brussels Bonn or Barcelona I'm in demand and quite at home
  there
'Adelante!' Through the door
'Un momento por favor'
This is what I get paid for
'Muchas gracias senor'
I'm a player in the continental game with unlimited expenses to
  reclaim
Information's easy
tapping at my PC
That is the frame of the game
I'm single bilingual
Single bilingual
I'm single bilingual
Single bilingual
'Hay una discoteca por acqui?' (sic)

The message of this song seems clearly to be that the new élite is made up of unattached young people who make a living flying all over Europe, attending meetings one day in Barcelona and the next in Brussels. Their position is due in no small measure to their mastery of more than one language.

This song struck me for two reasons. First, it is the first time in my experience of listening to morning radio that I can remember a popular song focused explicitly on multilingual repertoires; certainly multilingualism has made its way into popular culture before (notably in the new varieties of world music), but mainly in the form of multilingual practices produced by marginalized groups aiming at fragmenting the unity of the dominant group. But it was less clear to me before I heard this song that popular culture of the mainstream, morning-music variety had appropriated this notion and made it its own, that is, that multilingualism was becoming a marker of élite status in the new economic order, and was no longer only a strategy of resistance on the part of marginalized groups. Second, the message of the song touched something that I was beginning to understand about the Lucs and Sandras, the Farahs and Saïds of Champlain: language is becoming a commodity.

Many of the students at Champlain have little access to French outside school, although many do have one French-speaking parent, and some even come from homes where French is spoken on a regular basis, perhaps exclusively. For most of them, however, French is not about identity, or even about a politics of identity;

French is about the accumulation of the symbolic capital that will allow them to enjoy the fruits of what the French-Canadian politics of identity has won. These are not students who long nostalgically for close-knit communities and large families; like the protagonist of *Single,* they long for exciting careers and the world at their feet. This is not an unreasonable desire; it is what their parents and grandparents wish for them, too. Certainly, the politics of identity has made them sensitive to exclusionary practices, practices they have no wish to be victims of, and so will not condone. They have learned from the politics of identity that it is important to fight discrimination not on the grounds of collective rights, but on other grounds altogether. They prefer to alter the discourse, to move it to something pluralist which might be a way-station towards a situation in which they will no longer care about ethnicity, or race, or any other social category which might be used as a basis for social stratification. But they have no desire to alter the fundamental nature of the market they are engaged in; they are not trying to move into or build an alternative market (Woolard 1985; Bourdieu 1972), they are trying to get equal access to the dominant one.

This also helps to explain why language remains a potent tool for them. It is not inherently exclusionary, insofar as it can be learned, and many of the students at Champlain know this from profound personal experience. At the same time, it opens doors; speaking French allows students to reposition themselves within the dominant market, to bring to that market linguistic resources that have value there, and that therefore increase their chances of achieving their goals.

Because language appears democratic, it is difficult to see how it can act as a mechanism of social selection (hence, as Bourdieu would note, it has great force as just such a mechanism). However, we have seen here some ways in which it does just that. The most evident mechanisms of social selection have to do with the ideology of what being bilingual means. Setting up bilingualism as two parallel monolingualisms, in which each variety must conform to certain prescriptive norms, places some students at an advantage over others in terms of their ease of access to learning to be bilingual that way, and in terms of the relative cost and benefits to them.

The kind of bilingualism the school promotes makes sense to students who expect to place themselves as some kind of bilingual brokers, exploiting their linguistic capital to good effect in domains which require constructing relations with both monolingual francophones and monolingual anglophones, indeed, whose livelihood may depend on being able to forge a link between these two monolingual groups. Students who are freest to appropriate the school's linguistic resources for themselves are, in general, those for whom family practices and school practices coincide, or those for whom the school is in fact the major source of that resource in their lives. This is particularly true for the male members of those groups, who profit from gender ideologies and a gendered division of material and symbolic labour which give them freer access to learning and using linguistic resources outside their original repertoire. In some respects, not speaking French outside school may even be an advantage for some students; they can appropriate the school's capital without having to worry about what it means in relation to any other kind of sociolinguistic experience they may have. Their concerns about authenticity are in part alleviated simply by virtue of getting a diploma from an authentically Franco-Ontarian school like Champlain. They are also alleviated by the increased heterogeneity of that community's image of itself. There is much to be gained by working on downplaying authenticity in favour of internationalism, hybridity and diversity.

Students who bring to the school a different set of experiences are left to position themselves with respect to the prevailing practices and norms. All the native speakers of Canadian French, whether of the monolingual or the bilingual varieties, find things difficult. The major obstacle they encounter is the force of the school's linguistic norms. This is compounded for the monolinguals by the prevailing peer practice of semi-diglossia (the separation of domains of use of French and English) within the school milieu, which they find exclusionary, as well as antagonistic to their attempts (consistent with the school's political agenda) to find a monolingual arena in the school. For the bilinguals, obstacles are heightened by the rejection by both peers and school of the specific codeswitched forms that their bilingual practices take.

As is so often the case with marginalized groups, the particular practices in which these students have invested are replete with social significance for them. That significance is mainly one of group solidarity and ethnic identity. To abandon their own practices for those of the others or of the school is to betray not only values, but also people who are important in their lives, whether family or friends. Again, males and females are differentially positioned even within this group, as males have more avenues of flight or resistance open to them than do the females. Nonetheless, as has so often been noted with respect to marginalized groups, these students tend one way or another to collaborate in their own marginalization. Champlain never has to take up the challenge of including these students, since they tend to leave, always for reasons that make sense on an individual level and so do not challenge the school as an institution.

The kind of vision of what it means to speak French (and to be francophone) that the school has invested in, with the active collaboration of one set of students and the passive collaboration of another, constitutes, then, a process of social selection. This process reinforces the internationalization and diversification of sources of francophones, promotes the socioeconomic advancement of one set of francophones, but marginalizes another set and narrows and normativizes the definition of what it means to speak French. Champlain shows us the emergence of a new international *francophonie* and, within it, the rise of a new bilingual élite from the fertile grounds of minority education.

3   Discourse at school and other sites

This book has focused on the transformation of linguistic minorities, and the rise of a new bilingual élite, from the vantage point of an educational institution. Clearly, schools play an important role in this process; what we have seen at Champlain shows us how privileged schools can be as sources of the production and distribution of linguistic capital, and the critically important role they play in social selection. What schools do not show us, however (*pace* Bourdieu), is what the sources are of the definition of the value of linguistic capital, and how those sources articulate with the institutional processes of schooling.

This is, then, a methodological as well as a theoretical problem, namely, how to link up the kinds of things we have seen at Champlain with the reasons why Champlain representatives act the way they do and believe the things they believe. I have been able to invoke some broad influences, through the history of minority language education in Canada and of the political mobilization of its francophones, as well as some more local ones in the form of state-imposed constraints, on the one hand, and personal life experiences of staff and students, on the other. What remains to be done, it seems to me, is to explore the nature of communicative, discursive links among people (in the form of social networks and social categories) and among communicative sites.

All those whose paths cross Champlain's at some point bring to their school experience some set of values, orientations and knowledge (a habitus, in Bourdieu's terms) which may or may not endure. It remains to be seen in greater detail how people put together their experience of life in school and outside school. It also remains to see long-term effects that school events and school-related processes can have not only on the lives of individuals but also on the history of institutions like Champlain, and of the community it tries to help build.

Nonetheless, a sociolinguistic perspective on these processes is fruitful. It allows us to understand the scope of action available to individuals within the structural constraints which shape their experience. It allows us to discover the creative use of resources which escapes anything resembling deterministic models of social process and social change. We can discover something about how things happen, and start developing a sense of why they happen the way they do. Perhaps, most importantly, we can begin to track the connections among interactions, and the consequences they have for individual opportunities and for individual attempts to take advantage of open doors or to deal with ones that are closed. We can, in other words, put together what we see people doing with language with what we can find out about the resources at their disposal and about their access to communicative situations where their participation, of whatever kind, might make a difference (in a variety of ways, both short term and long term) to themselves and to others. We can understand language use as a form of social action, and link it, through discovering its distribution and its consequences, to social structure.

It is equally important to take into account the relationship between the kind of work I have produced here, and how it can be taken up in milieux like those of Champlain. From this perspective, the difference it could make if things were done in another way at Champlain remains to be seen. My own sense is that there is much in the story of Champlain which goes far beyond the scope of action of any given school (let alone any given principal, teacher, parent or student). Clearly, things can be changed within a school's culture; the *multiculturels* showed that more than convincingly. But the conditions have to be there; there have to be both structural opportunities and deep interests, and these things come from outside. The question for institutions (and for individuals) is, therefore, more than anything else, one of how to overcome obstacles and take advantage of opportunities. But it is also one of how to understand where deep-seated interests come from, and how to identify the consequences, and for whom, of doing things the way they are done.

Certainly we have seen here some important ways in which the people involved in Champlain have made creative use of the linguistic resources available to them to reinvent the school, and to position themselves well with respect to what the modern world has to offer. They have developed creative strategies for dealing with contradictions, and especially for reconciling the politics of identity with democratic values. They have opened doors, the existence of which was barely glimpsed when Champlain was first created. At the same time, opportunities create new choices, and the transformation of Champlain has different consequences for different people.

The community of Champlain will have to take its own position with respect to what I have written here; it will have to decide for itself how it feels about what it seems to be doing, and whether anything ought to be changed or not. But this I think is what a sociolinguistic, ethnographic analysis can bring us: an understanding of how things happen, and some sense of why they happen the way they do. The rest is up to all of us.

Bibliography

Anderson, B. 1983. *Imagined Communities*. London: Verso.

Balibar, R. 1985. *L'Institution du français. Essai sur le colinguisme des Carolingiens à la République*. Paris: Presses Universitaires de France.

Billig, M. 1995. *Banal Nationalism*. London: Sage.

Blommaert, J. 1996. Language and nationalism: comparing Flanders and Tanzania. *Nations and Nationalism* 2(2): 235–56.

Blommaert, J. (ed.) Forthcoming. *Language Ideological Debates*. Berlin, N.Y.: Mouton de Gruyter.

Bock, M. 1996. Les États généraux du Canada français, ou l'éclatement de la nation: une analyse des journaux de langue française de Sudbury. *Revue du Nouvel-Ontario* 19: 11–37.

Boudreau, F. 1995. La francophonie ontarienne au passé, au présent, au futur: un bilan sociologique. In: J. Cotnam, Y. Frenette and A. Whitfield (eds), *La francophonie ontarienne: bilan et perspectives de recherche*. Hearst: Le Nordir, pp. 17–51.

Boudreau, F. and Nielsen, G. (eds) 1994. Les francophonies nord-américaines. *Sociologie et sociétés* 26(1): 3–196.

Bourdieu, P. 1972. *Esquisse d'une théorie de la pratique*. Geneva: Droz.

Bourdieu, P. 1977a. L'économie des échanges linguistiques. *Langue française* 34: 17–34. Bourdieu, P. 1977b. The economics of linguistic exchanges. *Social Science Information* 16(6): 645–68; English translation.

Bourdieu, P. 1979. *La distinction. Critique sociale du jugement*. Paris: Minuit.

Bourdieu, P. 1982. *Ce que parler veut dire*. Paris: Fayard.

Cajolet-Laganière, H. and Martel, P. 1995. *La qualité de la langue au Québec*. Québec: Institut Québécois de Recherche sur la Culture.

Cameron, D. 1995. *Verbal Hygiene*. London: Routledge.

Choquette, R. 1977. *Langue et religion: histoire des conflits anglo-français en Ontario*. Ottawa: Les Éditions de l'Université d'Ottawa.

Choquette, R. 1987. *La foi gardienne de la langue en Ontario, 1900–1950*. Montréal: Bellarmin.

Clas, A. and Horguelin, P. 1979 (1969). *Le français, langue des affaires*. Montreal, Toronto: McGraw-Hill.

Clift, D. and Arnopoulos, S. 1979. *Le fait anglais au Québec*. Montréal: Libre Expression.

Crowley, T. 1991. *Proper English? Readings in Language, History and Cultural Identity*. London: Routledge.

Crowley, T. 1996. *Language in History: Theories and Texts*. London: Routledge.

Eckert, P. 1989. *Jocks and Burnouts: Social Categories and Identities in High School*. New York: Teachers College Press.

Éloy, J.-M. (ed.) 1995. *La qualité de la langue? Le cas du français*. Paris: Honoré Champion.

Fairclough, N. 1992. *Discourse and Social Change*. Cambridge: Polity Press.

Gal, S. 1993. Diversity and contestation in linguistic ideologies: German speakers in Hungary. *Language in Society* 22(3): 337–60.

Gee, J.P., Hull, G. and Lankshear, C. 1996. *The New Work Order: Behind the Language of the New Capitalism*. Boulder Colorado: Westview Press.

Giddens, A. 1990. *The Consequences of Modernity*. Cambridge: Polity Press.

Giddens, A. 1991. *Modernity and Self-Identity*. Cambridge: Cambridge University Press.

Gramsci, A. 1971. *Selections from the Prison Notebooks*. (Ed. and trans. by Q. Hoare and G. Nowell-Smith). London: Lawrence & Wishart.

Grillo, Ralph. 1989. *Dominant Languages*. Cambridge: Cambridge University Press.

Grisé, Y. (ed.) 1995. *États généraux de la recherche sur la francophonie à l'extérieur du Québec*. Ottawa: Actexpress – Les Presses de l'Université d'Ottawa.

Gumperz, J. 1982. *Discourse Strategies*. Cambridge: Cambridge University Press.

Haché, J.-B. 1976. *Language and Religious Factors in Canadian Ethnic Politics of Education: A Case Study in Power Mobilization*. Unpublished Ph.D. thesis, Graduate Department of Education, University of Toronto.

Heller, M. (ed.) 1988. *Codeswitching: Anthropological and Sociolinguistic Perspectives*. Berlin, NY: Mouton de Gruyter.

Heller, M. 1992. The politics of codeswitching and language choice. *Journal of Multilingual and Multicultural Development* 3: 1–13.

Heller, M. 1994a. *Crosswords: Language, Education and Ethnicity in French Ontario*. Berlin: Mouton de Gruyter.

Heller, M. 1994b. La sociolinguistique et l'éducation franco-ontarienne. *Sociologie et Sociétés* 26(1): 155–66.

Heller, M. 1995. Language choice, social institutions and symbolic domination. *Language in Society* 24(3): 373–405.

Heller, M. 1996. Langue et identité : l'analyse anthropologique du français canadien. In: J. Erfurt (ed.), *De la polyphonie à la symphonie: Méthodes, théories et faits de la recherche pluridisciplinaire sur le français au Canada.* Leipzig: Leipziger Universitätsverlag, pp. 19–36.

Higonnet, P. 1980. The politics of linguistic terrorism and grammatical hegemony during the French Revolution. *Social Theory* 5: 41–69.

Hobsbawm, E. 1990. *Nations and Nationalism Since 1780: Programme, Myth, Reality.* Cambridge: Cambridge University Press.

Hobsbawm, E. and Ranger, T. (eds) 1983. *The Invention of Tradition.* Cambridge: Cambridge University Press.

Jaffe, A. 1993. Obligation, error and authenticity: competing principles in the teaching of Corsican. *Journal of Linguistic Anthropology* 3(1): 99–114.

Juteau-Lee, D. 1980. Français d'Amérique, Canadiens, Canadiens français, Franco-Ontariens, Ontarois: qui sommes-nous? *Pluriel-Débat* 24: 21–42.

Kachru, B. (ed.) 1992. *The Other Tongue: English Across Cultures.* Urbana: University of Illinois Press.

Kuzar, R. 1996. Linguistic and political attitudes towards Israeli Hebrew: ongoing revival versus normalcy. In: J. Blommaert (ed.), *The Politics of Multilingualism and Language Planning: Proceedings of the Language Planning Workshop held at the Political Linguistics Conference, Antwerp, December 1995. Antwerp Papers in Linguistics 87.* Antwerp: University of Antwerp, pp. 143–83.

Laforest, M. 1997. *États d'âme, états de langue.* Québec: Nuit Blanche Éditeur.

Lash, S. and Urry, J. 1994. *Economies of Signs and Space.* London: Sage.

Landry, R. 1982. Le bilinguisme additif chez les francophones minoritaires du Canada. *Revue des Sciences de l'Éducation* 8(2): 223–44.

Marcellesi, J.-B. 1979. Quelques problèmes de l'hégémonie culturelle en France: langue nationale et langues régionales. *International Journal of the Sociology of Language* 21: 63–80.

Martel, M. 1997. *Le deuil d'un pays imaginé: rêves, luttes et déroute du Canada français.* Ottawa: Presses de l'Université d'Ottawa.

Martin-Jones, M. and Heller, M. (eds) 1996. Education in multilingual settings: Discourses, identities and power. Special issues of *Linguistics and Education* 8(1,2): 1–228.

Maxwell, T. 1977. *The Invisible French: The French in Metropolitan Toronto.* Waterloo: Wilfrid Laurier University Press.

McDonald, M. 1990. *We Are Not French.* London: Routledge.

Ontario Ministry of Education and Training. 1994a. *Aménagement linguistique en Français: Guide d'élaboration d'une politique d'aménagement linguistique.* Toronto: Ontario Ministry of Education and Training.

Ontario Ministry of Education and Training. 1994b. *Investir dans l'animation culturelle: Guide d'intervention.* Toronto: Ontario Ministry of Education and Training.

Ontario Ministry of Education and Training. 1994c. *Actualisation linguistique en Français et Perfectionnement du Français.* Toronto: Ontario Ministry of Education and Training.

Outram, Dorinda. 1987. Le langage mâle de la vertu: Women and the discourse of the French Revolution. In P. Burke, and R. Porter (eds), *The Social History of Language.* Cambridge: Cambridge University Press, pp. 120–35.

Pennycook, A. 1992. *The Cultural Politics of English as an International Language.* London: Longman.

Pet Shop Boys. 1996. *Single.* Cage Music Limited.

Phillipson, R. 1992. *Linguistic Imperialism.* Oxford: Oxford University Press.

Rampton, B. 1995. *Crossing: Language and Ethnicity among Adolescents.* London: Longman.

Schieffelin, B. (ed.) 1997. *Language Ideologies.* Oxford: Oxford University Press.

Sériot, P. 1997. *Ethnos et demos*: la construction discursive de l'identité collective. *Langage et société* 79: 39–51.

Swiggers, P. 1990. Ideology and the 'clarity' of French. In: J. Joseph and T. Taylor (eds), *Ideologies of Language.* London: Routledge, pp. 112–30.

Sylvestre, P. 1980. *Penetang: L'École de la résistance.* Sudbury: Prise de Parole.

Urla, J. 1995. Outlaw language: creating alternative public spheres in Basque free radio. *Pragmatics* 5(2): 245–61.

Welch, D. 1988. *The Social Construction of Franco-Ontarian Interests Towards French-Language Schooling.* Unpublished Ph.D. thesis, University of Toronto.

Wolf, E. 1982. *Europe and the People Without History.* Berkeley: University of California Press.

Woolard, K. 1985. Language variation and cultural hegemony: toward an integration of sociolinguistic and social theory. *American Ethnologist* 12(4): 738–48.

Woolard, K. 1989. *Double Talk: Bilingualism and the Politics of Ethnicity in Catalonia.* Stanford: Stanford University Press.

Author index

Anderson, B., 7, 67
Arnopoulos, S. (and D. Clift), 46

Balibar, R., 11, 115
Billig, M., 10
Blommaert, J., 10, 11
Bock, M., 9
Bouchard, G., 260–1, 264
Boudreau, F., 9
Boudreau, F. and G. Nielsen, 10
Bourdieu, P., 12, 14, 17, 60, 187, 265, 268, 270–1

Cajolet-Laganière, H. and P. Martel, 116
Cameron, D., 11–12
Choquette, R., 33–4
Clas, A. and P. Horguelin, 124
Clift, D. and S. Arnopoulos, 46
Crowley, T., 12, 59

Eckert, P., 21
Eloy, J.-M., 115

Fairclough, N., 12
Foucault, M., 12

Gal, S., 11, 115
Gee, J., G. Hull and C. Lankshear, 10
Giddens, A., 10
Gramsci, A., 12
Grillo, R., 8, 115
Grisé, Y., 34
Gumperz, J., 10

Haché, J.-B., 30, 34, 36, 45
Heller, M., 13, 15, 16, 34, 42, 77, 90, 92, 101, 116, 129
Heller, M. (and M. Martin-Jones), 13
Higonnet, P., 8
Hobsbawm, E., 8
Hobsbawm, E. and T. Ranger, 67
Horguelin, P. (and A. Clas), 124
Hull, G. (and J. Gee, C. Lankshear), 10

Jaffe, A., 13, 15
Juteau-Lee, D., 34

Kachru, B., 10
Kuzar, R., 11

Laforest, M., 116
Lambert, W., 97

Landry, R., 97
Lankshear, C. (and J. Gee, G. Hull), 10
Lash, S. and J. Urry, 10

McDonald, M., 15
Marcellesi, J.-B., 8–9
Martel, M., 9, 33
Martel, P. (and H. Cajolet-Laganière), 116
Martin-Jones, M. and M. Heller, 13
Maxwell, T., 47

Nielsen, G. (and F. Boudreau), 10

Ontario Ministry of Education and Training, 93–5, 98, 117
Outram, D., 115

Pennycook, A., 10
Pet Shop Boys, 266
Phillipson, R., 10

Rampton, B., 68
Ranger, T. (and E. Hobsbawm), 67

Schieffelin, B., 10
Seriot, P., 8
Swiggers, P., 12
Sylvestre, P.-F., 34, 42

Urla, J., 13
Urry, J. (and S. Lash), 10

Welch, D., 34, 42
Wolf, E., 10
Woolard, K., 15, 268

Subject index

Academic performance, 13, 64, 101,
    117, 142, 147, 166–8, 188,
    197, 203, 214, 219–20, 231
Academic streaming, 62–3, 132,
    222, 235–6, 241
Académie française, 8
Acadia, 91
African-Canadians, 65–6, 68, 80,
    128, 138, 172, 185, 198–9,
    208–9, 216, 222–4, 230–8,
    241
Anglicisms, 8, 123–4, 133, 147
Anglophones, 5, 11, 124, 213–15,
    218
Anti-racist education, 64–7, 90,
    210–11, 230, 256–7
Assimilation, 49, 75, 91–2
Authenticity, 59, 153, 178, 267

Bilingualism, 2–3, 13, 37, 39–40,
    47–8, 62, 96–7, 138–43,
    148–51, 162, 166, 168,
    187–8, 190–2, 198, 200,
    208, 210–14, 218–20, 231–2,
    257, 259, 271, 273
  academic success, 142, 231
  accommodation to bilingual
      practices, 140
  additive, 96–7

career success, 142, 231
code-switching, 13, 48, 75–6,
    114, 141, 151, 167, 200,
    268, 272
credentialized bilingualism,
    219–20
education, 39–40
gender, 3, 13, 190, 192,
    198–201, 209, 272
government and legislation, 42,
    47
identity, 208, 214, 218
ideology of bilingualism, 2, 151,
    271
job market, 38, 185, 266
markers, 151
meta-commentary or meta-
    discourse, 151
subtractive, 97
Britain, 10, 33
Business, language of, 185

Canada, 31–7, 42, 46–7, 49, 64,
    265
  BNA Act, 34, 42
Canadian Charter of Rights and
    Freedoms, 42, 49
Canadian French, 31, 34, 36, 44,
    47–8, 63, 75, 129, 140,

152–3, 160, 165–6, 169–71, 173, 175, 188, 232, 239–40

Capital, linguistic, 20, 59–60, 124, 144, 184, 266, 271–3

Catholicism, 4–5, 33–9, 41, 43
  Catholic school system, 36, 38, 40

Citizenship, 263

Class, 3, 9, 13, 40, 46–8, 61–3, 67–8, 76, 115, 124, 152, 166–7, 213, 216
  ethnocultural/ethnolinguistic affiliation, 68, 115, 124, 213
  gender, 62, 115
  linguistic minorities, 3

Codeswitching, 13, 48, 75–6, 78, 114, 141, 151, 167, 181, 200, 268, 272

Colonialism, 184–5

Commodification of language, 29, 271

Conversational structure, 131–2, 143, 163

Creole French, 175, 192

Curriculum, 63, 176, 182–4, 235, 237

Decontextualized language, 96, 98, 102, 116–17

Demographic change, 57, 61

Discursive space, 149, 190, 201, 209

Dissing, 223, 226–8

Diversity, 32, 50–1, 60, 67, 117, 211, 218, 236, 254, 272

English, 36–8, 43–4, 48, 54, 65, 68, 75, 84, 91, 102, 104, 123–4, 126, 132, 138, 140, 145–6, 160, 166–7, 169, 181–2, 184–6, 191, 200, 205, 218, 221, 235, 237, 243, 268

anglicisms, 123–4

common language, 38

English as a second language (ESL), 140

gender, 200

identity, 75, 160, 218, 268

ideology, 123

job market, 37, 184–6

learning English, 140, 169

music, 68, 243

pedagogy, 104, 126

schools, 36, 38, 43, 65, 91, 146, 166, 184–6, 205, 237

syntax, 123,

university, 104, 145

Equity, 4, 61–2, 64, 190–3, 257

Families, 40, 47, 49, 53–4, 63, 138, 148, 155–6, 238, 248
  family communication, 49, 53

Fieldwork, 61–4, 210–11

Flagging, 106, 124–7

Floor, 84, 89–90, 102–3, 148

Franco-Ontarians, 32, 34–6, 38, 42, 48, 50, 67–8, 91–4, 97–8, 115, 138, 210, 217, 259
  Franco-Ontarian schooling, 32, 34–6, 38, 42, 48, 50, 67, 90–3
  institutions, 69, 138
  music, 68
  post-secondary education, 138

Francophones, 2, 10–11, 90, 115, 134, 141, 165, 171–2

French, 13, 31–8, 41–2, 48–9, 50, 53–4, 61, 63, 75, 117, 123–4, 129, 134, 140, 144, 153, 160, 163, 165–6, 169–71, 172–3, 175, 177–8, 181, 188, 202, 218, 231–2, 236, 239–40, 242, 266, 271–2

anglicisms, 8, 123–4, 133, 147
brokers, 271–2
Canadian French, 31, 34, 36,
    44, 47–8, 63, 75, 140, 153,
    160, 165–6, 169–71, 173,
    175, 188, 232, 239–40
common language, 140
Creole French, 175
European French, 47–8, 162,
    240
la francophonie internationale,
    13, 69, 73, 98, 115, 171,
    188, 209, 273
French as a first language, 50,
    140, 162, 176–7, 188, 231–2
French as a second language,
    50, 177
gender, 192, 202
globalization, 47, 73, 98, 273
immersion programs, 48–9, 99,
    190, 202, 211, 218
intonation, 48
job market, 138
language quality, 115, 129, 176,
    188, 268
lexicon, 124, 175
monolingualism, 139, 178
morphology, 124
norms, 8, 48, 54, 74–5, 79, 98,
    114, 134, 139, 152, 191, 198
pedagogy, 176–8
phonology, 48, 124, 107
programmes, 42, 117, 137–8,
    176
'Québécois', 8, 16, 163, 165,
    171, 208
standard, 5, 8, 129, 139–40,
    151–3, 166, 169, 177–8
stereotypes, 153, 163, 188, 208,
    239–40
syntax, 48, 124, 129, 177
varieties of French, 115, 117,
    124, 138, 172

French-language education, 34–6,
    38–9, 42–3, 48–50, 54, 60,
    67, 91–5, 99, 101, 117, 122,
    236, 267, 273

Gay and lesbian students, 192,
    195, 201–2, 205–7, 209
Gender, 3, 13, 19, 38, 49, 54, 62,
    64, 115, 152–9, 189–211,
    237, 242, 271–3
    academic success, 13, 64, 197
    bilingualism, 3, 13, 190, 192,
        198–201, 209, 272
    class, 62, 115
    discourse, 189–90, 198, 209
    division of labour, 38, 54, 62,
        64, 190, 192, 209
    equity, 62, 190–2
    fashion show, 139, 195, 197,
        237, 242
    monolingualism, 13, 198, 200
    romance and sexuality, 190–2,
        195, 197–8, 201–7
    stereotypes, 13, 19, 190–2, 202,
        211
Globalization, 3, 8, 10–11, 32–3,
    47, 60, 67, 75, 127, 183,
    211, 264

Haitian students, 66, 188, 213,
    228, 236
Hip-hop music, language and
    culture, 199, 211–12,
    214–15, 221, 242–3, 245,
    248, 257
Hockey, 140, 156
Hyper-modernity, 3, 265

I–R–E (Initiation–Response–
    Evaluation) format, 79, 81,
    102–3, 113–14, 132
Identity, 1–2, 10–11, 20, 30, 46,
    60, 75, 97–8, 160, 208–9,

214–18, 221–2, 265–6, 268, 271–2

Ideology, 2–3, 5–7, 9, 13, 18, 33, 38, 54, 61, 66, 69, 75–6, 79, 90–1, 97–100, 115, 123, 134, 139–41, 151, 153, 168–9, 178, 187, 211, 236, 257, 271

Immigration, 13, 49, 50–1, 54, 156–7, 236

Institutions, 37–9, 44–5, 56–7, 61, 73, 75, 78, 226–9, 236–7,

Interactional order, 87, 89–90, 219–20

Intermarriage, 49

Job market, 37–8, 46–7, 138, 183–6, 231, 266, 271

Language norms, 8, 12, 48, 54, 74–5, 79, 98, 101, 114–15, 134, 139, 152, 191, 198

Language pedagogy, 11

Lexical gaps, 127

Linguistic capital, 20, 59–60, 124, 144, 184, 266, 271–3

Linguistic competence, 67

Linguistic deficit, 50

Linguistic insecurity, 13, 102, 166–7

Linguistic minorities, 1, 3–5, 9–10, 12–13, 20, 31–2, 34, 54–5, 59, 69, 74–5, 259, 265, 267, 273

Linguistic monitoring, 7–8, 75, 79, 90, 101, 187–8

Linguistic purism, 48, 124

Linguistic repertoire, 67, 95, 100, 116, 124, 188, 231–2, 243, 270

Literature, French Canadian, 117–18, 129, 173

Marginalization, 13, 33, 54, 124, 188, 190–1, 197, 199–203, 209, 211–14, 218, 227–31, 242, 256, 272–3

Methodology, 9, 14–20, 76, 80, 274

Mobilization, 10–11, 32–3, 48

Modernization, 37

Monolingualism, 2, 7, 10–11, 13, 32, 34, 37–9, 44, 46, 69, 74–5, 80, 90–1, 97–8, 100–2, 115, 117, 124, 138–41, 148, 154–5, 162, 178, 181, 187–8, 198–200, 228–30, 266, 271–2

Montreal, 33, 46, 62, 156, 223, 236

Multiculturalism, 3, 19, 55–65, 199, 210–14, 235–6, 242, 254, 257, 275
   anti-racist education, 64, 210–11, 235
   Canadian federal government, 64
   Ontario government, 64
   pluralism, 64
   policy, 235
   Quebec, 63–5

Multilingualism, 7, 11, 145, 257, 270

Music, 68, 138, 211–12, 214–17, 221–2, 242–4, 246, 248–7, 257

Nation-state, 1, 4, 7, 9–10, 32, 67, 69, 91, 265
   and linguistic minorities, 9–10, 32
   and monolingualism, 10, 32, 69, 91

Nationalism, 1, 3–9, 12, 32–4, 36, 38, 44, 46, 48, 67, 69, 91, 115, 155–6, 263–5, 267

Acadian, 91
civic, 263–4
ethnic, 1, 5, 264
ideology, 33, 38
institutional, 90–1
minorization, 12
Quebec, 33–4, 36, 46, 69, 91,
  156
territorial, 90–1
Networks, 54, 67, 102, 138, 147,
  155–6, 199–200, 202–3,
  211–13, 220, 231–2, 242,
  248, 259, 274
New Brunswick, 36, 49, 155–6
New France, 33, 69–70
Norms, linguistic, 8, 12, 54,
  74–5, 79, 98, 101, 114–15,
  134, 139, 152, 191, 198
North American Free Trade
  Agreement (NAFTA), 143

Ontario, 33–6, 39, 43, 46–7, 56,
  61–2, 64
Ontario Ministry of Education, 41,
  64, 67, 92–100, 116, 236–8

Pedagogy, 11, 76, 81, 84, 89–90,
  92, 104, 113–14, 122, 126,
  145, 160, 177–8, 221–2
ideologies, 90
social organization, 89
Pluralism, 19, 31, 64, 96, 98,
  190, 200, 265, 267

Quality of language, 75, 90,
  101–2, 115, 129, 133, 176,
  188, 268
Quebec, 5, 11, 18, 33–4, 36, 43,
  45–6, 49, 63–5, 69, 91, 140,
  156–8, 165, 172, 236, 248,
  265
Québécois, 8, 156–9, 163, 165,
  172, 174, 208–9, 217

Race (and racism), 3, 17, 33,
  59, 62, 172, 180–2, 187,
  210–16, 231, 253, 257, 271
Rap, 212
Refrancisation/Francisation, 93
Refugees, 50, 80, 155
Regionalisms, 124
Respect, ideology of, 79, 81, 84,
  134

School, 36, 38, 43, 54, 63–6,
  74–5, 90–3, 101–3, 115,
  134, 146, 166, 184–6, 205,
  237, 256–7, 272, 268
administration, 63–4, 74–5,
  256–7
board, 54, 65–6
English, 36, 38, 43, 65, 91,
  146, 166, 184–6, 205, 237
French-language minority, 32,
  34–6, 38, 42, 48, 50, 67,
  90–3
language norms, 74–5, 90, 92,
  101–3, 115, 134
normative order, 75, 102, 134
social order, 89
Sequential turn-taking, 84, 89,
  134, 141
and normative order, 134
and spatial organization, 134
ideology of respect, 134
Service and information economic
  sectors, 3, 47
Social order, 75, 81, 82, 83, 89,
  134
Somali-speaking students, 3, 61,
  63, 65, 80, 84, 88, 138, 167,
  171, 181, 187–8, 192, 197,
  199, 201, 209–12, 216,
  227–9, 230–1, 234–6, 257
Space, 134, 149–50, 190, 236
Sports, 156, 213–14, 216, 218,
  221, 230, 235

Stereotypes, 13, 19, 65, 153, 163,
180, 188, 190–2, 195, 202,
208–9, 211, 239–41
Stigmatization, 18, 48, 133, 188,
201

Turn-taking, 79, 84, 89, 134, 141

Unity, 31, 32, 61, 71–2

Vernacular, 18, 139, 152, 195
Voyageurs, 1, 30, 71

Workplace, 37–8, 40
English in the workplace,
37–8
English-dominated job market,
38
gender roles, 38